'Untitled' by Opriseo

Published by Little Toller Books in 2022

Text © Jay Griffiths 2022

Jacket and frontispiece photography © Oleg Oprisco 2017

Typeset in Garamond by Little Toller Books

Printed in Cornwall, UK by TJ Books

All papers used by Little Toller Books are natural, recyclable products made from wood grown in sustainable, well-managed forests

A catalogue record for this book is available from the British Library

ISBN 978-1-915068-01-9

NEMESIS, MY FRIEND

*Journeys through
the turning times*

Jay Griffiths

LITTLE TOLLER BOOKS

Contents

Compass

No god worth the name would choose a changeless heaven
If he could dip his wings to earth.
Part potter, part poet, divinity flies downwards
And throws clay to sound
An unfurled word —
A thought, fired, attracts.

The meaning is in the keening,
The direction of turning,
Tuning the inner ear
To the Earth's magnetic message:
This near-hearted alignment,
Undeniable as gravity or light.

A flit-compass in the swift
Tilts feeling feathers to the field.
The turtle knows its constant way to true.
Even in this torn world, magnetism vouchsafes us:
A geopetal force, an ancient love
Which tugs the lodestone of my soul.

Introduction

The Hourglass

This book is a journey through the turning times of the day and the year. It is a journey that begins at home, with the birdsong of dawn, morning rituals, the woodlands and flowers of spring. The book moves outwards into larger journeys across the world, the Alhambra, the early morning rituals of Bali, travels of noon in West Papua, summer in Mexico, and the evening of the year in the Arctic. As dusk deepens, the book turns back towards home, the hearth, and then to night and winter, a time for skating and stories.

The experience of the day's hours, turning light to dark to light, and the year's seasons turning spring to winter, is an almanac of the turning world.

This is not just a physical experience. Light is how we think. Noon-thinking is bright, seeing far, keen and quick, whereas night is a time of dream, of intuition and insight rather than sight. The psyche is responsive to the play of dark as much as to the play of light; storytelling is a winter art. Dawn and dusk are tricksier times, carrying a particular charge: enigmatic and chancey.

The day turns, runs like sand in an hourglass. We hold time in our hands. Fragile. Dear. The mattering world.

★

One moment in my childhood was momentous. I was in the garden of my parents' house. Alone. At night. Blanched by moonlight and terror.

Why? Because I was looking at the stars and was suddenly over-awed by the infinity of space, cowed and soul-broken to be so small and unmattering. I felt a pang, a sharp constriction of anguish at the centre of my being. Though it lasted only a moment, it was a total eclipse of the spirit.

I felt it again, recently, when I held in my hand an hourglass, containing only dust from before the sun existed. It makes me feel again what I felt that night as a child: the enormity of space, the eternities of time.

As a child, my mind would never have grasped that there was such a thing as 'Before The Sun.' My mind can hardly grasp it now. But it is real. Graspable. I have held it, this hourglass, part of Katie Paterson's artwork 'The Moment,' containing pre-solar dust. I have to go slowly with this phrase, *pre-solar dust*. The freight of it rocks me. All that it means, its reference to a time before anything.

Our sun was formed 4,567 million years ago, when a cloud of dust and gas (a nebula) collapsed under its own gravity; the cloud spun and flattened into a disk with our sun forming at its centre, while the disk's outer edges became the solar system. Dust, from that time, is in the hourglass now, and in that dust, all of life crouches like the Ur-hermit in the vast desert of desolate space. That dust comes from before it all.

Before Grief existed, or Laughter.

Before Light, Life and Love.

Before Breath, Thought or Spirit.

Before Sky and Cloud.

Before the sand at the seashore felt flecks of life pick its way out onto the land.

Before that Sea.

Before Ears to hear the music of the spheres.

Before Chlorophyll's love affair with sunlight to create green, green life.

Before Writing.

Before the Alphabet.

Before 'Before.'

Before Time, or any way of counting it.

Before the Solstice, times of prayer or my mother's watch.

Before Mothering.

Before Meaning.

Before Levity and Leverets: Grace and Graylags.
Before East and Easter: West and Westerlies.
Before Day and Daisies: Night and Nightingales.
All this, before Sun Was.
When the *All that Is* was still to come.

★

Nemesis is a goddess of Greek myth whose role is to give people what they are due. She looks at people's actions and effects on others and assesses the cost, and where humans display arrogance towards the gods, Nemesis steps in. Often pictured as a beautiful woman with bold white wings, she ensured that people had a balance of happiness and sadness: an equal measure of good luck and bad.

Her greatest gift is setting implacable limits and she is often pictured with an hourglass. The hourglass symbolises time past, present and future. The past is the dust below, the 'dust to dust' of a life past; the future is the promise of time to come; the present, at the hourglass's centre, is where time is most alive in the racing, tipping, collapsing sand. All the lines of the hourglass point to its centre, the small aperture of Now, the passing moment when time is most charged with life.

The heart of an hourglass is its narrowest point, and the Latin for 'narrow' is *angustus*. It means not just narrow but limited, constricted, choking. *Angustus* gives rise to many words: anxious, angst, anger, anxiety and indeed angina, that painful constriction of the heart.

Ours is the Age of Anxiety, and the hourglass expresses it. The sands of Time seem to be running out. Individuals feel hurried, pressured, driven by speed, and many people feel the angst of angry stress. Pervasive anxiety is the signature emotion of modernity, and there is a longing for time to be sustained and sustaining, for the future to be infinite again: the sand of time stopped in its cliff-edge rush, the hourglass held gently and laid down on its side, sleeping easy in the symbol of infinity, the ∞, the 8 on its side, the hourglass's opposite.

An hourglass is different from other traditional time pieces. The sundial shows time's constant cycles, as does a clock face. Myth shows time as an infinite, self-replenishing thing: the Greek sun god Helios drives his horse-drawn chariot across the sky each day and the horses are refreshed by night. The river is a universal symbol of time passing, and crucially it flows and runs, but does not run dry. Unlike these, the hourglass carries a warning: time is short and can run out. Contemporary protest symbolism casts the hourglass in a circle as the symbol of extinction, wherein the circle represents the world, with the stylised X as the hourglass, the two together showing how time is running out for so many species. Creatures are being crossed out — forced into extinction at the fastest rate ever. The life-spirit of this mosaic world is being plunged into starving darknessbefore our eyes. It would sadden the very sun.

Young people are suffering a never-before-known sickness, eco-anxiety, as time is running out for the climate, the soil, the oceans and creatures. The Dominant Culture is breaching the limits of what the world can stand, a transgression like no other in its consequences. In a few decades, it has seized resources, broken the wise and necessary limits, taken more than its due, stolen life itself from the future. In its greed and in its hubris, it has endangered the coral reefs, the bees, the Everything.

Nemesis is the goddess for this moment.

She is a goddess who gets a bad press. She is maligned and misunderstood, spoken of as if she were spiteful, vengeful and punitive, as if she relishes the retribution she serves. Not so. She represents divine justice, specifically the importance of respecting boundaries. If you cross the line, if you break the laws that are inherent in physics and metaphysics alike, you will suffer Nemesis, swift and certain. Where there is hubris, Nemesis will follow. Her symbol, the hourglass, is the exact emblem of a defined and foreseeable limit. This is an age that fatally refuses to recognise limits, that rages against them. The teaching of Nemesis is an ethics lesson taught in physics.

We know our individual lifetimes are limited. It is harder to think larger, to imagine a species having limited time: nothingness on either side of being. The cold, dark eternities of that nothingness filled me with dread as a child, seeing the Earth, sunlit and bubbling with life in a vast abyss. The terror taught me that life is sacred and time is short and precious. When I was a little older, I read a line from the *Rubaiyat* of Omar Khayyam and felt my anxiety was articulated: 'One moment in Annihilation's Waste. One moment, of the Well of Life to taste.'

The hand may hold this hourglass but the mind staggers under its symbolic weight, because right now, those of us alive today are holding the future in our hands. The power — to destroy or protect — lies in our hands, and at this acute moment in history the sands of time are at their tipping point, falling fastest and most alarmingly. We know we could turn the hourglass back again — that is its grace — but there is no certainty that we will. It is in our hands. Half gasp, half siren-cry, anguish combines fear, remorse, pain and anger: we are collectively at the heart of the hourglass, its tightening, constricting chest pain is a world-reckoning anguish as the narrowing chance of change is closing, moment by moment by moment.

Dawn

The Ethics of Fire

At dawn, the sun is young. It is interested in everything, quick and open. The sun, first flame, is reflected in a myriad of ways, including every match, candle and fireside.

When I light my wood stove, the flame begins its life as every young thing does: sensitive, curious and light-hearted, licking at paper, trying the sawdust and tasting the kindling. And, like every young creature, it is also fragile, easily dampened, needing tending and encouragement. It gets to its teenage years in teenage minutes. Thirteen minutes on from its baby steps, it is leaping at slim, quartered logs. By thirty minutes, it has reached its middle age, and is confident to take on medium-sized logs. Then, a few minutes older, it is a mature fire, breathing in and basking in its own warmth. It sighs and glows, satisfied in its largesse, giving out heat in open-hearted generosity. It represents both the physical and emotional warmth of home.

So come in, please, be welcome. Tea? Earl Grey, Lapsang Souchong, or Ordinary? There are also about twenty different kinds of herbal teas in the kitchen. If you're lucky, you'll see my cat's best trick: he stands on his back legs on the sideboard and with one front paw works his way along the herbal teas, flicking the packets off, one after another.

Sit with me by the hearth. I've just lit it: it'll take the chill off the early spring dawn. This is my snuggest place, tucked up by the wood stove set safely in a stone hearth which is folded into the earth of a hill. A hearth is a good place to talk. Welcome, it says. Make yourself at home, I say. I'll put some music on.

If I am at home without human company, two things stop me feeling lonely. One is my antic cat, Otter, and the other is my fire. Both need air, food and attention, and die without them. Any flame adds vitality to a room. A prayer in church, or any ritual of tenderness, even an everyday supper, is given an especial significance if it is witnessed by candles, inviting a divinity, no matter how humble, to attend the moment with keener spirit.

In terms of domestic ethics, the hearth in someone's home is an invitation to kindness: the flames of anger or rudeness are held in check. No emotional arson here: arguments should be defused before they explode. Most individuals want their homes to feel safe for themselves and for their guests, aligning with the simple ethics of the hearth's welcome. My wood stove is generous with its warmth, but its rules are strict. The chimney has to be swept each year. The wood has to be dry. I am careful that nothing can ever fall onto the stove, that its fire is contained at all times. A fireside is heaven, a house-fire is hell. Both are fire, but one breaches the limits.

A few years ago, a friend of mine went for a walk in the hills for a couple of hours. All was green and serene. Turning back towards her house, tucked into a hillside, she noticed smoke coming from somewhere. She was curious but undisturbed until, her steps taking her closer and closer, she saw it was her own house that was on fire. The shock was appalling, the damage enormous. A little cat died in the flames, which were thought to have started with an electrical fault. Fire engines arrived, and in time, the whole inferno was hosed down to blackened smoky rubble. The following day, a team of us arrived to help clear up. Almost all of the house was burned, and everything was soaked with water. My friend asked me to look after the books, so I carried armfuls to the barn, and stood them up, their pages fanned open to attempt to dry them. On one of my trips back towards the house, I saw a half-burnt page on the ground, just a single leaf with all its edges singed brown. It was beautiful. I picked it up. What book had it come from? Dante's *Inferno*. God's own truth.

Once, in days of late summer sun, I canoed down the Wye with a friend, and we camped on the riverbanks. We set up our tents, mats and sleeping bags, but it was only when we lit a campfire that we could feel properly at home. All night, this our tiny sun burned and its embers were still glowing in the morning when the real sun rose and the river suddenly lit up as if someone had spilt a pint of sunlight in the water and it splashed liquid gold.

One morning on that trip, we briefly paddled out of the Wye to canoe up a tiny tributary, with curtains of willows from both banks reaching together in midstream. As the canoe parted the leaves, just then, in a lightning-quick dart, a kingfisher flew right in front of me, barely two feet away, from one bank to another.

The sky and the kingfisher share a secret. The bird's turquoise feathers are actually not blue at all. Remove it from sunlight, and its feathers are brown, because the blue only appears as a result of a phenomenon called structural colouration, the same process by which we see the sky as blue. Search for the blue in the kingfisher feather, and you'll never find it. The magic is a gift from the very fire of the sun. They are birds of flame, the exact point where, in a hearth, ordinary orange flame becomes extraordinary blue, right at the vanishing point of beauty. A kingfisher belongs partly to the element of fire, burning so briefly but so brightly that they leave the very air purified by their flame.

These birds of blue flame are as magical as a firebird to me, flashing sky in its wings.

The widespread myth of the Firebird speaks of humanity's ambivalent relationship to fire, as the story shows both the allure and the caution; the beguilement and the bewilderment. The Firebird attracts people, setting a fuse of desire burning. The desire burns along the fuse, further, faster, into fascination, then obsession, and then the inevitable explosion. The story often begins with the hero finding just one feather. He is captivated, charmed. Wiser voices, including a horse in one story, caution him. Stop at this point, the stories suggest, and you could have the firebird *of the mind* forever, for in terms of the psyche, just one feather *is* enough: it is the name 'Firebird' that fires the imagination, the idea of it, light as a feather that sets light to our delight. The feather is fractal fortune, already containing within itself the idea of the whole. So the hero is warned to heed a limit and not to look for more. Defuse the desire and preserve the beauty. But, true to human nature, the hero is heedless of the advice and deliberately breaks the limit, moving into a place of jeopardy as he seeks the bird. The Firebird is a marvel, highly coveted, representing treasure that is rare and hard to possess. Often, the hero wishes to hold or cage the bird but, as the story shows, the one who thinks he possesses the bird is, in fact, himself possessed, captive to his own greed. Going too far, the hero crosses the line.

In one version, the hero is told that he can take the Firebird one night as everyone is sleeping, but that he must not touch its golden cage. As ever, the prohibition acts as command. Of course he cannot resist the gold, and as soon as he touches the cage, bells ring, everyone wakes and the hero is taken prisoner.

Folktales often caution against breaking rules and crossing boundaries. Nemesis is everywhere, though not by name. The idea that there are set limits is embedded in ancient wisdom and in language alike. To transgress is to behave wrongly in the specific sense of crossing a line. 'That really is the limit,' we say in anger, or 'you've overstepped the mark.' An old term for a badly behaved man was a 'bounder,' breaking the bounds or limits. Indigenous Australian culture has a strong sense of the Law greater than any human law that does — and must — govern human acts. These are fundamental laws, ones that exist before us and after us.

The sun is the universal fire, of course, the prime quickener of life, the central hearth which makes the Earth a habitable home. Its fire creates the almanac of time, making days, shaping the seasons. The sun's heat, the very fire of fires, giving light and lightness, creates the carefree and happy-go-lucky nature of summer. Because heat and light and time will never run out, the world dances in summer. All the gravity and mahogany of winter is dispelled by the warmth of the sun.

One summer when I was eighteen, I walked and hitchhiked and camped with my boyfriend. We were dizzy with sunshine, drunk on camomile tea, chirpy as sparrows, penniless as daisies, rich in the commonwealth of summer. It was a time of utter innocence, guiltless, insouciant and as generous as the feeling of summer itself. The world has never felt so right as it did that summer, nature so safe and soft, entwining and embracing, so perfectly right that it could be taken for granted that every summer would be like this, forever and forever until September when everything would — just as rightly — cool to luminous mists of gold and that particular scamper in the breeze when sunshine turns seeds into harvest and fruit.

Then autumn would fall, just as rightly, to winter and the certainty of seasons would never, could never, be shattered or even doubted because the seasons exemplified the balance of things, the right proportion of the sun and its seasons in harmony with universal law. Perennially in accord, the sun's fire, heat and temperature would run fluent with Ecclesiastes: to every *season* there is a season. In winter, fire festivals coax the flame of the spirit, longing for light in the bleak days, needing candles, hearthsides and the cosy *hygge* of domestic warmth.

But all is not right with the world. We have blindly become arsonists. The climate is like a parasol or umbrella, protecting the world. Our generation has set fire to the very thing that was our defence.

Collectively, we have lit bushfires, taken some sixty thousand koalas and have thrown them into the flames. Disoriented by terror, some koalas stumble *towards* the fire, driven, who knows, by an instinct to go home, bewildered and crying in agony. Nearly three billion animals were killed or displaced in the Australian bushfires in 2019 and 2020.

In the Arctic, temperatures are rising fatally as the Earth runs a fever. Ice disintegrates, wildfires burn across the tundra, permafrost melts. The perfectly balanced geography of the world, with its ice cap at the north and south and the temperate and tropical zones between, is thrown off balance.

A new dissonance wrecks the harmony of aeons. The rhythms are broken: melodies howled out of tune. The seasons are colliding like delinquents, driving time into a vortex. The certain leaf-time knowledge of trees is turned to chaos. Birds starve in the confusion. The choreography of mating, flowering and egg-laying is smashed. The birds flee to nowhere: their feathers scorched, they are dying on the wing. The roses are evicted. Butterflies are banished and a wren is flung out with the garbage. The flowers hate each other as they fight over one last bee.

No one ever said we couldn't break the limits. No one said excess couldn't happen. No one ever said we couldn't act with the reckless arrogance which the Greeks called hubris. But such transgressions are implacably punished.

The laws of physics correspond to the laws of metaphysics: where mortals overstep the mark, they will be struck down. Justice is implicate with the laws of the universe that even the sun must obey, for no one and nothing is above the fundamental laws of nature. According to Heraclitus, justice is exemplified by those laws: 'The sun will not go beyond its bounds, for otherwise the Furies which watch over justice will find it out.' Natural laws *are* divine laws. The gods set limits for humans but those who ape the gods in arrogance, and overreach those limits, face a reckoning.

Where hubris, there Nemesis.

Wrongly referred to as goddess of retribution, Nemesis is better regarded as goddess of limits, proportion, proper measurement and rightness. Her many symbols include a measuring rod, scales of justice and a bridle. Her name is related to the Greek *nemein* meaning 'to give what is due': she metes out justice that punishes disproportion and guards right distribution, the apportioning of what is duly owed.

Nemesis is our friend. She knows how things function well, and how they malfunction. She is like a doctor using wise medicine to draw down a fever. She is a good judge on the side of life.

Animals like her. Dogs want to know the rules of the pack, and keep them. Kingfishers love her. Territorial, kingfishers measure their limits along riverbanks: a mile or so belongs to one bird before the next bird's territory begins. Canoeing, you can measure the miles in kingfishers for the bird may (seen or unseen) accompany you along a stretch of river, stopping at the point which marks a boundary known only to the brilliance of birds. Then the next kingfisher catches the thread of your path.

The living world is desperate for Nemesis to tug on her bridle and rein us humans in a little. If they could speak, imagine how the polar bears would plead with her. 'Step in, ma'am, please tell these humans that their unbridled sense of entitlement is going to kill us.' Whales would want Nemesis to right the sense of apportion that gives to the sea creatures a chance of living in their living waters. The Amazon, and everything it sustains, would have given anything for the principle of due and right apportioning; it could have thrived forever without this one crazed subsection of humanity who recognise no limits. How might a turtle pray for Nemesis to restore the only order that works for all: ecocratic, natural laws?

Nemesis, though, is viewed as vindictive because modernity dislikes facing consequences, despises limits, loathes the idea of punishment and disdains boundaries. Collectively we have come to feel entitled to live like gods, burning as much from the fossil fuel realm as we want, and heedless of the punishment it inflicts on generations to come, and indeed on current generations in the unwealthy world. We have turned a goddess of right limits and due care into a caricature of vengefulness.

This isn't only about the damage that excess brings. It's about the gifts of limits, because here's the thing: the principle of Nemesis is what gives us *beauty*. The measure and metre of music. The golden ratio of art. The strictures of the sonnet compressing beauty in its lines. The rhythm of the dance, the drum, the dervish.

Limits matter, whether physical or cultural. In a creative sense, we know that the constraints of form create a tension with the force of the artistic spirit, and from that tension, great art comes. For music to be able to withstand the outrageous genius of a Mozart or Beethoven, it needs to give them rules: the outward form is limited so that the inward spirit may be unlimited.

When I think of a visual example of the tension between obeying the rules of form, and the force of the creative spirit, I see the Alhambra, the Moorish palace in Granada in southern Spain. The palace is set in exquisite gardens, whose green contrasts with the snow of the Sierra Nevada behind it. Walking into the Alhambra, I could almost hear it, as its intricate sculpture and symmetrical patterns, its arabesques and decoration, are at once leafy and limitless, yet exactly and perfectly obedient to the limits and rules of art.

Doorways and arches give onto courtyards, pools and mosaics of turquoise and lapis lazuli, everywhere a lapidary gift: a palace fit for a kingfisher. Every fountain is an arabesque of air, made visible by water. Every carving unfurls endless geometry, and those patterns cast a trance spell, bewitching the senses.

Inside is poetry, the spirit spelled in curving calligraphy. Outside, the flowers and herbs scent the air in filigreed breeze. There is one bee. So delicate is the whole edifice that it is like the architecture of the mind at its most sensitive. Water cascades in carved runnels and the flow is channelling not only living water but more: it channels the *All* that flows close to the divine. And yet the weight of all this stone seems no more than the weight of that one bee on that one flower.

The framing of views at the Alhambra concentrates the mind, as all frames do. Look long enough, and the arches inscribe themselves in you so you frame with your attention everything beautiful that you see. As a frame physically contains the artwork within it, so form creates the necessary bounds around expression: this is how the constraint of form gives tension to the artistic endeavour. The fire-spirit duelling with the strictures of form, becomes ever tenser until it explodes an object into significance.

My spirit soars. I want to *be* the Alhambra. Entranced, the psyche is given its wings. The effect results from recognising the exacting geometries of form and, by respecting them, surpassing them. The confines of form are never broken because they are precisely the kindling of intensity by which the Divine appears. I catch fire.

The Alhambra is flame at its most exquisite: the fire of the senses. But it was once threatened with arson. Napoleon's troops were stationed at the Alhambra in 1812, and had been ordered to blow up the palace as they left. In the early hours of 16 September, some of it was indeed destroyed in a series of explosions. But beauty such as this also provokes defenders, and one soldier, José García, remained behind. He had been wounded in 1808, had lost a hand and limped badly, but that morning, alone, he stayed to put his life on the line. Dragging his injured leg as he walked, and fearful of reprisals for going against orders, he removed the fuses and saved the palace. Some grow strong in the presence of beauty, and García stood like a lone David against the Goliath army of destruction, recklessly defending what the heart holds dear.

Wild animals are lit by the fire within, vivid and intense, instinct blazing. A hawk in yarak knows it. Cats know it, their eyes glittering in the hunt. The kingfisher knows it as it flies with a streak of pure sky. The phoenix condenses ideas of fire and flight, and does so drawing a distinction between the realm of humans and the realm of the gods. According to the legend, the phoenix lives in the immortal world but flies to the mortal world in order to die and be reborn. On Earth, it makes its nest from cinnamon and other spices and herbs, then sings a haunting melody, settles down and waits for sunrise. A spark from the rising sun sets fire to the nest and the phoenix dies in the blaze. Three days later, however, it rises again from the ashes.

Of course we humans want to fly: that is why we have metaphor, to give our minds wings. That is why we have those soaring emotions of hope and love and sheer sunrising splendour. But in mythic truth, we have overreached ourselves by making flight literal. In the many stories about the theft of divine fire, the flame is often stolen by a bird whose wings allow it to reach the realm of the gods without overreaching its physical being. The Firebird is of course winged, magical and made of fire, a mythical creature with heaven in its feathers. Birds fly according to the laws of nature. Humans don't. Nor do horses. When the Greek hero Bellerophon tried to ride his winged horse to Mount Olympus, the seat of the gods, Zeus was angered by Bellerophon's hubris and sent a gadfly to sting

Pegasus, causing him to plunge from the sky. Pride, we say, comes before a fall. The agent of divine justice sent to temper hubris is a little insect who flies according to natural (in other words divine) laws as if to prove that a tiny mite is right if it lives according to universal law. A gadfly is small, but a virus is smaller. In our times, the gadfly of Covid has stung us for the most ancient of reasons.

So many pandemics are a result of quite literally overstepping the limits of those natural/divine laws, the laws which kept the habitat of wild creatures separate from us, safe from us, apart from us: boundaries that we transgressed. SARS was a virus from a horseshoe bat. Cholera jumped to humans when, in the 1760s, the East India Company cut down the mangroves in the wetlands of Bengal and the Sundarbans. Perhaps if we had collectively not sought minerals and timber from the forests, regardless of how vulnerable the forest was, perhaps if we had collectively worked out ways to share the home, the great home of the Earth with every creature, we would not be facing the fearsome results of Covid-19 which resulted from similar invasions into the natural world. Modernity's relentless desire to fly everywhere then ensured that the virus spread rapidly around the world in the worst pandemic in a hundred years.

What is it with wings? Nemesis herself is often pictured with wings, as if the human imagination has been uncannily prescient, reading ahead from the far past into our contemporary world. Flying is for the gods, the birds and the insects. Respect the limits, the myths say sternly. The gods use a winged creature, the eagle, to punish Prometheus for stealing the fire that properly belonged to the gods. The eagle pecks out his liver every night, but his liver regrows and is endlessly pecked out again, for eternity. (The liver is the organ associated with fire — ill-tempered anger, for example, was known as being 'liverish.')

A question.

Where is there redemption for the human desire for the fire of the gods? Are there ways in which we humans can draw the divine fire down, in ways that are not hubristic and do not offend the ancient ethics the myths hold? Can humans channel it, being the green fuse through which that fire is driven? What divine flame can we hold for a moment?

It is there, in works of spirit, imagination and the arts: it is in that authenticity, the burning passion, the smouldering vulnerability where brokenness is a proof of truth. I think everyone feels it when they are in its presence, and I imagine every culture knows it, though few may have named it and perhaps only in Spanish has its meaning been so well explicated. The force that in Spanish is called *duende*.

Singers may have it: shamans can: artists and writers may be touched by it.

The term possibly comes from *Duen de casa*, the lord of the house, but it makes more sense as the spirit of the Earth: a touch of the Daemon, neither devil, nor angel, nor commanding god. It is more like Pan or Dionysus, but it really lives without a name, because its spirit is the essence of fire.

It drives performers or artists of all kinds to a place of electrifying emotion, lightning-struck, damaged, defiant and transcendent. The singer sources her song in some deeper, older fire. She doesn't give a fuck what she looks like: this is not about what is pretty or about style or virtuosity. It isn't polite. It isn't about pleasing but about burning. It is incandescence and a high-wire act, taking risks in poetry, dance, and all the arts that seek their truths in higher skies, living in the moment of the flame.

Flamenco — the flame dance — is of course a prime art form where *duende* may be glimpsed. It looks like a performance of sexual fire in the rhythmic concentration that flamenco shares with sexual ecstasy. As the crescendo comes to climax the dancer almost appears to catch fire. So concentrated are the performers in their intensity that they cannot smile. It is trance, it is longing. The dance is the flame, and the musicians kindle the spark for the dancer who almost shivers in the heat until she catches herself alight. Raise the bar higher: tangent tension. The most accomplished flamenco artists don't care if their contortions make them ugly for the resulting beauty. That they lose themselves, that they are taken over by *el duende*, that art will kill if necessary because art burns.

It is a flame dance and a risk, as every fire is a risk, either that it won't catch (being out of step in flamenco, or having too cool a spirit) or that it will catch too rapidly (performers as arsonists, burning down the house).

Apollo and Dionysus duel. Apollo, all rationality, order, logic, prudence and purity. Dionysus, all wine and dance, irrationality, chaos, emotions and instinct. The *duende* must struggle with death on the one hand and with geometry and measure on the other. The strict rhythms of Apollo are known, but the rapture of Dionysus must take over, letting the wild spirit guide. In Lorca's famous essay *Theory and Play of the Duende*, (from a lecture he gave in 1933,) the *duende* is an earth spirit who helps the artist see the limitations of intelligence. There must be earthiness and an awareness of death. It isn't about disintegration or chaos, but struggle. There is a severity here: this is not a party. This is love and hate, life and death, fire and ice, an extremadura of the emotions. Can you risk the high notes? It is intensity performed. It is gunfire and martyrdom and brinkmanship.

Lorca mentions flamenco artists, singers, bullfighters, guitarists and other performers as having the capacity to channel the *duende*. Amy Winehouse, Leonard Cohen and Nina Simone all had it. The Pogues. Billie Holiday. Keith Jarrett. Allen Ginsberg. The howl in the breath, the catch in the note, the break in the voice, the magnification in the tears. The audience knows it in that place of primal feeling, the body, when words or voice make the hairs stand up on the back of your neck, when, without knowing why, you cry, when the song makes you gasp because the singer has touched the note that makes the moon weep, and you feel all the griefs of your life, and within the artist, the pain and the gift are fighting to the death and you fear for them.

Listening to gypsy music in Quetta in northern Pakistan, Swiss writer Nicolas Bouvier describes their 'equivocal, allusive, tremulous music.' In Tabriz, if a woman sang an Armenian ballad or unearthly Azeri lament, it was, he writes, 'as if the windowpanes had been shattered and everything that was powerful, lost and irreplaceable about Tabriz seemed to burst into the room.'

Lorca refers to the 'dark sounds' that are so characteristic of *duende*: it is a spirit of intensity and passion, not the vaunted and cheap energy of many performers but the almost unendurable authenticity of Enargeia: not emotion recollected in tranquillity but the burning here, now and before our eyes, experience heightened in the dark sounds and against the backdrop of the night the flame grows brighter, the spirit right at the fire's centre, the tongues of flame. Then the moment of incandescence as the blue flame appears — the blue note.

Lorca writes, 'So, then, the *duende* is a force not a labour, a struggle not a thought. I heard an old *maestro* of the guitar say: "The *duende* is not in the throat: the *duende* surges up, inside, from the soles of the feet." Meaning, it's not a question of skill, but of a style that's truly alive: meaning, it's in the veins: meaning, it's of the most ancient culture of immediate creation.'

It is the *cante jondo*, the deep song, the song of the earth, the earth of darkness and eternity, the earth which gave us life and which will hold us again when we are dead. The *duende* gives us a veiled glimpse of something between those two moments, created by the tension between life and death: sheer flame.

Duende, says Lorca, 'won't appear if he can't see the possibility of death, if he doesn't know he can haunt death's house.' By coming so close to death, it throws life into sharper relief, the black grate against which the flame blazes. So the *duende* sings along the veins the suicide poet will slice. It exults in the voice of someone who cannot speak for the agony, and yet can sing for others. The *duende* performs right at the edge of death and life, honouring the sacrifice that the gift demands. Every song has a price and sometimes the price is too high: in the taut and terrible bargain between the gift and the price, the artist may die, and the *duende* hears and attends.

It is the art of the ecstatic, standing outside oneself. Something from beyond possesses the artist, speaks through them. Singers, players or dancers sublimate themselves in the moment, a poignant ecstasy of unrehearsable emotion.

An artist through whom the *duende* lives plays a role which is the inverse of the hero in the Firebird myth. The performer does not, will not, cannot, trap and cage the Firebird but rather lets themself be taken in the talons of the bird, carried away, ecstatic. The performer does not want to possess the magic feather but to be possessed themselves. It isn't about expressing the ego but rather expressing the *duende* by abandoning the ego, about being possessed by the *duende* in mind and body. The opposite of hubris, the artist sacrifices the self on this divine fire, honouring the *duende* whose service is that suffering passion. Not wanting to own the flame but rather to give its flame away as the gift of the spirit, catching from one spirit to another to another, the eternal fire of the gods, lit, for one moment, on the Earth.

It is about authenticity that is utterly natural, to exist as utterly within the heart of the moment as the animals and birds and plants. The nightingale sacrificing its strength for its song; the bat pulsing its sonar presence; the otter giddy with the delight of play right in the moment; the daisy keeping time with the sun; the flash of a kingfisher fishing for fire in lively flame, finding the constituents of the life force, the quick of flame that drives the love of life.

The Grace Notes of Birdsong

I am thirsty for this music. I lean nearer. The tiny twig of a tail juts up — the wren stops. I freeze. He sings again. It is as if my listening is stretching out through my fingers to hear more nearly this mini-Paganini, and of all birds this one sings like the sweetest, highest string of the violin, known as the singing string, the chanterelle. (Its vocal range is one of the highest-pitched of birds, singing up to one full octave above the top note of a piano keyboard.)

My ears, though, are perplexed by him. I cannot hear fast enough to keep up, so the last notes of his cadence fall silent before I have properly heard the first, and by the time I deeply hear his song, he has already finished. If starlight is emitted light years ago, and we may only see it after a star has ceased to shine, so I seem to hear this bird only after it has ceased to sing, its song emitted just sound-seconds ago but always uncatchable.

It is both fleet and fleeting, fast and evanescent. Quick and quickening, it touches the quick of the spirit, in the acuteness of time. It quickens the woodlands with liveliness, as to be quick also means to be alive, as in 'the quick and the dead.' Birdsong is the very quick of music, the poignant nerves of sound germinating its seedling songs in the leaves, inseminating the air. The lack of birdsong unnerves a woodland. Birds embody the very quick of things, vitality or the life force. A world without birds is not only silent, it is dead and deadening. We humans need their singing.

It is dawn in the woods near my home. I come here most days because the birds, chissicking and fluting, enliven me, quicken me. A little riff-raff of sparrows chitter in the hedge. Blue tits and great tits chip in a divertimento in hemidemisemiquavers. he crow's croak cauls around the dark branch. A robin fills its little red jib with wind and sails into the day, all keel, no anchor. (Not solely a metaphor, that: a bird's flight muscles are attached to what is called a keel bone.)

As soon as I hear it, I want to describe it, as if once I have breathed in birdsong, I must transpose it into a human key and breathe it out in language. This imitation seems to be a perennial human desire, from childhood stories with the owl's *to-whit, to-whoo*, or John Clare's transliteration of a nightingale's song, '*Chew-chew chew-chew... jug jug jug*,' as if to set a filigree net of little letters to catch a song without breaking its wings. It is sweetly futile: the ineffable may be indicated but not reproduced, but still we try and birdsong seems to turn us all into diligent but endlessly frustrated secretaries to St Francis, missing his knowledge that the only way to speak with birds is simply to laugh (aloud: silently) and to let the birdsong blow across his strings.

John Bevis's book *Aaaaw to Zzzzd: The Words of Birds*, a compendium of the notation of bird sounds, dedicates itself humorously and eagerly to the acknowledged impossibility of the task, but ever willing to give it a try. *But-but* is a bullfinch, *chack chack* a field fare, *zzzzd* is the lazuli bunting and *aaaa* is a jay, not to be confused (clearly!) with the *aaaaw* of the black skimmer. Mnemonics also mimic the songs, such as the wood pigeon's 'take two cows, Taffy,' or the great tit's 'teacher, teacher!' The yellowhammer's 'a little bit of bread and no cheese' is thought to be the reason why Brexit-wary civil servants called the planning for a worst-case exit from the EU Operation Yellowhammer.

Onomatopoeic naming evokes birdsong on the instant, as the cuckoo calls its name in its two-note pan-pipe, or the owl (*ule* in Old English, *ulula* in Latin) softly cries its way through all the nights of the world: owl, howl and ululation are all thought to be from a Proto-Indo-European root, *u(wa)l*, created in imitation of the owl. The chiffchaff chatters its way to day unless it hears the sinister mew of the kite keening its onomatopoeic name overhead, while the stonechat does what its name tells, making the sound of two stones clacking against each other. The hoarse cries of the crow (*crawe* in Old English) or rook (*hroc* in Old English) or raven (*hræfn* in Old English) speak their own names. Ornithologist-poet

Don McKay captures the latter in metaphor, describing the call of a raven as 'doorbell/crossed with oboe.'

The words peep, pipe and pibroch are onomatopoeic, from Old English *pipian*, to play on a pipe which derives from Latin *pipare* 'to peep, chirp' of imitative origin, because the word itself derives ultimately from the peeps of birds. Sardinian has *pibiare*, retaining a form closer to Latin than Italian does, and Sardinian children, chicks nestled in bed, are told: '*Como muda, mancu unu pibiu*' 'Now be quiet, not even a peep.'

The Indigenous Maya-K'iche' poet from Guatemala, Humberto Ak'abal says, 'to name a bird is to sing with it' because each name for a bird is its song. In his poem 'Songs of Birds' he demonstrates this:

Klis, klis, klis...

Ch'ok, ch'ok, ch'ok...

Tz'unum, tz'unum, tz'unum...

B'uqpurix, b'uqpurix, b'uqpurix...

Wiswil, wiswil, wiswil...

Tulul, tulul, tulul...

Many collective nouns for birds paint a sound picture: a murmuration of starlings; a bellowing of bullfinches (that's not kind, now, is it? nor true); a dole of turtle doves; a clattering of choughs or jackdaws; a gaggle of geese; a storytelling of crows; a tittering or a tidings of magpies; a quarrel of sparrows; a clamour of rooks; a party or a scold of jays. (That's unfair too: they're too much like Sid James to be cross.)

Whether it is whistled, written, copied or played, birdsong seems compulsively mimicable — in visual form too, and there are artists who have tried to draw birdsong, or use computer-generated images to evoke it. Seeing birdsong written on a musical score is like concrete poetry, a graphic score, a fizzy dizzicato pizzicato of acciaccatura — that species of grace notes theoretically timeless.

Every dawn they sing up the sun in a vivace creation. Woodpecker braggadocio on the castanets of a chestnut tree. Four finches fiddling fugues in F sharp for a fiddlehead fern. Urchin sparrows flicking cheeps as a fox trots past on a dawn errand (*get* that pheasant, *get* that pheasant).

If I offered my notation, birds seem to sing the names of composers (particularly Russian) — 'Stra*viii*nski, Stra*viii*nski' or '*Tchai*kovski, *Tchai*kovski, *Tchai*!' Sometimes chirping 'Tippett, Tippett, Tippett' then calling low and sweet, 'Keeats, Keeats, Keeats.' This is my scherzo giocoso, undisprovable glee to my ears, and meanwhile the madrigal widens to a crescendo of coloratura as each bird becomes the maestro of its own cadenza into full morning.

Musicians and composers have an elective affinity with birdsong. Human music has entwined with birds since the earliest records of culture: a flute made of a hollow bird's bone, from a griffon vulture is one of the world's oldest recognisable musical instruments (the other is a flute from the bone of a cave bear.) The cellist Beatrice Harrison famously performed with a nightingale and the duet was broadcast on BBC from 1924 until 1942 when it was interrupted by the drone of aircraft on the Thousand Bomber raid.

Olivier Messiaen's work is famously bird-canted, including the score for *Visions of the Hereafter* which makes the calls explicit: *Il imite Scrub wren... Il imite Magpie... Shrike tit... Rosella... Grey Thrush... Il imite le Kookaburra...* 'In my hours of gloom,' Messiaen wrote, 'when I am suddenly aware of my own futility... what is left for me but to seek out the true, lost face of music somewhere off in the forest, in the fields, in the mountains or on the seashore, among the birds.' Vivaldi composed his flute concerto *Il Gardellino* (The Goldfinch) in 1702. Or so they say. But when you listen to that flute solo you know, of course, the bird composed it first. When Beethoven composed part of his *Pastoral Symphony*, he said, 'The yellowhammers up there, the quails, nightingales and cuckoos around about, composed with me.' Mozart had a pet starling, and when it died, the composer held a full funeral for it, which has a certain sad prolepsis for a genius who would himself have a pauper's funeral. Vaughan Williams's *The Lark Ascending*, that sheer saturation of joy, was inspired by George Meredith's poem of the same name, which was inspired, of course, by the bird itself

— what a trio! Respighi's *Pines of Rome* requires a recording of a nightingale, and Magnus Robb's piece *Sprosser: Hallucinations of Purity* (1998) uses percussion to imitate the rhythms of the thrush nightingale, the *Sprosser*.

'Through all the woods they heard the charming noise
Of chirping birds, and tried to frame their voice
And imitate. Thus birds instructed man,
And taught him songs before his art began.'
Thus Lucretius, poetic and prescient.

Humans have been recording birds since 1889 when an eight-year-old boy, Ludwig Koch, recorded an Indian shama at Frankfurt Zoo, the vibrations of the song cutting grooves into a wax cylinder. But birds have also recorded humans, and did so nearly a century earlier. In 1799, the German naturalist Alexander von Humboldt was seeking the source of the Orinoco River. Along the way, he stayed in a Carib community and acquired a parrot. But the parrot was not speaking in the Carib people's language. It turned out the Carib had massacred a neighbouring tribe, the Maypuré, wiping them out. They had taken the parrots as trophies. No one was left alive, no shred of their existence. All that remained of the Maypuré language were fragments spoken by the birds. Death, it is said, always leaves one singer to tell the tale. Von Humboldt, meanwhile, took notes, and made phonetic transcriptions of the words the birds spoke. Fast-forward two hundred years, and the artist Rachel Berwick was enchanted by this story, and used von Humboldt's notes to teach two Amazon parrots to speak Maypuré: the parrots had vouchsafed the only surviving remnants of a human culture.

There is a case, some linguists say, for arguing that we sang before we spoke, that the emotional content of our language, in pitch, timbre and musicality came before the lexical part. Shigeru Miyagawa, a linguist at M.I.T., suggests that, between 50,000 and 80,000 years ago, humans merged the expressive songs of birds with the information-bearing communications of other primates to create the unique music of human language.

Was it their grace notes that sang at the very source of our language? Is it possible? Is that part of the reason for my keen and keening listening, as if I am not just learning to hear but dimly remembering how we first learnt to speak? As if humanity's compulsive imitation of birds is because, collectively, we are unable to forget that we may have learnt language from the birds?

A world without birdsong strikes us as grievous. We would be bereft in the subsequent *Silent Spring*, as Rachel Carson's 1962 book demonstrated, an early warning call for a more ecocratic philosophy. Perhaps there never was a more poignant sense of collective love for birdsong as in the early days of the Covid pandemic in the spring of 2020, when the birds could be heard without traffic, when the sheer soaring spiritedness of their music was calling a kinder tune. They blessed us. We loved them, openheartedly. Nemesis, in friendship, gave us a calling song, a prompt to act on love. And yet, in this as in so many other ways, we have collectively offended the laws of Nemesis, stolen from the birds their due allotment of habitat, and directly or indirectly slaughtered them. Between 1967 and 2007, the number of nightingales in the UK fell by 91%. According to the RSPB, in 1966 there were forty million more birds in the UK than there are today. 800,000 turtledoves are killed each year in Spain alone.

*

I am drinking the wren's silver laughter, thirsty for its liquid song. I'm not alone: 'One moment just to drink the sound/Her music made,' writes John Clare of the nightingale. George Meredith pictures the skylark's song as a jet of water soaring 'With fountain ardor, fountain play,' this carefree — spilling — overflow as if the bird's song in its pure liquidity dissolves all the dry distinctions of joy and light, the listener and the singer, in an aural alchemy.

I listen soundlessly. I breathe in for this wren but then I am rapt in beauty and each note reminds me of the jewels I had in my hand as a child when I pretended that drops of water were diamonds and I was surrounded by priceless treasure. Our best applause: first silence, then song.

In Western myth, the figure behind every poet and musician is Orpheus, singer in the woodlands, whose music is so sweetly compelling that the trees uproot themselves to come closer to him, the stones hop nearer like birds while the birds become as stones, transfixed. According to Ovid, the shrieking maenads who tore Orpheus apart killed the birds first, and as his spirit vanished down the wind 'the birds, lamenting, cried for you, Orpheus.' As if Ovid heard what so many people do, a melancholy in birdsong, longing for the very soul of music. That poignancy is reflected in a scene in a Haida story, reported by Canadian poet Robert Bringhurst:

> After they'd travelled a ways,
> a wren sang to one side of them.
> They could see that it punctured a blue hole through the heart
> of the one who had passed closest to it, they say.

It seems we humans sing most like birds when we sing most in our Orphic keys of music and poetry, as if to be a poet is to be part bird, and poets have long made the comparison resonant. Shelley's skylark is 'Like a Poet hidden/In the light of thought.'

To me, the skylark high in the sky is the cloudless psyche at noon, and yet it has a tension of pleasure which can feel bittersweet. The speck of a bird, a punctuation of pure joy, pierces the sky and my heart. Birdsong, like poetry, tends towards poignancy, sharp, quick and deep: the beak is a flint which strikes the heart of feeling, so Robert Burns hears in the woodlark 'nocht but love and sorrow join'd.' The nightingale, its nocturne a solo sung in the dark, rhymes with the twilit knowing of poetry's shadow vision and Keats tends the night of both nightingale and poetry. The word 'nightingale' means night singer, for 'gale' is from Old English *galan*, to sing, which also gives us *galdor*: song, spell or enchantment. The song of the nightingale releases the song of the poet. To me, every blackbird is John Donne, singing a tender confluence of beauty without knowing whether he sings for the female or for the divine.

Why do they do it? The obvious answers lie at my feet like litter: courtship, mating, territory. Because they are machines for survival: mechanical embodiments of genetic compulsion. Oh, I know these things are all true, I know it well. I have watched a woodpecker almost sheepish with horniness until, in order to broadcast his message louder, he became a metalpecker, clinging to a telegraph pole, rattling the metal strut with its beak, and I thought he would get a terrible headache as he tried to drum up a mate from thin air: roll up, roll up, can't hold on much longer. *Drrrrrrrrum* úp. (Pause.) *Drrrrrrrrum* úp. (Pause.) *Drrrrrrrrum* úp. (Please?)

But here's the thing. Birds are known to sing beyond what is necessary to find, impress and keep a mate, beyond what is necessary to get and hold their territory. They sing long after the chicks have flown the nest, right into autumn, so late and so well. And this is the gap to watch, the opening which begs that the question is asked again, and willingly: *why*?

The gap between need and achieve that lets the beauty in. The eager profusion, the unmeasured abundance. You can't miss them, the ones which tickle the leaves of the woodlands for joy, tinkling the ivresseries, the ones which can't stop themselves, whose songs run rings of bright sound around themselves like otters chasing their own tails at a noon tide high as — ha! not kites, please god, not if you're a small bird in the woods, a wren hushed in quick quiet. The journal *Science* reports that male zebra finches sing — silently — in their sleep. They dream of singing.

The musician, philosopher and writer David Rothenberg, author of the beautiful book *Why Birds Sing*, argues that as well as the obvious reasons, birds sing for joy. As a musician himself, he feels a camaraderie, an understanding that birds, as much as humans, are musicians and they sing for the sheer pleasure of performance, far over and above their need. 'Music is a songbird's utmost desire, an endless yearning to sing.' Rothenberg plays music with birds, a gift between players, an exchange of beauty.

Gift culture takes many forms and in my garden, it is strawberries. I give the blackbirds strawberries: they give me song. I think this is a good exchange. Joseph Addison gave his blackbirds cherries for the same reason. Hans Christian Andersen explores the nature of gift in *The Nightingale* where the bird works within gift culture, singing free in the woods, responsive to wishes, seeing tears as true treasure. The ethic of the gift is dramatised: it cannot be bought, should not be sold, and must not be caged or held, meanly, in a tight fist. The emperor is sent an artificial nightingale, covered with diamonds, rubies and sapphires and when it was wound up, it would sing. The court decides the birds should sing a competitive duet and, while the real nightingale sang its own song, the artificial bird sang only waltzes. Yes, I thought, reading that: I have never heard a waltzing bird. The real nightingale is scorned, despised and banished, yet only she can save the life of the emperor when he is ill, but only if she is allowed to sing for him as a gift, and only if he conceals the story of her song.

Beauty is in truth, this story says: truth, not artifice. It lies in the true and natural gift, not in pretence or pretension. The recognition of a gift often provokes first pathetic mimicry, then spite and banishment. And what is truly of value? The priceless things: tears, gratitude, freedom, gift.

★

The wren is watching me. I breathe out as quietly as I can. His tiny eyes are a brilliant, liquid black — he blinks. He is the smallest bird I see in these woods, but his song is the loudest and this is why, open-heartedly, simply, gratefully, admiringly, I love him. He dazzles my ears. There is courage here: cocky, proud, brave and beautiful. This is undaunted gift; how much sheer magnificence can you pack into one tiny wren?

Other songs nearby include the nuthatch — *do it, do it* — and the *yip yip yip* of the great spotted woodpecker, with the chiffchaff chafing at the *bit bit bit*. Together, they are getting the dew giggling and creating a pointillist painting in sound. Their calls are so familiar to me in the woodlands where I live that they are my belonging — and it was the wood pigeon which signed the title deeds of my heart's home, as a child. Chaffinches have dialects: the male sings a variation on a shared theme, depending on geography. A Kentish chaffinch is different from a Welsh one, while chaffinch song in Scotland can alter from valley to valley.

There is an interdwelling of birds and time (dawn and dusk) and also of place, for birds co-create the atmosphere of the woods they sing in. A blue tit banks sharply to perch, an arpeggio in motion. A blackbird glides a glissando stream. A buzzard swoops an octave between hillsides. A pied flycatcher hops a staccato twig. To imagine one's landscapes without their soundtrack of birdsong is a bitter desolation, a fearful silent spring in truth. Air without birdsong is like a garden without flowers; nights without dreams; language without metaphor. Our woodlands would be, year-round, 'Bare ruin'd choirs, where late the sweet birds sang,' as Shakespeare wrote.

'If you want a red rose you must build it out of music by moonlight, and stain it with your own heart's blood,' wrote Oscar Wilde in *The Nightingale and the Rose*: the nightingale must sing with its breast against a thorn. This, poets know as well as birds, is the willing though poignant sacrifice. But can you price the sacrifice, or measure this cost?

Could you weigh a nightingale's song? The very question delights me: there is something joyously pure in its superfluity of curiosity; this is science for science's sake. And someone has indeed tried to do so. Robert Thomas of Bristol University measured nightingales before singing, at dusk, and after singing, at dawn. The birds that sang more lost more weight: it costs them dearly to sing.

It is not the weight which fascinates, of course, but the lightness of the birds themselves which is part of their appeal, their almost weightless flight contrasted with our flightless weight: the light lift of a bird, yet full of such weight of emotional message.

Imagine how different it would be if they sang without flight? The flight makes visible the gap of yearning, the leaning longing which humans feel for their song, trying to get ever-closer to the bird as it flies ever further away, trying to hear the song more closely even as it escapes our human ears. The feathers are the nearest tangible thing to their near-immateriality of music, the blue note of the song dropped on the path, and the mind has feathers which, unfurled, can sing our thoughts soaringly. In a beautiful rhyme of pragma and poetry, a bird feather quill is a pen for the plumage of the writer and in myth, the god of writers, Hermes or Mercury, is feather-capped with wings at his heels. Feathers are to the air what individual private thought is to public meaning, and a word is like a secret feather of a hermeneutic language, placed carefully, winged to fly, free.

The word for 'wren' in Welsh is *dryw*, meaning (according to Robert Graves) the soul of the oak and is cognate with 'tree' and 'truth.' Each word is freighted with its meaning and fretted too with its etymology which draws lines, fret-marks scored to the word's biography, as a bird's feathers can have fret-marks, showing for the rest of the bird's life its history of stress or hunger.

I hate the idea that I am making this wren fret. While it sings, I know it is okay, and if it peeps its alarm call, I will step away. Even as I want to be nearer to it, I do not ever want to catch it, hold it or cage its elemental freedom. Injured or caged birds, birds kept indoors, trapped or killed, can disturb me to the point of panic. 'He who binds to himself a joy/Does the winged life destroy,' in Blake's words.

I have, of course, tried to get close to birdsong by listening to it online, to the great perturbation of my cats. (When it is running at actual speed, they go glittery as predators and pounce on my computer; when it is slowed right down so that a nightingale sounds like a humpback whale, they become fear-warped like prey and hide under the bed. Sorry.) When I heard wren-song slowed down nine times, my ear could finally catch up, and weigh the song's beauty recalibrated to human scales. In a glorious duet of bird and human voices, Marcus Coates first recorded birdsong then slowed it down up to sixteen times, and asked different humans to take different bird voices: their singing was then played at bird-speed, so the humans sound like the chirping birds.

The gifts of birdsong are given even in our inattention, and sometimes in the woods I have become aware that I have been lost in myself and have not been listening. Then, letting their windfall song wash over me again, I feel as if they had been pouring out a blessing, playing softly on, pedalling the priceless whether I noticed them or not. And what am I to the wren, after all, whose audience is other?

Birdsong seems inextricably linked to a sense of spirit, of beneficence, of the divine. In traditional Persian culture, all birds sing their own *zikr*, a praise-poem for the world and for god, and the nightingale is especially honoured because his *zikr* never repeats itself, endlessly creating newness. Angels are usually pictured winged like birds, flying to deliver their messages. Birds, meanwhile, have long been thought to be messengers, whether it is the casual remark 'A little bird told me' to augury, or birds in folktales offering wisdom or advice, and the birds' manifold messenger-role in myth. Their very presence in a landscape is a message, speaking of the health or otherwise of the natural world for when a place is empty of birds, it is also empty of insects and flowering life. Birds intensify and quicken the air that is their element.

There is a *leitmotif* of longing when we humans hear birdsong, whether it is science's longing to measure, record and question, art's longing to translate the music, or the human spirit keening for all that quickens the soul. The same tangent of longing is there, yearning for the beyond. Hearing the song without seeing it, seeing the bird without touching it — the quest, not the destination.

The skylark circling higher and higher in the air becomes an invisible source of song — always beyond — and a line of Browning comes to my mind:
'Ah, but a man's reach should exceed his grasp,
Or what's a heaven for?'
What the senses can actually grasp is overtaken by the yearning to reach beyond them. Height beyond sight. Pitch beyond hearing. The song beyond the reasons. Reason not the need, Shakespeare wrote, as if only humans yearned for The Beyond. Birds, we know,

sing beyond needfulness, and to the human mind they are the angels of abundance, creating and reflecting joy.

Birdsong seems to happen on the horizon of the human mind, just beyond the extent of our senses. Immanent but untranslatable — the dash — ! — the glimpse, the hint, the ellipsis. All birdsong is always partially eclipsed to us, as if it is always leaning towards the leading note, the seventh keening for the tonic, as a skylark, self-leading, rises higher and higher, to the high-octane octave — yet — always — leggerissimo — as lightly as possible, where light is both weight and sound, both brightness and joy, and the octave is reached only at a point of silence created by the very quintessence of its own music.

'Till lost on his aërial rings/ In light' writes Meredith.

Till lost in light. The quality of the silence after Mahler's Ninth symphony, the silence into which we pour our hushed applause of the heart. Between sound and silence. Between earth and sky. Between visible and invisible. Between literal and metaphoric. Between seeing and dreaming. Between sight and insight. Shelley and Keats alike write between waking and sleeping, as the skylark flies higher, sings its furthest reach yet, 'Until we hardly see, we feel that it is there,' writes Shelley. I am drawn out of myself into its ecstasy of sound, and I have become the tangent of my yearning. Between all categories, this, before memory and beyond longing, both the nostalgic possibility and the charisma of loss at once, a synaesthesia of the soul.

Coda. A blackbird is serenading the dawn, distilling the day to rhapsody.

Rituals at the Doorway of the Psyche

My father died during lockdown. There was no funeral.

Those nine words are like nine bells tolled.

My father died during lockdown. There was no funeral.

Heavy, iron words.

Nearly ninety, he died during the first spring of the pandemic. Although he did not die of Covid-19, it was the pandemic that choreographed his dying and that denied him a funeral.

He died among strangers. His last few days he lay in a hospice. No one was allowed to visit. No goodbyes. He was cremated by strangers. With no one in attendance, there was no ritual to mark the moment.

If one chapter does not end, the next chapter cannot begin. Without a funeral, he remains, in my mind, in a strange un-place. My father is Schrödinger's dad: he is both dead and not-dead at the same time. He has vanished into thin air.

Usually, with a death, it is as if the air is not thin but thick — heavy, intense, with clouds boiling and raging — and the funeral is the release of a storm. The intoned words, *earth to earth, ashes to ashes*, roll like thunder, words that get heavier over a lifetime with the added weight of every death you have known. Then comes the gash of lightning straight through your heart, that exact electric moment, the lightning strike that connects heaven and earth, the ordinary and the extraordinary, as the body is committed to flames or to the earth. The Thing is Done.

Then it *has* happened. Past tense. The sob. The tears like rain. And, like rain, tears clear the air. The mourners begin to see again. To look, to move, to be jolted out of the funeral and into the wake. Death's darkness is over and life can reawaken. Drink. Eat. Talk.

Having no ritual is eerie. It is a place of hollowness and echoes, a vacant but permanent emptiness, an ever-unfinished symphony, a story with no final chapter, an abeyance that will last forever.

In lockdown, there were a million missing rituals. No funerals. No church rites. All those eighteenth birthdays cancelled. No sweet and daft rituals at the end of a young person's schooldays, no popping the cork and pouring pints for the end of university finals. The wedding bells were silent. People obeyed the rules, even though, as for my mother, it cost them dearly.

It was Easter when my father died. My mother could not be with him in his dying days because of lockdown rules, and she was in agony. But she was from the war generation that believed in acting for the greater good, even if it meant sacrifice to the level of utter heartbreak. So she obeyed the rules strictly, in good faith that so would others. No one, she insisted, should travel anywhere for fear of spreading the virus: including her. And over those very days, as my father lay dying and my mother weeping for the man she loved for sixty years, over those exact days of Easter, one of the men who had put the rules in place set himself above those rules. Dominic Cummings was celebrating the ordinary domestic ritual of his wife's birthday, taking her out to bluebell woods, after he had driven halfway up the country knowing he was carrying the virus. Soon after that, dozens of people including the Prime Minister Boris Johnson gathered for a drinks party at No. 10, Downing Street. They partied away the night before the Duke of Edinburgh's funeral while the Queen wept alone. There is offence that can never be forgiven or forgotten.

I held a miniature funeral for my father, a funeral for one. The time set for his cremation was early morning of an early spring day. It was a moment sweet as a flower, in that the day and the year were both opening their petals to the sun, to all that would come. I went to my favourite stream. There were so many bluebells it was as if the skies had fallen to earth. I picked some, and tucked them into a little terracotta pot. I lit a candle. I — in my own way — prayed. Earth the flowers. Fire the candle. Water the stream. Air the whispered words.

★

When it comes to rituals, it is the smallest that I like the best. And of them all, possibly the loveliest are the tiny, everyday rituals in Bali.

I had been in Bali to speak at the Ubud Writers and Readers Festival, and I was wonderstruck by ubiquity of ritual, so much so that on the pavements it is hard to avoid stepping on offerings, *canang sari*, these beautiful little baskets of flowers in front of shops and restaurants. Ritual vitalises the smallest of places. Any little nook may be sprung with a still-burning joss stick or a staircase lit with the bright beauty of marigolds: everywhere has a quality of having been acknowledged, so it is twicely alive, actually and then symbolically. Ritual quickens the place, the person and the moment.

There, any tiddly doorway may have an offering: a one-pump petrol station, a shrine. At a waterfall, the spray is incense-scented, and a banyan tree is garlanded with flowers. The Balinese year is drunk with feast-days (over sixty in a year), yet every morning women also make up to fifty small offerings. Every house, they say, has a security temple rather than a security guard, and the family temple is always decorated with offerings. Each offering is made of a base of coconut palm containing petals of hibiscus, hydrangea and marigold, a few drops of water from a frangipani flower and a whisper of a prayer. The offerings, *canang sari* (pronounced 'chanang sari'), may carry a little metonymic prayer too: a bus ticket to ask for safety on a journey, some small change representing the hope for a little more money, or a condom, suggesting, I was told, 'more sex: less children.' They are a kind of gossip to god, a hint let slip.

No culture and few individuals live without ritual. In public life, rituals include the inauguration of a president, student graduation, the rituals of temples, mosques and synagogues, Christmas lights or the Easter ritual opening of the doorway of spring. While larger rituals may be vulnerable to commercialisation, tedium or cynicism, they can also shine with what Émile Durkheim called the 'collective effervescence' of ritual and be freighted with significance. In Japan, the ritual of viewing the cherry blossom is famous for its celebration of the transience of life and beauty, because the blossoms teach the importance of the *now* as the way to the sacred.

For Indigenous Australians, ritual is so important that it sings the natural world into continued life, in a diffuse, enchanted and enspirited relationship between the Dreamtime and the present. The Dreamtime past, which created the landscape and order of the world, surrounds the present, giving significance and profundity to life, and reflecting cosmic order. Crucially, rituals are necessary to sustain the Dreamtime in turn: the ordinary present co-creates the extraordinary and numinous Dreamtime order.

In a ritual, dating from at least 1443, Shinto priests in Japan performed the rite of recording the freezing of Lake Suwa. The manner of freezing created ridges of ice and, when the world is viewed with twice-sight and nothing is only what it seems, such ice-ridges were seen as the footsteps of the gods. Since rituals both create and reflect order, the record of freezes suggested an accustomed order and divinity apparent. For 250 years, there were only three years when the lake did not freeze. From 1955 to 2004 there were twelve years without freezing, and from 2005 to 2014 there were five years without freezing. It did not freeze from 2013 until 2018 and now freezes on average just two years every decade.

Small rituals can also enhance social order, vitalising the moment. Ritual is alive in the slightest of phrases, a 'thank you' which increases gratitude; a ghost of a god in 'goodbye' (god be with you), the grace spoken before eating, the little personal talismans touched a certain way for luck. Habits, given half a chance, seem to want to augment themselves into ritual: embellish a habit with attention, stylise it slightly and it will elbow its way into the domain of rites, until even a cup of tea can be accustomed and ceremonious.

In lockdown, while the plague raged across the world, my partner and I split up. The sadness of that together with my father's death hurt my heart, and I found comfort in turning habits into rituals. I needed rites like a set of stepping stones across the tumult of the day: an antidote to crisis. Obviously a schedule is not a ritual but, in those days, the intensity with which I believed in its power was what turned it into a protective rite. I needed the consolation, and I needed the sense of meaning I could attribute to these rites.

My lockdown ritual was an augmentation of the rituals of my writing day. Like many people, rituals garland my mornings more than any other time of day. I like waking up about six. I drink a bucket of lapsang souchong tea with a delight that borders on ceremony. I read. I light a joss stick and do some yoga. I do something with my spirit that other people might call prayers. I go for a run or a bike ride. Then I write.

In the first lockdown, my mornings were as usual except I couldn't write for grief, and the bike ride became a daily ritual of exhausting labour, cycling the huge hills of mid-Wales, its forests and lakes, in that surpassing springtime.

In the afternoons, I went into my garden and dug out weeds. Correction: I dug out just one weed, actually. One weed took me six weeks. This supposed ornamental had gone rogue and overtaken half of my garden. It had climbed through a brick wall, cracking slate, and cemented itself to a wall, three feet down and twenty feet in all directions. I attacked it, weeping, sweating and with my hands bleeding, as if it was pure evil that I had to eradicate. I found out later it was called Devil's Tears. Indeed.

I spent every afternoon gardening until, as the town hall clock struck six, I downed tools and drank a beer with ferocious gratitude for having made it through another day. My days were ordered by these offices of hours.

Tiny, everyday rituals are a hand-crafted prayer to domestic order, beckoning the divine to step inside a moment. In Bali, the *canang sari* are offered individually but its effect is a collective efflorescence. *Canang* means a basket of flowers, while *sari* means essence, and what is essential, I was told, is the purity of right intent, paying heed to the *Bhagavad-Gita* where Krishna describes what god requires of an offering: 'Whosoever offers to me with devotion a leaf, a flower, a fruit, or water, that offering of love, of the pure heart I accept.' As in so many small rituals in so many cultures (including the funeral I held for my father) an elemental grammar of the natural world is used: flowers suggesting earth, candles suggesting fire, a little holy or purifying water, and the air made visible by incense, with the ethereal element of prayer.

Do you pray? It is one of the most intimate of questions. Do I? I do not pray to any off-ground god, but yes I pray and, though I cannot tell you the words I use, I will tell you their core is beauty. Though I use household words, these prayers are the strongest elixir of my language. I put the essence of myself into them but if anyone was looking, they would see no drama, no props, just breath and a certain abstraction from the mundane for a sweet minute.

The rituals of morning seem to ready oneself to steady the day. We have rituals of exercise, yoga, meditation, journalling or dream diaries, rituals of washing and rituals of eating (breakfast is the most habit-bound of meals). Creating internal order before the day unleashes its chaos, through ritual one attempts to decrease one's own missteps, placating chance. In Bali, I spoke to one woman, Kadek, about her experience of making these offerings. Laying the *canang sari* out early, she said, made her feel ready to start her day but by contrast: 'If I don't do *canang sari*, I feel a bit lost and a bit dark. I feel that my step is not firm.' Making the offerings is like building cairns for the mind, walking its path through the day.

Yesterday's wilted flowers and burnt-down joss sticks, yesterday's miniature plates of rice are swept away, then the women dress in their temple-best, doing their hair and make up with great care. When the incense is lit, a woman will take a frangipani flower, dip it in holy water, hold it between index and middle finger, sprinkle the shrine and then tuck the flower behind her ear. 'That way,' a woman in a guest house tells me, 'its scent goes through your words.' I went with her as she put the *canang sari* around the family compound, the guest rooms and her corner shop, placing one on the shrine, another on the crisp shelf and one between the beer and the biscuits, while a tinny radio advert was telling us to buy chocolate coffee and a gecko zipped across the shrine. The shop, perhaps three metres square, was given six offerings.

The *canang saris* last just one day, tracing the ephemeral as a breath clouds a mirror for a moment and is gone. The joss stick smoke in the breeze enacts the memory of a prayer prayed a minute before you came while a wish tucked into a petal still swings in the air. In their slight grace, momentary and unsigned, they are the absolute opposite of the vast and vatic arrogance of an Ozymandias. The *canang saris* should include something edible for stray dogs and monkeys, sparrows, ants and butterflies, and one ex-street dog I met had survived solely thanks to the morsels scattered so widely on the pavements. At the edge of survival, the edge of the gutter and the edge of importance, the offerings are as unmonumental as the sparrow that feeds off them: precisely because they are not precious, I prize them.

It is often the smallest of prayers that move me more than those intoned by priests or cathedralised in stone. When, in 2013, I walked the Camino de Santiago across northern Spain, I came upon a ruined stone hermitage that was completely empty of any kind of furnishings but full of prayers — hundreds of them — written on scraps of paper, on the backs of biscuit wrappers, paper bags, rizlas, handwritten, fluttery, forlorn and imploring. In Aberdaron at the end of the Llŷn Peninsula in Wales, in the church where the poet R.S. Thomas used to be vicar, prayers are written on pebbles from the shore. The intimate prayers, sequestered in the secrecy of the heart, have an intensity that evaporates in larger ritual oration. 'Pray to your Father who is in secret,' says St Matthew's Gospel, 'And your father who sees in secret will reward you in secret.'

Rituals are the doorways of the psyche, between the sacred and the profane, between purity and dirt, between beauty and ugliness; and a ritual is an opening out of the ordinary into the extraordinary. *Canang saris* are routinely placed at doorways, in an unobtrusive hospitality to those who enter, blessing the spirit via the doorway of the senses. The front door is the most ritual-surrounded aspect of all domestic architecture, from horseshoes, Christmas wreaths, the Jewish *mezuzah*, or the traditional strings of chillies and limes at Indian doorways. Even the aesthetics of doorway decoration work as unconscious ritual, whether it is a Welcome mat, a pot of geraniums or lion gateposts. Doorway rituals separate the intimate from the public, the hearth from the outdoors and the clean interior from the dirt of the street but also the doorway is the place of arrivals and departures, beginnings and endings, place of most chance, good or bad. As with most rituals, the *canang saris* are offered at the doorway of the day: morning.

In a culture of ubiquitous ritual, rice, that most ubiquitous of food, is attended by rites in Bali, and every rice field has a sequestered place for rituals. Rice production demands exact irrigation and the paddy fields are strictly regulated to distribute water fairly according to social justice and as needed by the plants. The water is metered by rite. 'Ritual' and 'rite' are from *ritus* in Latin, meaning the correct way of doing something, while the related Sanskrit term *rtá* means regular order or indeed meter. Ah Lovely Rita, meter maid.

Nemesis, wise friend, is here. Ruling always for fairness, and just regulation, she pours what is due, consorting well with ritual.

And here's the thing: rituals work. Rituals alleviate grief, reduce anxiety and increase confidence, and they seem to work even for people who say they do not believe in them. Rituals also aid self-control, as *Scientific American* reports on experiments using ritual to regulate over-eating patterns. Unmetered unregulated behaviours can be metered by lovely *rtá*.

Some rituals can have a profound and negative aspect. In times of epidemic, for example, there have long been rituals of scapegoating so in Ancient Greece, beggars, criminals and the disabled were used as scapegoats in rituals of purification, and were attacked, ritually stoned and driven out of society. They were called the *pharmakoi*, a word related to both remedy and poison. Healthcare workers in the Ebola epidemic in West Africa in 2014 were often assaulted for their work attempting to safely remove corpses. During the Covid-19 pandemic, there were numerous accounts from Argentina to Australia to the UK, of health workers and pharmacists being attacked for their perceived complicity: their work to bring care and remedy was mistranslated into being bearers of contagion, poison and death.

In the Dominant Culture, ritual is often a stale, wilted word, as dusty and songless as Christmas decorations in midsummer. Many people profess no clear religion and lack formal rites and yet, even in the midst of such ritual-poverty, a yearning persists to rekindle it from a stub of a candle, a petal and a word. There is a perceptible need for that numinous Other Place, where no one is exiled and none ever a foreigner. The passport to the numinous is ritual. We need it because we need to give our wishes wings, even in the prayerless times. And there is today a defiant fecundity in contemporary ways of answering that need.

In Bali, at the Temple of the East where people greet the sunrise, a woman sprinkled me with holy water and then did her make-up: *surya namaskar,* then mascara. But beauty rituals are not as skin-deep as they may appear. Animal behaviourists view grooming as the earliest of all human rituals, and suggest that much of human culture may be rooted in early animal ritualisation: courtship, mating, play, dance, art and education. There are numinous themes in grooming rituals, according to human behavioural scientists, including the belief in a 'before and after' transformation, the healing qualities associated with grooming routines, the cleansing and purifying taking place in sequestered, restorative places of contemplation. Beauty rituals may thus be primal rather than superficial and perhaps not something to be despised, especially when people know no other rites. 'The meaning of ritual is lofty indeed. He who tries to enter with the violent and arrogant ways of those who despise common customs and consider themselves to be above other men will meet his downfall there,' said the Confucian philosopher Xunzi.

The offerings are about making beauty, one Balinese woman emphasised to me. *Making* beauty, not possessing it, and the poiesis of beauty is the kind of making associated with art or poetry. Meanwhile the effect of making beauty, a Balinese taxi driver said to me, is that 'your mind is surprised and happy. Beauty makes you feel pure, and purity is necessary for prayer.' In lockdown, I was struck by how much people missed the hairdresser, priest and florist or garden centres. They are all purveyors of ritual things: beauty, flowers and the gods.

Flowers attend rituals all over the world: flowers for birth and death — those doorways of life — flowers for social doorways, for guests and hosts, flowers to honour and to thank with the lightest touch — a petalweight of unimpeachable beauty. You don't have to believe in god to believe in the divinity of flowers and their efficacy. You can scorn the angels, refuse prayer and disprove to your own satisfaction the very worth of credence but it makes no difference to the radiance of flowers and their beneficence.

Lovely *rtá* is never so needed as now. Through the unregulated, unjust and unmetered use of resources we have collectively created a cosmic disorder and perhaps the loss of ritual thinking is part of the reason. Some argue that the loss of effective ritual leads to destructive behaviours, while anthropologist Roy Rappaport called for a collective responsibility to ecological order, and for that vision to be vitalised by ritualisation. Confucius considered that ritual propriety guides humanity into authentic goodness (*ren*): 'If for a single day one were able to return to the observance of ritual propriety, the whole empire would defer to *ren.*'

The sweet paradox of small rituals is that the sacred is reached through the commonplace. The ordinary is quickened and intensified into numinousness. It is an illustration of immanent divinity, demonstrating that all it takes to find enchantment is a tender attention: the living world is blessed by the psyche which blesses nature in return. Ritual sculpts, shapes and polishes the spirit and the heart is made more tender by the delicate touch of something little more than a thank-you. So the slightest of rituals which turns on a breath could open doorways onto a future, the footsteps of the gods crossing lakes of the human mind, and life might be protected by a petal and the holiness of prayers.

Things at their dawnings and dyings seem to ask for ritual: births and deaths, a girl's first period, a first kiss, a first solo journey. Both marriage and divorce ceremonies may be individually designed: today, rituals are composed for grief at the destruction of the Amazon.

The doorway signals closing as well as opening. My father's last words were threshold words of sweet simplicity: '*I'm going now.*' We notice things more when they are ending. Frame anything with death or departure and it will focus our attention. All the last things are etched more keenly: a last look, last book, last kiss, last work, the last notes of music, that threshold moment of disappearance, a swansong.

The Language of Flowers

I have an annual ritual, every spring, when I put out the pots of geraniums that have been sheltering indoors all winter. I like to choose a day in spring where there is the first promise of warmth and I like to do it when dawn is offering its first promise of day. Flowers are an almanac of themselves, and I want my timing to coincide with theirs. So from spring onwards, my front door is garlanded with geraniums, always deep red, against a black wall. This annual habit is steeped in gratitude because from then on, these geraniums speak a welcome to me whenever I come home.

Flowers are companions for us. They can be company in a lonely present, witness to memory and a promise for the future. They are characters: the geranium is warm-hearted and friendly; the chalk pale snowdrop is courageous; the daffodil is irrepressibly sunny; the fuchsia is a flamenco-dancer and the nasturtium is loyal as a dog.

Flowers mesmerise the senses. Their translucent colours seduce sight, their velvet petals petition our sense of touch, their presence in food is an especial grace to taste and their scents beguile that most elusive of senses: smell. For hearing, meanwhile, bluebells, canterbury bells and gentle harebells work a synaesthetic enchantment as their shape rings out. 'The temple bell stops but I still hear the sound coming out of the flowers,' wrote Bashō.

Flowering plants are quite literally a source of life: as botanist Walter Judd at the University of Florida (a university named after flowers) says. 'If it weren't for flowering plants, we humans wouldn't be here.' They are necessary, but they also illustrate the margins of grace beyond necessity — a rhapsody of colour where life sings: such is the veridical beauty of flowers. In terms of evolutionary aesthetics, the beauty of flowers is primal — they have sung a soft serenade for 130 million years and their beauty was there before we humans were there to see it. And perhaps after.

People want to give and receive flowers, to paint them, photograph them, grow them and arrange them. We play with buttercups and dandelion clocks from childhood; we cultivate them, gaze at them, write about them and send them as messengers. But why?

Flowers are healing, as gardeners in physic gardens and monastery gardens knew and as research demonstrates today: patients in hospital rooms with flowers need less pain medication, are less anxious and have lower blood pressure and pulse rates than patients in rooms without. The melancholy thistle just for one, was so-called because historically it was used to treat melancholia or depression. Florence Nightingale, whose very name is healing, with flowers in 'Florence' and birdsong in 'Nightingale,' wrote in 1859 how bright flowers aid patients' recovery: 'I remember (in my own case) a nosegay of wild flowers being sent me, and from that moment recovery becoming more rapid.' In *Losing Eden*, Lucy Jones describes how during the First World War, 'men grew flowers in the thick, damp soil on the front line or in makeshift pots made out of spent German howitzer shells. Forget-me-nots, cornflowers, Sweet William, poppies, primroses and other wild flowers were planted from seeds collected in French villages or sent over by relatives.'

A study by the University of North Florida found that being given flowers was a powerful way to lower stress levels, particularly for women, to the extent that the study's author, Dr Erin Largo-Wight, concluded flowers represented a public health solution to stress. Meanwhile, in research at the Mizuho Information & Research Institute, Inc., in the Tokyo metropolitan area, 31 male office workers were studied and 'exposed to 30 unscented pink roses (Rosa, Dekora) arranged in a cylindrical glass vase for 4 minutes... Data support the presence of physiological and psychological relaxing effects of being exposed to flowers on office workers.' All the more poignant a result for the unflowery language in which it is delivered.

Flowers, simply, make us happy. 'The earth laughs in flowers,' said Ralph Waldo Emerson. Studies in evolutionary psychology show that giving flowers to women elicits the Duchenne smile, the true smile, not the merely well-mannered smile, and that women who were given flowers reported more positive mood three days later. Further, gifts of flowers also improved episodic memory for older people. Research from the Netherlands shows that restaurant diners with fresh flowers on their tables seemed to be in better moods. During the isolation-times of the Covid-19 pandemic, my elderly neighbours made muffins and passed them to me through their kitchen window, which looks out onto my lawn and I gave them a little bouquet of flowers from my garden in return, a gift for a gift, because we need both food and beauty.

'When you have only two pennies left in the world, buy a loaf of bread with one, and a lily with the other,' according to a Chinese proverb. We humans depend for our very lives on food from flowering plants but it is an emotional as well as physical need. 'Just living is not enough... one must have sunshine, freedom, and a little flower' — Hans Christian Andersen.

In writing of the Japanese Way of Flowers, *Ikebana*, Robert E. Carter describes how flowers, used ritually, can 'electrify the entire room, just as a single individual entering a room can make his or her presence felt intensely without uttering a word. What presents itself is charisma, *ki* energy, radical authenticity, compassionate goodness, and they are uncontrollably contagious.' In *Zen in the Art of Flower Arrangement* Gustie Herrigel writes, 'it is as though people could not behave meanly in the presence of flowers, and as though their nature were refined by having to do with them.'

As bees are for flower's pollen so are we for their beauty. Some evolutionary psychologists argue that cultivated flowers have evolved to induce positive emotion in humans so that we will assist their propagation in seed or tuber dispersal and in protecting the plant from predators or dangerous environments. We protect what we love. As author Michael Pollan comments, floral attraction may be an evolutionary strategy for our 'pleasure, memory and maybe even transcendence.' A wildflower meadow, full of buttercups, eyebright, red clover and wood crane's-bill is a paradise on earth, comments Hugo Rittson-Thomas, who has photographed many.

To illustrate transcendence, the Buddha gave a flower sermon in which he spoke no words, but simply and silently held up a flower. The flower was the teacher: so beautiful, so entirely present, a perfect example of the enchanted moment which is a gateway to the eternal. A flower is a way to truth, a manifestation of the divine.

★

Wood sorrel which blooms at Eastertide is called Hallelujah in much of Europe, for the radiance of its flowers and its leaves that lift a praise to the skies. Like beloved friends, we give flowers eloquent nicknames. Honesty is so-named for the transparency of its seed pods. Biting stonecrop, which grows on house roofs and walls, is also called 'welcome-home-husband-though-never-so-drunk.' The chutzpah of Antirrhinum is captured in its common name, snapdragon. The bright blue speedwell is truly a walker's companion. Like many people I have always found it easier to learn flower names from a person than from a book, but it was a book that properly introduced me to the daisy, 'the poet's darling' according to Wordsworth. 'Daisy' is from 'day's eye,' reflecting the eye of the day, the sun itself, its gold centre and rays of petals, and also the eye that opens at dawn and closes with the dark. Chaucer's narrator, in his *Legend of Good Women*, deliberately sleeps out on the grass on May Day morning so that he can be there to see the daisy opening at dawn.

Of all flower names, my favourite is one known across many languages. *Ne m'oubliez pas* in French, *nontiscordardimé* in Italian, *nomeolvides* in Spanish, and similarly in Dutch, Norwegian, Greek and Swedish. What is its story? In a German folk tale, a knight picked a bunch of small blue flowers for his love as they were walking beside a river. But he slipped and fell into the water and, drowning, threw the flowers to her, crying *vergisz mein nicht*. So it remained in German as the name of the flower and Coleridge transplanted the name to England: the forget-me-not.

The language of flowers (floriography) assigns specific meanings to certain flowers, far more diversely than a red rose for love. Violets suggest faithfulness; daffodils symbolise domestic happiness; larkspur suggests levity and lightness while gladiolus speaks of strength of character. 'Pansies, that's for thoughts,' says Shakespeare's Ophelia, and they are so-named from the French *pensées*. She speaks in flowers: giving fennel for infidelity, columbine for flattery or insincerity and rue, of course, for rue, regret and sorrow.

Floriography and floral dictionaries flourished in the Victorian era, and people could convey a coded message through the selection of flowers while the recipient could translate the meaning of these talking bouquets.

The Japanese language of flowers is eloquently precise. Amaryllis: shy. Red camellia: dying with grace. The egret orchid: 'my thoughts will follow you into your dreams.' Lotus: 'far from the one he loves.' Cherry blossom represents transience, but the beauty of all flowers is partly because they are ephemeral, and their opening is a sudden glee on one unfolded day. They are profoundly associated with time and timing: Linnaeus created a flower-clock using the different times that flowers opened, so goat's beard was at 3am, morning glory at 5am, scarlet pimpernel at 8am and the day-lily at 8 in the evening.

To each its due allotted hours, so Nemesis here, gently noting the flowers as the highest of judges, their beauty as reckoners.

'Th'industrious bee,

Computes its time as well as we.

How could such sweet and wholesome hours

Be reckoned but with herbs and flow'rs!'

In my garden reading Andrew Marvell's lines of poetry, I am flowerswept, drunk as a bee in reverie, deep within the very quick of things. It is now, it is here, in this flower's blossoming and that bee's perfect timing to attend.

Then the facts wrench the time out of joint.

As the National Trust says: 'The seasons are becoming less distinct and more jumbled. Plants don't know what season they are in.' Flowers needs to be timed with the presence of bees, butterflies and other pollinators but as plants are flowering earlier, this timing is broken. In the UK, there is already a greater separation between the moment of fullest florescence and the timing of butterfly abundance. A further result of climate change is that flowers will lose their scent molecules as a result of increased groundlevel ozone. Around one in five of the world's plant species are threatened with extinction and 97% of UK wildflower meadows have been lost since the Second World War. Nemesis in despair.

The *New Monthly Magazine* in 1847 commented, 'Frankly do I confess that I dislike a wanton floricide. He has robbed the world of a pleasure; he has blotted out a word from God's earth-written poetry.' There is something profoundly shocking about a hatred of flowers: when Chairman Mao denounced gardens and declared that flowers were feudal, something deep in the psyche is offended, yet modernity is committing a crime of floricide beyond anything in history.

What is a flower? Strictly defined, it is the seed-bearing and usually petalled organ of reproduction. Flowers flush and blossom in amorous, generous abundance. They make us gasp with pleasure, all of Namaqualand on our lips and in our eyes. In a flower bed, a proud tip of stamen pokes up and all around, half-laughing, half-longing, the flowers turn like lovers towards the sun, stretching, curling and entwining, in drifts and sprays. It is silk, it is dew, it is the lightest touch of a breath across lips that know where pleasure lies.

Artists have long been enraptured by flowers. Flowers are used aesthetically all over the world in profuse variety, in pleasure gardens, the hanging gardens of Babylon, the Alhambra, gypsy and barge art floral traditions, Frida Kahlo's rampant flower portraits, William Morris's floral designs, the flowers in stained glass (the lily crucifix, for example) and indeed flowers described as glass. The poppy, wrote Ruskin, is 'painted glass; it never glows so brightly as when the sun shines through it.' At Kew, the contemporary artist Rebecca Louise Law created cascades of beauty, hanging hundreds of thousands of flowers in garlands alongside preserved Ancient Egyptian funeral garlands from 1300 BCE.

Flowers are an inherent part of rituals the world over. Pollen found at ancient graves suggest that flowers accompanied Neanderthal burials. Ancient Rome held festivals for the goddess Flora. In Britain, flowers have been used since time immemorial for spring traditions: marsh-marigolds strewn on doorsteps on May eve, and wildflowers such as moondaisies, harebells, boozie ganders, pots-and-pans, clovers, ragged robin and quaking grass for ceremonial garlands. Flowers accompany us at times of high emotion, in birth, illness and death, for weddings, birthdays and anniversaries. 'The Amen of nature is always a flower,' wrote Oliver Wendell Holmes.

And they mean it. A flower cannot lie. It is an ineluctable emissary of beauty, tendrilling itself in arabesques of visual poetry. Flowers are our primal aesthetic and in their symmetry, their radiance, and their almost weightless delicacy they are the incarnation of beauty, effortlessly speaking the language of grace — any old dogrose a benediction — they are a remedy, healing as dreams and yet, miraculously, real.

The Gladness of the Woods

On a spring morning after rain, the smell is electrifying. I feel as if my veins are running with sap, and my brain is turning into chlorophyll: I want to eat this light. The leaves are greener than at any other time of the year, and the soil is aching to be appreciated. Petrichor, the smell after rain, includes geosmin, whose bacterial workings in the soil has a direct effect on the human mind, raising serotonin levels. It makes us well and happy, filled with the gladness of the glades.

In the pandemic, the natural world seemed to speak with an ever more necessary voice. People were newly enraptured by birdsong, counted the lockdown weeks by the flowers coming into season, and craved time in woodlands. The news was full of headlines about timeless healing in the living world, anciently-known, newly-reported. Smelling cedar wood relaxes people. After 'awe walks' in nature, people find not only that their spirits are lifted, but that they respond more ethically, kindly and generously afterwards. The Japanese art of forest bathing (*shinrin-yoku*) was given attention: it was reported that even thirty minutes spent in woodlands could boost the immune system for up to a month, while a deep bathe of two hours is recommended, engaging the five senses, tasting a leaf, listening to a bird, touching the petal of a flower, or the prickle of holly, smelling the peaty air, and deeply seeing the outline of a tree. So important is it that doctors in Japan will prescribe 'forest medicine.'

It was as if humans, locked indoors away from nature, were experiencing a fresh love for something previously taken for granted. More poignantly, given the condition of the living world, it was as if humanity were realising at the eleventh hour how precious that world is, how real, how utterly necessary. Perhaps we collectively are seeing with a kind of eleventh sight at that eleventh hour, tipping into the too-late. Perhaps in a mythic sense this is part of the kindness of the workings of Nemesis, giving us a last chance to understand our role, and appealing not only to a sense of fear but to our sense of happiness.

If you bend a willow branch back and let it go, it will twang back. So it is for characters entering Shakespeare's Forest of Arden, in *As You Like It*. Rosalind, in particular, finds a release of sheer exuberance in the forest: she is made of rubber — as a boy, she is buoyant and boisterous, made to bounce, cocky as a sapling sprung in green.

If ever the gladness of the greenwood was written out for us, it is in this portrait of a forest. It suggests the workings of natural law (as opposed to the merely human law of the city), it offers healing and goodness, the trees themselves doctors of souls. Nemesis is here, with her sense of due and proportion. No one lives in excess in the forest, and the *here* is enough for all. Enough food, enough love, enough happiness, enough wellness. This, too, is Nemesis as friend, showing us the gentle obligations of both giving our due and getting our allotment.

The court speaks the language of intimidation and imperative, its trappings are constrictive, inhibiting and cruel. The forest speaks of freedom and the characters move from inhibition to exhibition, from restriction to a gentle wildness as the forest ripples its open-heartedness ever outward.

Away from the threatening court, the forest quickens and energises the characters with explosive dynamism, at once tough and tender. Arden is a place of encounters and chance meetings: serendipity may (almost) be expected because there is constant movement in the forest like wind blowing through innumerable leaves.

Arden intensifies the life force which cannot help but grow towards the sun, a force radiating out from a centre which is everywhere: the naughty, dirty, chthonic earth chuckling with rude life. Something scintillates — sensually — somewhere within people, and the forest represents the convivial glow at the heart of it all: Arden is ardent and asks human nature to align itself with forest nature, for this play is not an idealised pastoral but an idealised portrait of the human heart — open, ancient, friendly and deeply gentle. Edmund Spenser called Shakespeare 'that gentle Spirit' and gentle, at that time, had a chivalrous overtone: courteous but not courtly. Ben Jonson described Shakespeare as 'honest, and of an open and free nature.' Like the Forest of Arden.

In a paradox of belonging, the characters are banished from unnatural cruelty to come home to a natural kindness, to a sense of true humanity, a shelter offered even to the grumpy Touchstone and the restless Jaques, a temporary but trustworthy refuge in the natural world. Despite the pretence that culture is antagonistic to nature, it never really has been. Take the Forest of Arden out of Shakespeare, shake the linnet from the leaf, snatch the moon from Neruda, silence the Rite of Spring, take, in other words, nature out of culture, and what do you have left? A few shoddy catalogues and a tax return.

There is an ethic of fluent commonality in Arden, where characters cannot help but intertwine, depending on each other in a common good. Yes, there is dispute and disaffection in Arden, but tougher than that is kindness, not as a milky meekness but kindness as a force of nature so strong it will fight a lioness and win: fierce kindness, ferocious kindness, kindness that re-finds kinship relations with even those — like Oliver — less than kind. Kindness kindles humanity to see itself akin to nature so Rosalind can say she is native to Arden as much as the cony or rabbit, while Jaques empathises with the dying stag, gentling his way into the mind of the animal. Gentleness in Arden has a generous, flexible strength. It overcomes Orlando's aggression at the Duke's feast: gentleness, the forest suggests, is the heartwood at the core of humanity.

People thrive like trees in the forest: with a sense of sheer vivacity, the forest invites verve, encourages élan, the word-play of many characters is a verbal ricochet in a forest which resounds with many voices — including its own. For the forest is an actor in the play, it has a speaking part: there are 'tongues in trees, books in the running brooks, Sermons in stones, and good in everything.' It is a mindful place, a philosophical one, and there is inter-intelligence at play when human thought plays over the forest which speaks itself and tells its stories. It is a playful place, and it invites characters to play — Rosalind playful as a kitten.

If it is a place of sinuous playfulness it also suggests a serious magic. The forest guides, teaches and reveals. It is not a backdrop but an ethical place of transformation with its particular grace of light-hearted gravity. The characters may joke that Jaques is transformed into the stag, but the forest itself transforms Oliver, shocking him into his truer and better self. Duke Frederick is transformed at 'the skirts of this wild wood' where he met 'an old religious man' who deflected him from his plans and converted him to a kinder path.

On the edge of perception, out of the corner of the eye, we see the glowing green core at the heart of it all, and perhaps the key personification of the forest is the one character we do not meet, the mysterious magician 'most profound in his art' with whom Rosalind says that she conversed from when she was a tiny child, the character then reported by Orlando as 'a great magician, Obscured in the circle of this forest' and indeed the power of the forest itself. Shakespeare himself, of course, was the mysterious magician most profound in his art.

A light shines through — a dancing, changing light of morning sunshine through spring leaves, like light through stained glass, radiating on the radiant. Some force like a heartbeat at the core, emanates from the centre of Arden, the quick of things, the core of it and the *cœur* of us all, the heart, reaching ever outward, touching even those previously estranged from the magnetic, ancient heartwood of Arden which is — still — where it always has been: within us all. To grow is to green from within, and Arden's heartwood of love spreads ever outwards inviting not just the characters but the audience to belong, to be a playful part of the ardent forests of the human heart.

★

One day in late spring, when I was out running in the hills, a buzzard flew low overhead as it often does, and settled in the branches of one particular tree, as I had seen it do countless times. That day, though, I looked with more care: it was an ash tree. The tree's branches, upswept at the ends, were a visual rhyme with the flight feathers of the bird. The bird chose its perch well, for it was a lookout point on a hillside over the valley. The buzzard was watching me, hopping around and tilting its head down under the branch to keep an eye on me. And I, in turn, began to look deeply at the tree.

John Clare writes of the ash's hospitality to humans, describing a hollow ash in which ten people could shelter from the rain, and how an ash was where a gypsy chose to make his bed: a hospitality echoed by Edward Thomas, telling how a grove of ash trees 'welcomed me.'

The ash is the gladness of the woods. Lithe and lovely, pliant in lightness, it is a cascade of grace. Its wood is light in colour, the ash tree giving its name to hue ash blond, and its branches weigh lightly on the air. Its airy, light canopy gives light for woodland flowers to grow: snowdrops, wood anemones, ramsons and bluebells. It seems a tree of hospitality.

Versatile, flexible and fleet, the ash is the last to leaf up, and first to drop its leaves, a quick changer from summer to autumn, swiftly moving the story of the seasons forward as the Trickster does. The ash in autumn has a fling with the wind and ash keys helicopter in the air. It is a tree with wings at its heels.

Ash is the wood of travel. The wheelwright, wainwright, cartwright, wagonwright, ploughwright, harrow-hewer, oar-carver, barrow-bodger, axle-grinder, walking stick-wangler, aircraft-crafter and bus-builder all blessed ash for its strength and flexibility. Lorries, wooden aircraft and timber-framed cars such as the Ford Woody and Morris Traveller all used ash. It is the wood of wheelings and dealings.

Ash is associated with the threshold and was sometimes used in doorways for ritual reasons. Ash is the second most common tree species in the names of the early hundreds or wapentakes and often the ash was a landmark at a crossroads.

The story of Odin — trickster, shapeshifter, warrior and poet — is the most telling legend of the ash. Odin, in the beautiful enigma of myth, sacrificed 'myself to myself' in a nine-day passion, in order to find hidden knowledge. He hung himself on the World Ash, Yggdrasil, in voluntary anguish, to discover the secret of the runes by drinking mead from the well where the ash was rooted. 'From a word to a word I was led to a word,' says *The Poetic Edda*. To gain his insight, Odin sacrificed the sight of one eye. One-eyed but twice-sighted: it exemplifies the relation of sight and insight, of beholding and seeing.

Yggdrasil had three roots: the one in water, the second in air and the third in the otherworld. Its roots were watered by three fates: past, present and future. In its branches lived four deer and as I write this, with an ash twig in my left hand, I am struck by how the buds of its twigs are like tiny, delicate, velvet deer-hooves. The tree is the Axis Mundi, the spine of the world, for it extends from roots in the underworld to its branches in the heavens, a linking thing, a conduit between worlds, between times, between minds. The ash was used both as literal transport and symbolic communication.

In Norse myth, the gods held council under the canopy of the ash: a squirrel ran up and down the tree, carrying messages. Associated with both the secret and the spoken, the lost and found, the hidden and revealed, ash is a messenger tree, and its resin (or mead or ambrosia, or Odin's wine) was said to facilitate communication between gods and humans.

Odin is a wild god. God of war and wisdom, shamanism and poetry, his name comes from the word *wōd*. *Wōd* is a word and a half, a word on fire. It means frenzy, and the furore of poetry or the fury of war. Odin, inspired poet and fierce warrior, who carried a spear of ash, personifies the word. The first spark is *wet* in Proto-Indo-European, which means to 'inspire, spiritually arouse.' It took flame, running through Latin (*vates*) meaning a 'seer or poet' and then in Old English it crackled into 'melody' and 'song.' It set alight a series of need-fires in the human mind, connecting ideas of frantic, mad, furious, with words for mind and soul, and also words for music and song and the singer.

In John Evelyn's seventeenth-century book on British trees, *Sylva*, he comments that the ash tree 'serves the Scholar, who made use of the inner Bark to write on, before the invention of paper.' Literacy is power. The Old English *rūn* means mystery or secrecy, connecting script with magic. In an interplay of sight and insight, the visible knowledge of a character carved in bark yielded invisible wisdom beyond the literal and obvious: the insight of symbol and metaphor. 'Grammar' originally meant 'learning, incantation and spells,' before it thinned into the diluted meaning left today.

An old ash tree on Torberry Hill in Hampshire is known as a trysting tree, and I once saw an ash betrothed to an oak, on the path to Aber Falls above Abergwyngregyn between Bangor and Conwy. The roots of the ash embrace the trunk of the oak and the branches of the oak hug the ash back, leaning on each other in inseparable tryst.

Mythologist Mircea Eliade comments that the ash was 'symbol of life, of inexhaustible fertility, of absolute reality.' David Nash, whose own name is ash-rooted, from Middle English *atten ash*, meaning 'at an ash,' created his Ash Dome of twenty-two ash saplings in 1977, a living sculpture, now dying. When he began the project, he expected it to outlive him. To endure is a property of trees, both actually and linguistically. Envisioned to be true to the material and true to the roots of both word and wood, now, as a result of ash dieback, it is a ruined rhyme.

Tree pests and diseases are spread around the world by mass commercial transactions in the live plant trade, introducing disease to trees which have no previous experience of them, and therefore no resistance. Privileging profit over plant health in countless collective choices means sacrificing the natural world for the short-term artifice of commerce. In almost-silenced reproach to the mechanical and irreal malice of the profit motive, the absolute reality of tree and truth stand rooted in something deeper; the felt world, feelingful, sensed, sensing and sensitive. The writer Mike Parker tells me of the Welsh idiom *dod yn ôl at fy nghoed* — literally

I 'return to my trees' or figuratively 'come to my senses,' or 'fall into balance.' To stand under that absolute truth of trees.

A particular ash tree was the site of Wordsworth's 'tranquil visions' of 'bright appearances' which he described in *The Prelude*. It is thought that he referred to this exact same tree in his *Ode: Intimations of Immortality*, writing 'But there's a Tree, of many, one' which speaks 'of something that is gone' asking, 'Where is it now, the glory and the dream?' It spoke of endings and he listened. He both saw and beheld with the double-vision which William Blake possessed, both the outward eye and the inward eye with which he beheld the inner life of nature.

Many cultures have a version of the Tree of Knowledge but scientists today are discovering that trees have memory and, effectively, mind. Their roots are aware of stimuli and can send electrical signals that alter the behaviour of the root tip. Trees communicate with others, giving off warning gases to neighbouring trees when there are foragers about. Tree roots emit ultrasonic crackling and other seedlings' roots turn their tips towards these messages. Thirsty, they cry at ultrasonic frequencies. Trees care for injured companion trees, giving them sugars in a kind of tree hospitality.

The ash was John Constable's favourite tree, and he loved one in particular. When it died, he noticed it with especial care and grieved its death. A parish notice forbidding 'all vagrants and beggars' had been nailed to its trunk and almost immediately it began to wither and within a year had to be cut down to a stump. 'The tree seemed to have felt the disgrace,' said the painter. For a tree of surpassing grace, noted by poets for its hospitality, the graceless inhospitality of that parish notice cut to the quick and, said Constable, 'she died of a broken heart.'

When things are dying, or failing, we humans seem to notice them more. I have never noticed familiar things with such newness of sight as when the coronavirus outbreak began, and everything looked vulnerable. I didn't know when I was going to see my friends and family again. Or if. The last concert. The last visit. The last apple in the shop. And at the same time the sense of kindness overwhelmed me, kindness as if the Forest of Arden was greening us all, a force of human nature which silenced the stupid, fantastical world of money and profit. We became trees, in the sweet grass-roots world of neighbour to neighbour, people doing shopping for the ill and the elderly, like tree roots from healthy trees offering sugars through their roots to injured and sick trees.

'The eye should learn to listen before it looks,' said the photographer Robert Frank, and with poignant timing a recording of an ash tree's interior song has been made, just as its death is foretold. In a piece entitled *Heartwood*, Adrian Newton made the first-ever recording of interior sounds generated by an individual tree, and ultrasound detectors were used to make its voice audible. It crackles, and then echoes, it snaps and creaks, a gyre of knocking, then a wash of waves, the sound of water rushing over pebbles, then that of a violin bow played across a branch; it is intensely moving to hear the voice of this tree.

If you could hear the stretching torsion of thought itself, twisting, questioning, wondering, waiting, cogitating, it would sound (to my ears) just like this. And endings give a different dimension to the quality of our attending: hushed, ultra-aware, listening to its dying cadence, its final, falling song.

Time turns, of course, and this spring will come to fall, as today's dawn will become evening. This is just, it is due. It is the measure of Nemesis. And how would we appreciate summer without winter, or day without night? But it is deeper than this. That time turns — this too will pass — is both a comfort and a caution. Good times will not last, it warns, just as it consoles with the fact that bad times will pass. But the ash tree speaks of something grievous and inconsolable: not that one individual tree may die eventually but that they may die in their millions, unnaturally and unfairly. These trees feel wronged. The poignancy of it is that the goodness of the woods is healing for humans but collectively we have responded with poison. And the ash, the gladness of the woods, becomes instead its sadness.

A Trouserful of Wantonness

It is spring in Wales and it is raining, springing the springs, making the streams overflow. Young rains for a young year, they ripple and spill, chattering in the leaves. It is raining on the hedgerows, raining on the hills, raining on the rivers, raining on the kingfishers, raining on the grave of that most beloved of the old poets, the undying Dafydd ap Gwilym. One morning, daybright, fresh with rain and light, I pack a picnic and leave my house, looking for his home.

He is buried at Ystrad Fflur, the flower-strewn vale which shelters the remains of a Cistercian abbey. Just down the road from Ystrad Fflur, or Strata Florida as it is known in Latin, is Pontrhydfendigaid, a village of pebble-dash council estates, parents in too-thin jackets smoking at the school gates, the Spar-boys kicking a can, the nowhere-else-to-go days and the chips-with-everything TV nights of rural poverty. There is wealth here, too, in the countryside beyond the towns: the undwellings of second homes. And there are memories of other homes: Dafydd wrote of the 'houses of the glade' where he made love in the surrounding woodlands.

Moss on the abbey's stone walls is damp and bright, and the fiddlehead ferns are tuning up for spring. Dafydd's grave — and, yes, all his readers are on first-name terms with him — is marked by an ancient yew. There are in fact two ancient yews in the churchyard and he may be buried under either, but one in particular is where his memory lodges, a focus for his lovers.

Both yews are likely to be some 1,400 years old, predating the abbey itself. Yews can live more than 3,000 years, and are the longest-lived of all native trees. Roman legionaries would have sheltered under them from the Welsh rain of 2,000 years ago. Often found in churchyards, yews are, in many traditions, connected with the journey to the underworld, the soul's passage from one life to another; life always, even in death, a generous and regenerative association.

Yews, they say, are loners amongst trees. I prefer to call them soloists, as Dafydd was, a soloist poet and harpist. Dafydd's fourteenth-century contemporary, the poet Gruffydd Gryg, wrote of 'the voice and that great heart' of Dafydd, whose voice still calls, whose heart seems to speak across the years. I am not alone in being a little under his spell: George Borrow, on his walking tour through Wales, knelt and kissed the root of his tree.

Bounded now by a low wall, there are a couple of simple stones to mark his grave, and his name, roughly etched. I regret not having brought some gift. Others, heart-enchanted by this poet, have left the odd candle. Lying around on bits of broken concrete, five tipped-over jam jars once held flowers. The flowers are gone and muddy rainwater silts the glass. His grave is quick with life, studded with messages and gifts as tribute for the way his words quickened the living world into its second life: words in the human mind. Precisely because it is an untidy grave, it is therefore full of life. The drains on the chapel-of-rest are more tidily kept than Dafydd's grave and I like that: the church can keep its tidiness.

Fire has burnt out the trunk of the yew — lightning, people say, in a storm in 2002 which struck the tree. Possibly it has also caught fire from a candle left burning in a naughty wind. Please, let it not be deliberate. 'No love shall break you, nor fire consume,' writes Gryg, speaking to the tree where Dafydd was buried — but it almost has. Almost but not quite, for while flame has hollowed out the yew, yet, living up to all its associations, the yew is still sprouting, greenly alive, rising again, quickening like the phoenix from the ashes. Revivification.

> ... And the fire that breaks from thee then, a billion
> Times told lovelier, more dangerous. O my chevalier!
> ...and blue-bleak embers, ah my dear,
> Fall, gall themselves, and gash gold-vermilion.'

> G.M. Hopkins, from 'The Windhover'

One arch remains. When the lightning struck this yew, the fire that followed had, with uncanny precision, transformed the tree into the shape of a harp. I crawl through it, beneath its twisting striations of yew-wood like the curls of a treble clef, or the waves of smoke in the wind, to sit right inside, leaning back against the heart of the tree, all charcoal now. With that charcoal, I write in a page of my notebook 'Thank you, Dafydd' and tear out the page and bury it. My gift a note. Someone else's gift is a tiny, bleached bone, almost hidden, wedged between two stones in the wall. Fox shit triangulates the grave, a fox-homage which seems entirely apposite for this wild old fox-poet.

Tucked inside the tree's hollow, the wind hardly reaches me and I'm out of the rain. The yew, wrote Gryg, is 'the house where Dafydd is,' the tree is 'consecrated for his home.' If it is a home for him, it is an hour-shelter for his visitors, a day-dwelling, a hearth. There is a tradition, around here, of the *Tŷ unnos* the 'one-night houses,' which depended on speed, night and friends. If a person could rig up a house overnight, and have a fire lit with smoke billowing from the chimney by dawn, then they were granted squatters' rights to common land, as far as they could throw an axe to the four directions. Dafydd, meanwhile, wrote of the 'house of leaves' he made for his trysts in the woodlands: 'a living-room is better if it grows.'

Like any good hearth, this place offers a long welcome, for it seems to me that Dafydd would have loved people coming to sit by him and have a think. How many come here for a chat with him, I wonder? Or a spliff. Or a kiss. I want to sleep here, my face nudging into his yew-shoulder, as the harp yearns towards Dafydd's chest in the statue of him in Cardiff. Dafydd went on a pilgrimage to the Welsh patron saint of lovers, Dwynwen, and asked her to be messenger between himself and Morfudd, a married woman he was deeply in love with, and the subject of so many of his lyric poems. ('Play me like your harp, Dafydd,' I can imagine Morfudd chuckling, with Chaucerian sauciness.) He courted her and made love with her 'under the greenwood tree,' according to George

Borrow, their handfasting presided over by a bard and friend. It seems fitting for Dafydd who was himself, they say, a love child, 'born under a hedge,' the wilding son. Morfudd, though, was forced to marry another man, and Dafydd tried to take her back but was imprisoned for his audacity.

Just then, a man opens up a side-gate and comes into the churchyard. For a moment, I'm a little anxious that he has seen me and will tell me to get out of the tree. He walks right up to it, then jumps back startled. He hadn't seen me, and I needn't have worried: it is no concern to him. I apologise, though, for shocking him. 'S'arright, s'arright — I never thought to see anyone sat there, s'all,' he says, with a wide smile and waves as he leaves.

In the tawny bracken on the hill, light blurs into almost-sun. If I stayed long enough, everything would happen here: an argument, a shag, a snooze, a joke, a day of sunshine. Leaning forward, I realise that the charcoal has traced its black lettering lines over my coat. I've been written on.

Ystrad Fflur, or Strata Florida, has a long history of writing. It was a home for manuscripts and it hosted resident bards. It had a herb garden outside, a 'wort-yard,' as 'wort' means a 'worthy' plant, thus liverwort or lungwort or St John's wort. As well as the wort-yard outside, it had a word-yard library inside, and the abbey brought out an anthology of poetry. Appropriate for Strata Florida, the flowered vale, the word 'anthology' derives from a 'garland of flowers.' The abbey was noted for its hospitality to poets: dead and living alike. Dafydd, who is both, is the poet most linked with the abbey, with the surrounding hills and the land beyond. He fully lived, bursting at the edges, deepening the meanings of this land in which he was so at home. If ever a poet belonged to one allotted plot of land, it is him, both in life and in death and he could have said with Rosalind that he was native to this place: 'As the cony that you see dwell where she is kindled.' (Rosalind was being deliciously sexual, worthy of Dafydd, in this line, for 'cony' was slang for cunt, and 'kindle,' the art of making fire, has erotic overtones. She dwells where she is pleasured.)

With five toes and the mysterious heel of a goat, Dafydd leaves his footprints all over the literature and the woods of Wales. He is thought to have died of an earlier pandemic, the Black Death, but he is one of those ancient writers who never died: Montaigne, Omar Khayyam, Ovid, Virgil and Dafydd. Lascivious, mischievous and hot-blooded, barging his way across more than six centuries, his glad eye catching a girl's glance in a pub, we hear him shout 'fuck' as he bashes his shin in the dark on his way to her room; hitting his head on a table; knocking over a brass bowl; waking the whole innful of angry men who would suppress his urgings. Irrepressible as the cock of dawn, he writes elsewhere of his fantasy of seducing an abbess, for no other reason than 'because it is May.'

How many men have sung a mock-reproach to their own cock (in English this poem is translated as *The Penis* but surely Dafydd would have talked to it in the vernacular) for the trouble it has caused them? 'You are a trouserful of wantonness... pod of lewdness': lines so vibrant you can still see his rueful smile. 'It is imperative that I become a hermit,' he writes, even as he was rubbing his acorn till it sprouted. Dafydd, generous, genial, he of the jaunty genitals, was the cunning genius of the germinal. When the striking of a wretched clock woke him from an earthy dream, or when a horrible rattlebag of pipes interrupted a shag, we see him bursting with wry frustration all over the page, hundreds of years later. Garrulous, he was, you can tell, as generous in scattering his words as his seed, invoking the saints to help him in his love affairs, conjuring voices of the greenwood in his love for birds and trees.

He was a troubadour, for sure, and a poet who sung himself into his harp, but something more. He sung himself into the land, asking birds, animals and the wind to carry his messages to all his well-beloveds. More yet: the now-printed words echo the print of his body on the land, as he tells of the way that the places where he made love, the crushed leaves and grass, the bed-shapes under the saplings, will remain imprinted on the landscape forever, and on the landscapes of the heart. (He was right, and it is a harpist who confirms it to me.) With a copy of Ovid, the great love poet, in his hand, he says, the trace of his lovemaking 'will for evermore be seen,' in the 'place of trodden leaves, like Adam's path.'

> There is no hillock nor deep hollow
> on either side the valley of Nant-y-Glo
> whose twists and turns my passion does not know

from 'A Lover's Journey' translated by Rachel Bromwich

By a kind of shamanism of the centuries, he seems to have sung himself into the month of May — his cherished month — with its tumescence of buds and its tumult of green, as if each new-fledged dawn chorus gives him a new-fledged chorus of his own. He was a reveller, rooting for life with all his ruddy geniality, gorging himself on it, eating it and so sharing in its vitality. (And so would I, here at his grave.) He boasts gloriously of his sexuality, and it is easy to imagine he littered the land with offspring, saucy Dafydd a source, a wellspring. The spring was his season, his reason and his emblem, green and cocky as the new leaves of May. He was radiant, too, leaving the land of mid-Wales shining with the light of his love for it, so that even now, here in the lovely, low-down, warm and dirty earth, his words gleam. Wood, in Chinese philosophy, combines the elements of earth, air, water and (in the form of sunlight) fire. The element of wood stands for springtime and the colour green, heralding the beginning of life and fecundity. In wood, Dafydd is in his element.

In the green valleys, in the high hills, the ages sleep while the old language turns its phrases to describe the land. Penrhyncoch, a 'ruddy promontory,' is a fitting place for Dafydd to be born. He wrote in Welsh, Britain's oldest language, one entwined with Latin, and the abbey's formal inscription to Dafydd is a quote from Virgil, written in Latin and in Welsh:

> My heaven-born poet! To me, your song is like sleeping
> On the grass when one is tired, or quenching thirst
> From a gentle brook of sparkling water in the heat.

This is old land. In geological terms, some of the oldest rock of Europe is to be found here. The old maps warn you away from

Pumlumon, a wild land where even tomorrow is already old, and in its rain shadow, the rain of ages falls, as it always has, ceaseless, changeless, constant, obscuring the velleities of the hills, their slight inclinations, the gentle rise of the will to higher things. It is a land of old animals, too: the last wolves of Britain were thought to have roamed the Powys hills in the seventeenth century, and badgers, whose very teeth look mediaeval, are the last of Britain's bears. Last and loathed by many, be it said, falsely blamed for carrying disease, and found mysteriously dead along roads and paths.

Spring, though, is when mid-Wales comes roaring to life. Merry with — drunk with — daffodils and their burst of open-hearted sunshine, spring ransacks the land for every bit of glee. In the sky, Dafydd's 'wild untrodden land,' skylarks sound the measure of blueness: the bluer the sky, the more they sing. In the woodlands in May, the hedge-music of the finches, sparrows and blackbirds is a realm of its own. It is like listening to Allegri's *Miserere*, before any score of it circulated, when publishing it was banned, when it was only played in spring, in Easter week, in the Sistine Chapel, in the days before fourteen-year-old Mozart's audacious genius wrote out the whole score after just two hearings.

If you sleep out in the woods in spring, the dawn birdsong wakes you, song made sunlight, sunrise made audible. In the dawn chorus, it is hard to know exactly which bird is singing exactly which song: the dawn breeze seems to shake the song from the bird, and the woodland is like an aeolian harp, apparently played by no one except the wind blowing across the strings of the world. 'And what if all of animated nature/Be but organic Harps diversly fram'd' suggested Coleridge, while Shelley, invoking the wind, asked it to 'make me thy lyre, even as the forest is.'

Harp music was the 'craft of the string,' in Dafydd's time, and those strings are unbroken, for the harp has had an uninterrupted history in Wales. Memory, history, the past and the harp seem like ideas strung together in the human mind. Orpheus, the god of music and poetry, played the harp, enchanting humans, animals and gods alike, and with his lyre evoked memory from the underworld past.

When Shakespeare's evil Richard III tells Elizabeth to be silent about his murder of her children, his phrase is, 'Harp not on that string, madam, that is past.' She responds: 'Harp on it still shall I till heart-strings break.' For there was, in Shakespeare's time, an idea of the correspondence between the heart's strings of emotion and the actual harp's strings. The strings are metaphoric paths of memory, but harp songs themselves have literally been passed down over the generations, the unbroken strings of time, with harpists memorising music before any notation was used, and it is still a current practice.

The harpist Harriet Earis, who lives near Dafydd now, holds history in her hands with the music in her fingers learnt from this oral — and aural — tradition. All the past is not only within the harpist but also the harp, for her harp has a small piece of yew embedded in the frame. It is from that yew tree where Dafydd, the Welsh Orpheus, is buried. Given that molecules of a man will gently snuggle down into the earth, and swim with rainwater when a thirsty tree draws them, then she is, in some infinitesimal but quintessential way, making music which resounds with him: an Orphic resonance, if you'll excuse the pun. (She tells me about going running in the hills of Nant-y-Glo, following his call, and I know he has enchanted us both.)

Dafydd was master of the Welsh poetic form, *cynghanedd* or 'word-harmony,' fluent with its alliteration, assonance and half-rhyme. It is a mesmerising, enchanting and entrancing form, one in which Gerard Manley Hopkins was also fluent, and influenced by. 'As a skate's heel sweeps smooth on a bow-bend,' he wrote in poetry which was partly inspired by Wales: by the Welsh language which he had learned, and by the landscape landscape of mid-Wales close to where I live now, and where he made his home in 1877. That was his year of miracles, when he wrote most of his best poetry.

The oral transmission of songs, music and poetry is an unbroken path, a kind of songline over time which is known to musicians. The songlines were made famous by Bruce Chatwin, writing of Indigenous Australians, but there are aspects of songlines all over the world, a music of the land, passed from singer to singer, held in mind by memory.

I was once told that the Gaelic word *fonn* means 'song' and 'state of mind' and 'land,' suggesting the idea of a songline, a song of land, held in mind. Here, the land near Pontrhydfendigaid is criss-crossed with lines and paths and ancient tracks. The three-day pilgrim route, called the Monks' Trod, from Abbey Cwm Hir to Strata Florida, which I walked some years ago, has been sung with feet and with music for hundreds of years. Few people walk these footpaths now, although the aggressive *Trespassers Will* and *Private Keep Out* signs, so common just across the border, are not much in evidence here. It is more likely that you'd see a wonky-lettered plea: 'EweS in Lamb Dogs on Lead Please' but the council's rights of way department will tell you that the footpaths which are blocked most vehemently are those which cross the land of second-home owners.

Fields of thistles speak of a farmer in trouble: the 'tallest thistle competition' at a village fête suggests the sometimes-desperate attempt to snatch the flower of fun from the thorns of despair. The scruffy outbuildings of the smallholdings are ramshackle and untidily alive. Brambles nibble at rusty prams, while a yellow toy tractor is a saucer for rain. Dumpy-bags of cement rubble mooch by mossy feedbags. Cartridge caps punctuate the mud: an old kite is tangled around empty oil drums and blue plastic piping coils around a rusting car door, while a one-legged wheelbarrow whiles away its retirement as a nest for a puppy.

★

Dafydd's grave nestles between the Glasffrwd brook and the Teifi river, famous for its salmon. On a windless day, you can hear the Teifi chirruping on the edge of the graveyard. A wellspring, the 'well of the silent grove' (*Ffynnon dyffryn tawel*) a mile from the abbey was possibly honoured long before the new religion of Christianity, as many water-sources were, suggesting the revivifying waters of life springing from the underground past. The land of mid-Wales has liquid songlines in its rivers, and my favourite is the little river, the Clywedog, which means 'heard from afar' – sending out into the world its brave signature of significance, though it's little more than a stream. The Clywedog is the underdog of the mid-Wales rivers; it cannot compete with the Severn or Wye, but by god, it will do its best to be heard. I like that in a river: 'Myself it speaks and spells, Crying What I do is me: for that I came' — G.M. Hopkins.

Alive with sound in spring, a woodpecker knocks a peg into the dawn, hammering *Listen to me*, while in the rabbit-rustling and sheep-snuffing fields 'no sound is dissonant which tells of Life,' in Coleridge's words, one who had not heard the vile ferocity of the military jets which tear the sky apart with their low-altitude flight-training in these hills. From a fox's point of audience, or an owl's ears, or a deafened robin or a silenced wren, this land has more-than-human songlines. In ways beyond our human senses, too, songlines are traceable across these lands. Salmon leap the Teifi and other rivers in their sudden salmon-run days, finding their paths in scent. It is impossible not to respect their mysterious and extraordinary ability to smell in the ocean water the precise trace of water from the exact rivulet of their own home and, following that scent, like a line on a map, doggedly making the journey back home to spawn and die.

The mythic Welsh poet Taliesin was, he wrote, born from a leaping salmon, eaten by his mother, and his poetry is fluent with a riverrun of metamorphosis.

> The second time I was charmed
> I was a silver salmon,
> I was a hound, I was a stag,
> I was a mountain buck.

This metamorphosis is ancient, Ovidian, full of pre-Christian ideas of rebirth and reincarnation, the spirit re-housed in the dwelling of a cat or a chough or a man, part of the long pagan tradition which softly, stealthily survives. The last time I walked to the source of the Wye, a chaplet of flowers had been tucked by the tiny spring of its source. A local manufacturer of wood stoves gives out a leaflet with hints on woodburning: don't burn the elder, it says, it is a fairy tree. One local farmer I know adamantly refuses to honour any midwinter festival except the solstice, and this area was full of pagan tales until Methodism tried to hush the storytellers. The stories live on, if told in quieter voices.

In Dafydd's poetry, the Christian element looks suspiciously well-behaved. Proper. Minding its manners. As if he did it partly to please his parents and partly as a piece of poetic diplomacy: as long as he threw in some churchy numbers, his resplendently pagan poems, where his true poetic – shamanic – heart lies, might be admitted without too much botheration. His tradition is not only that of poet and harpist but also that of the Welsh wise man or woman, the shaman, also known as the *consuriwr*, conjuror, whose work was to *con-jure*, to bring about, or to constrain by a sacred invocation, to enchant. One who conjures the spirits of the land as Dafydd conjured the mistle thrush, the wind, owl, fox and roebuck. The conjurors were enchanters. Re-enchanters. And they were invoked by metaphor and mouth, as the spirit of Dafydd is now.

Snug in his tree, I pull out his poems to read and to dwell on a while. In the cold, they warm me. 'Poetry first causes dwelling to be dwelling. Poetry is what really lets us dwell,' wrote Heidegger. For an exile, a traveller, a soldier, a refugee or the simply unfathomably lost, one book of poetry can be the single most cherished treasure, because it is a pocket hearth.

Poetry is home: a shelter for the soul. Every beloved poem is an hour-shelter or a day-dwelling, a one-night house. Poetry offers a lodging, the smoke from its chimney tells of a hearth indoors and the warmth of habitation. Poetry is snug with welcome, and nested with significance. Poetry is where dwelling wells with meaning; a defence against the arbitrary, where the psyche, seeking a hearth, uncurls and stretches like a kitten. The eighteenth-century French poet Jean-François Ducis conjured for himself the beloved home in the country that he had always wanted and never had. When he was seventy, he decided to give himself this home, so he wrote little poems to his flowerbeds, his kitchen-garden, his wood- and wine-cellar. It never existed, except in poetry, and yet, like the best homes, it has provided a warmth and a welcome to those who come upon the image of his inglenook.

The old monks at Ystrad Fflur were kind to poetry, giving it a home — Dafydd more than any, whose grave here is a focus for his memory as a hearth is the focus of a room. Dafydd's grave is a hearth, a passing-hearth, a way-hearth, with its charred hospitality. His hearth-in-death, his old yew burns in spirit. Dafydd lives, alive, thriving, green and invoked.

As Omar Khayyam wrote,

Here with a loaf of bread beneath the bough,
A flask of wine, a book of verse — and thou.

Sometimes Orpheus is enough. It occurs to me how the yew at Dafydd's grave has been fed, over the years, by his body and here, with the earth partly-peat and root, and partly charcoal from the tree, I take a peck of earth and eat it. Another kind of dispersal, another kind of metamorphosis of earth.

*

I went back to Dafydd's grave on May Day Eve, with the ineffable novelist Niall (no relation) Griffiths and his darling Deborah. Harriet Earis would meet us here in the morning with her harp. Our evening had been generously convivial, and after several glasses of wine, I found that I had to fight Niall to sleep in the tree.

You'll be cold, he said.
I've got my Norwegian sleeping bag. (True.)
There's a hooligan storm. You'll get wet, he said.
I've got a tarp. (True.)
It's a cemetery. You'll be scared, he said.
No, I won't. (False.)
Anyway, I said, it was my idea in the first place. (Two kids in the playground. I won.)

So, later, I lay wrapped in tarpaulin, sleepless in my sleeping bag, hollow-eyed inside the hollowed-out yew as the gale drove through the cemetery. Niall and Deborah were snug in their tent, yards away but seemingly a hundred miles. Darkness and tempest will do that to distance. The storm was ripping off branches, flinging slates from the chapel roof, and tearing at the ancient abbey stones like a ravenous god. In a storm, everything is cut down to the quick, to the living. Deadwood is swept away in storms: only necessity and will remain. I admit I was scared. Nothing was untouched in this storm-changed night, drumming its imperative: transformation.

Storm is a catalyst of havoc, a twister in the plot, a tornado turning and turning time forward in the story. Demanding with Lear that things must change or cease, storm is a kinetic trickster. In *A Tempest*, a political retelling of Shakespeare, Aimé Césaire added the Trickster to Shakespeare's cast of characters: Eshu, the gatecrashing and border-crossing god, a force of turbulence against Prospero's rule.

Seeming more than weather, storms suggest a crisis when the gods rip open the backdrop and demand a speaking part. They may voice vengeance in the Kamikaze, the Divine Wind which destroyed the Mongol fleet, or the storm voices may repeat the trespass which stalks the thoughts of Alonso; dark, electric, guilty.

Lear's realisations are storm-driven: storms transform perceptions with sudden blue flames in the rigging of the mind. During the gale at Dafydd's grave, in a flash of illumination I understood how mediaeval people would have beseeched the volatile gods for day and summer. Lightning quickens the mind to shocked sight.

It is in a lightning flash that Doctor Frankenstein truly sees the monster he has created. Lightning storms transmute: in the alchemy of atmosphere, leaden night is galvanised to gold vision. The science of electrickery crackles through Mary Shelley's work; the trickster which entices the natural philosopher into the tradition of alchemists, of Faust and of Prospero, where science had its roots in magic. A magician, Prospero conjures the storm till the clouds are shuffled in the legerdemain of a sky-conjuror.

Storm is an act of ur-theatre: Ariel 'perform'd to point the tempest.' With the ancient force of tragic theatre, storms drive situations to catharsis. In storms, everything howls *now*; screams *here*. Everything is tornadoed into utter immediacy, and from Conrad's *Typhoon* to Kurosawa's film versions of Shakespeare, storms are theatrical, those gods demanding their dialogue with humanity. It is impossible to reject the facts of storms now, the storm-surges, the increase of hurricanes, the hurling fury of an increasing number and worsening force of tempests as the climate moves towards its crisis. This too is Nemesis at work through and on behalf of natural laws to draw attention to limits that have been crossed: 'Stop at once. Turn back now.' Nature speaking.

Storms are the 'language of the ancient earth' wrote Wordsworth, and he was not alone. In Navajo philosophy, the four winds are also known as the four words, and are associated with language, communication and thought: the psyche. More painful than the actual storm, for Lear, is 'this tempest in my mind.'

If ever the storm-force psyche was written into human form, it is in Heathcliff and Catherine in *Wuthering Heights*: their souls made of lightning and fire. They are not *like* storm: they *are* storm. When Catherine's ghost hand grasps in through the window during a storm, her passion smashes through the etiquette of walls. Heathcliff dies in a storm, the windows wide open with rain driving straight in: a tempest transgressive to the end. 'Ambience of a psychodrama' is the stage direction which opens Césaire's *A Tempest*. Storm words speak the language of the psyche: to storm is to rage, to be tempestuous, to be turbulent, 'minded like the weather' — the tormented mind, like *tormenta*, a storm, in Spanish.

Césaire also uses the storm as an element of political transformation — in its aftersurge both Caliban and Ariel plan their political independence from Prospero the coloniser, recalling that for Shakespeare the inspiration for *The Tempest* was the 1609 shipwreck that led to the colonisation of Bermuda. From Shakespeare's tempest where a storm wrecks the characters into restitution, to the hurricane which strands the boys in *Lord of the*

Flies, storms transform the old order; tempests subvert the status quo in the thunder-carnival of a savage sky.

Meanwhile, at Dafydd's grave, the gale howled, the yew tree was shaken to its roots and my resolve shaken to its quintessential granite form: my will versus the storm's wildness. I don't make a habit of sleeping with the dead, quiet or unquiet, but I had so wanted to be here for May Day dawn, when Harriet-the-harp would arrive and play, and I would read Dafydd's love poems which so dizzyingly describe the sensual, green month of May.

At last, daybreak. And something utterly unexpected happened: the twister in the tale. As Harriet took her harp out of its case, the wind blew through it, every string resounding, from the highest to the lowest, from infrared to ultraviolet. The Greeks called the god of tempests Aeolus, from which we get the term Aeolian harp, an instrument played by nothing except the air itself — an Ariel enchantment. The storm was outstormed. The force of transformation was itself transformed. As rain is transformed by sunlight into a rainbow, so the gale swept through the strings, wind on one side, transformed on the other — to music.

Noon

Prague

The world has turned more than a year since my father died. The intensity of what I felt has lessened, while my wish to understand him has increased. Yet if I look for him now, his essence or his spirit, where might I find him? I've searched in a few places, but although there are clues of him, and footprints here and there in the genetic heritage, I cannot find him.

My mother tells me that she and my father went to Prague some years ago, and she includes a detail: they went to a cafe hidden in a bookshop behind Wenceslas Square, or Wenceslas-the-lazy, as the king was known. The cafe served only Czech beer and Czech sausages which was perfect for my father. My mother, more a light side salad and a glass of chilled white wine kind of person, would have preferred a different menu, but her memory is my quest.

What is it with Prague? I love Czech films: *The Ear*; *Closely Observed Trains*; *Capricious Summer*; *Daisies*. I adore *The Good Soldier Svejk*. Reading Kafka as a teenager left me bug-eyed with delight. There is something endearing in the Czech sensibility, something tender and daft, a tragicomic, piebald humour, a playful sadness that draws me as well as that subtlest of filaments: the way that people who have visited go misty-eyed, saying fondly, as of a beguiling and mischievous friend, 'Oh Prague, yes, *Prague.*'

So I would set out to find someone who no longer exists, in a place I had never been to, and to which, having described it, I can faithfully inform you that I still have not seen. It is better to travel than to arrive. In the pandemic when travel was for the most part neither safe nor legal, it is better to travel in the mind. I phoned a friend and borrowed the idea of his horse for a month.

I have always wanted to go to Prague and I will go with someone I have never met. It is not possible to fly because of Covid restrictions, so I will ride there, across Germany, on a horse with no name called Herbie. It will be a picaresque — even quixotic — journey into dream and reality and I would rather travel with Herbie than arrive with any other horse. A herbivore, like my mother, Herbie can graze through the forests but I will need travel costs for stabling him in small towns. Prague is one of the greenest cities in the world, with 56% of its area covered with grass or trees, which is good for a herbivore. (A friend's friend, who wants their cat to be vegetarian, has ended up with a very sick cat. I suggest we do a carbon offset-type thing: Herbie will eat more grass so the cat doesn't have to.)

My editor, for it is he who I have never met, covers our expenses by sending Herbie a drawing of Don Quixote's horse, Rocinante. Both Herbie and Rocinante are a little bit thin, a lot bit old, but very willing to take on adventures too much for them. 'Herbie is a gentleman,' says my friend whose father owns the horse. I have ridden him many times, always greeting him nose to nose, a bee-breath between us, letting him smell me. He is white and covered in straw. He has a wry intelligence although he gets scared of unexpected things like plastic bags, witch's knickers in trees. He is indeed a gentleman when he is not nervous. He is chivalrous, courtly, even.

He is also huge. I am not. It is sometimes hard for me to get on him. I fell off Herbie for the first time ever, just as I was about to leave for the idea of Prague. I tried to mount him by standing on a bench. One foot on the bench and one foot in the stirrup. 'Careful,' said my friend, 'that could go horribly wrong.' It did. I fell between bench and horse. I — quite literally — fell through the gap between dream and reality.

I look at the guide-books my parents took with them and I'm drawn to the house names including the White Turnip and the Green Crayfish. My father has marked At The Golden Pear in green highlighter and the guide-book describes this as a 'Baroque house with a cosy restaurant.' I look it up online. It is 'frequented by locals and visiting dignitaries' (my father would have liked that) and has a 'wood-pannelled gourmets' corner serving Bohemian fish, fowl and game' (my father would have *loved* that.) But hang on —

Bohemian fish? The shores of landlocked Bohemia were previously only reachable in Shakespeare's *The Winter's Tale*.

On TripAdvisor, At the Golden Pear has been splattered with a spiteful review headlined 'Disgusting' from someone who visited one Christmas Eve. In a spirited response, the management tells us that the Disgustant did not pay the bill, and they suggest the team at At the Golden Pear would happily visit the reviewer at his home next Christmas to experience his hospitality at no charge. *Touché*. I like them already. But the restaurant is now permanently closed.

Unfortunately, so is my father.

Angelo Ripellino is the author of *Magic Prague*, a love letter to the city. Ripellino wrote it when the occlusions of Communism made it impossible for him to be there in reality. Missing the city terribly, he wrote the book to recreate it for himself. In his map of Prague at the front of the book, the map legend marks places as either:

1. Existing
2. Existing under a different name
3. No longer existing.

I do not know in which category my father belongs. Not 2. Terminals 1 *and* 3 perhaps.

I buy *Magic Prague* from a second-hand bookseller called Olaf.

Gustav Meyrink, author of the novel *The Golem*, had a friend who was a second-hand bookseller in Prague. The bookseller only sold rare books with the consent of his tame raven, who perched on the counter and signalled Yay or Nay. My editor, Mr Crowe, might appreciate that detail. I ask Herbie to remind me later. He responds: 'What is the difference between a canary? One wing is yellow: the other is also blue.'

I write to Olaf saying I have a question. He responds: 'Olaf here, eagerly awaiting your Prague question. Regards, Olaf.' I ask where he'd recommend I visit. He suggests the Jewish Quarter, and the paradoxically-named Old-New Synagogue. In the Jewish Quarter the clock runs 'backwards' but only depending on your point of view. Reading Hebrew, your eyes move from right to left, hence this clock runs forward in Hebrew, telling the right time. There could only be one right time to go to Prague whose very name is followed by the word 'spring.'

A phrasebook tells me that the best way for an English speaker to say 'thank you' in Czech is to look them in the eye and say 'dickweed' really quickly. I really will not be able to thank anyone in Prague. I think I speak no Czech, but I find that 'robot' is a Czech word. Good start. I plan my cultural diet and read an interview in *Prague Morning* of an artist from Bangladesh called Soumik whose 'ongoing art journey' is called *Alien in Bohemia*. I like the sound of it but I get sidetracked by the font. It is called 'Roboto; sans serif.' I understand robot and I know that Sans Serif is the island most favoured by printer's devils on April the first.

Mr Crowe writes to me at thirteen minutes to noon on April the first. 'Did you get to Prague? Are you there now?' I am there now. I am also here now.

Where will I stay in Prague? Since I won't actually be there, I can stay literally anywhere. There is a hotel called Miss Sophie's Downtown. Mind the gap. Apostrophes can be dangerous: the misuse of the grocer's apostrophe leads to rotten tomatoe's. Is this one a possessive? Miss Sophie's place? Or does it mean that Miss Sophie is downtown? Their advert features what male writers in a pre-feminist time would have called a leggy blonde (but I am not so I won't) lying upside down (which you can do if you put your feet on the pillows). She has amazing tattoos and then I am engulfed with envy because she has a European passport casually tossed beside her. Prague is the capital of what used to be called Bohemia, and I have a Bohemian passport, enabling me to travel freely in the Imaginosphere and the Past, but no Bohemian passport will ever be as good as an EU one. I was a European without realising it until Brexit stole my nationality. It stole all of Europe and gave me back a bunch of liars. Dickweed very much, I mutter to the duplicitous robber barons. So I will need a visa. Herbie, Celt to his whiskers, and unwilling victim of Brexit, recognises no borders except the sea.

Olaf writes to me: 'Have you heard Christopher Hitchens' Kafka anecdote? It's on YouTube. Worth a listen.' I do. Hitchens describes going to Prague for a long weekend. He promises himself he will not use the word 'Kafkaesque.' (Key example: in Kafka's *The Trial* the police have the criminal, but not the crime.) But on the Friday evening, at a literary event, Hitchens is arrested. The police refuse to tell him on what grounds he is detained. Under the circumstances, thinks Hitchens, there is only one word to use. 'Fuck.'

Olaf follows this, saying: 'At the risk of being too Kafkaesque, I am not Olaf but Michael...' Olaf exists, and is Michael's partner in an online shopfront, but this is not him. We are in Terminal 2: 'Existing under a different name,' swimming along the seafront of the surreal.

Speaking of Prague, my mother smiles gleefully as she says two words. They pop up, cocky, bright and oxymoronic. *Pink Tank*. My father, an architect, was interested in Goethe's colour theory and he would have appreciated the acute humour of that colour choice. The Tank was erected as a monument to Soviet tank crews in 1945. In 1989, the Velvet Revolution led to the collapse of Communism in Czechoslovakia and in 1991, the artist David Černy and his friends painted the tank pink and erected an eloquent middle finger. (My mother doesn't mention that bit.) Černy was arrested and the tank was repainted green. However, fifteen MPs took advantage of their official immunity from arrest and painted it pink again. It went back and forth, green to pink a few times. Then it was moved, and in 2002, a fountain called 'Trapdoor of Time' was installed in the place the tank had formerly occupied. The place my father had formerly occupied is a different kind of Trapdoor in Time. Is he in Prague at all? Is he anywhere now, except the past?

The novelist Karásek in 1907 writes: 'only the Past is present in Prague.' All I will say is Karásek hasn't been to Wenceslas Square recently.

Ripellino fills *Magic Prague* with the past, focusing on Rudolf II (1552-1612), Holy Roman Emperor, King of Hungary and Croatia and Bohemia, Archduke of Austria. Rudolf, great-grandson of Joanna the Mad by two lineages, who looked like 'a god in need of help,' according to Max Brod. Rudolfine Prague was a city of distillers, astronomers, soothsayers, charlatans, sages who sold 'turpeth and rhubarbe-hermodactyl pills,' a plethora of alembics, mandrake roots and a turtle chockful of clockwork. With a gorgeous sense of *noir*, Ripellino describes one casino, with a foul basement called *Zblunk*, 'a word meant to imitate the sound of a body falling into a swamp' with 'swarms of squalid scoundrels, thieves and counterfeiters.' In 1893, the innkeeper hanged himself.

I have a feeling that I will meet the Baroque painter Petr Brandl, who walked across Bohemia one summer, tavern to tavern, beer to beer, ditch to ditch. Petr will appear briefly when the beer is flat and the geese have logorrhoea, when the past flows into the present and out again in under three seconds, according to Czech poet Miroslav Holub. I have a date with Heraclitus on the riverbank in central Prague, where St John of Nepomuk, the patron saint of drowning, was thrown to his death.

Heraclitus has upped his game. 'You never step into the same Vlatava twice,' he says, 'but Schrödinger's cat did and didn't at the same time. Twice.' Schrödinger's dad didn't too.

The guide-books say: 'At the House of the Black Cat, if you order a beer, further half-litres come willy-nilly until you decline.' My father would have liked that. Not just the beer, but the phrase 'willy-nilly,' which made him giggle. He would also have liked the idea of the Church of Our Lady Under the Chain and would have twinned it with St Andrews by the Wardrobe. He would have photographed the Street of Political Mistakes, its now-permanent name after years of political shenanigans. He would have saluted Peter Parler, architect of genius, who built St Vitus cathedral, 'that vertical sonata, that druse of crystalline stone, that triumph of the ogee arch,' according to Ripellino. An old Czech proverb says, 'You won't fry a weasel in a flying cathedral,' but on a hot day my gourmand father would tell me that you could fry an egg on a flying buttress.

On Petrin Hill, Prague, there is a labyrinth, a maze made of mirrors. I wonder briefly if my father is there, but I do not remember him ever, not even once, looking into a mirror. Do you ever find yourself in a mirror? Honestly?

Karl Kraus says that in Prague 'poets multiply like muskrats.' Blame the statues which people the city, particularly on Charles Bridge. Modern Czech poetry is full of sculpture, languorous statues or speaking ones. The poet Vladimír Holan writes to one statue: 'My last dear illusion is that when your pedestal is removed you will remain for an instant in the air.' In April, says Ripellino, 'when even stones fall in love, the pedestrian has the illusion that they are stirred by the warmth of spring and their lips whisper sighs of love.' My father, who never willingly read a poem, was chary of sunshine, and ticked the love box once and forever with my mother, would have been far more interested in the great engineering of Charles Bridge than the statues on it. He would also have appreciated Prague's tiniest feats of engineering: the flea circuses, for example, of which all Bohemia was proud, populated by acrobat fleas, high-wire fleas, flea ballerinas in tutus, fleas that duelled with paper sabres, and a flea orchestra.

The Good Soldier Švejk is over a hundred, being first published in 1921. My father was first published in 1930 and went out of print in 2020. He is a clown, a beer-loving clever fool. (Švejk, that is. My father shares some, but not all, of those qualities.) By following orders to the letter, Švejk creates havoc for his superiors but retains his innocence. He pronounces that he is a '*blb*,' an idiot, with bulbous, bibulous boasts. He is not just any old pseudo-idiot, he is 'an official idiot... a genuine idiot.'

Švejk's first cousin, the Prague Golem, is truly a dim-witted mud puppet, a leaden lump of reverse alchemy. The Hebrew word 'golem' in Psalm 139 means a rudimentary thing, an unfinished mass of clay. Rabbi Jehuda Loew ben Bezalel created his Golem in the Prague ghetto: a robot-prototype, existing to serve his master. A giant, he was, with nostrils like sewers. My father, not one to dwell in the Imaginosphere, would have only wondered whether the sewage pipes could be made to modern specifications with materials fit for purpose. One day, the Golem goes on the rampage. 'Things take a woeful turn when the idiot himself falls in love,' writes Ripellino. 'A whiff of cunnus arouses even clay.' (My mother says, 'I hope you don't put that in your piece' but I tell her I was brought up to think for myself, knowing she can never have an answer to that. My father, still on the whiff-bit, is trying not to smirk out loud.)

I don't remember my father ever relating any dreams, and yet — and yet — something in Prague's dreaming would have intrigued him, the ambiguous Traumwelt, the 'absurd oneiric reality' according to Czech surrealist Jindřich Štyrsky. Absurdism suited my father and surrealism (which happily took root in Prague) was a trick of the light he saw out loud.

★

Why do I want to go to Wenceslas Square?

Because it is wintry, with soft snow falling at twilight, slightly yellow under the lampposts, and there is a scattering of old benches around this small square, while eaves overhang the winding alleys that ribbon off and away into darkness like cooking smells. Old waiters, serving beer and coffee together at breakfast, smoke mournfully between customers, at their own special bench where they feel no need to be polite.

Because tucked behind Wenceslas Square is a bookshop. Because tucked inside the bookshop is a cafe. Because tucked inside the cafe is a plate of sausages and a pint of beer which is now tucked inside my father who is now tucked inside the ruck of a map.

Tracing his steps on Google Street view, I see many beer-bellied middle-aged tourists and I wonder if I am weirdly — actually — going to find my father. Actually is actually a little too much. Not IRL but at least Google-real.

I find the bookshop, called Academi. The plot where the bookshop is now was a brewery in the late fourteenth century. Then it was a Renaissance property, then a neoclassical house. In 1895, it was demolished and the current house was designed for the architect Antonin Wiehl.

I look up. All the building's upper storeys are painted with scenes and portraits, extravagant and spirited. There are scenes in alcoves, one *trompe l'oeil* after another. Figures of naked men like Atlases carry the weight of the upper storeys on their shoulders. One scene shows a citizen being knighted for his achievements and another shows the Slavic goddess of winter and death, Morena, with the tagline 'Against death there is no cure.' The murals depict the Ages of Man and allegorical figures. My father lurks, photographing the drainpipes rather than the art, but he is not really here. In the cafe, the menu has expanded: it is not the place it once was.

Prague is a hybrid place, a melting pot of languages, a mixture of cultures — mainly Czech, German, and Jewish in its jostling heyday. It excelled in cabaret, that most hybrid of shows, gleefully called the Tingeltangel. Prague is famous for its *tandlmark* or *tarmark*, the flea-markets where you could find shoes, clocks, daggers, mirrors and parrots, pancakes, pork and peas, puppets, metaphysical clowning, fake jewels and real gems. A flea-market is the emblem of the hybrid.

Hybridiana. Hybriderie. Could there be a collective noun for a group of hybrid things? I ask Herbie who gazes at me and replies: 'What's the difference between a joke and a rhetorical question?'

One of Prague's most famous painters, Giuseppe Arcimboldo, fashioned portraits in hybrid collage, making human faces from fruit and vegetables. Arcimboldo's 'The Librarian' makes a portrait of a man out of books, and *The Good Soldier Švejk* doffs his cap to him as he encounters characters in the insane asylum: 'the wildest was undoubtedly a gentleman who pretended to be the sixteenth volume of Otto's Encyclopedia and asked everybody to open him and find the entry "Cardboard box stapling machine" otherwise he would be done for...'

Švejk's creator, Jaroslav Hašek, born in Prague in 1883, was said to be a regular at over a hundred Prague taverns, and had a hybrid career as apothecary, dog seller, tramp and clown. As an apothecary's apprentice, he set fire to a barrel of petrol in the cellar and the building burnt to the ground. He became editor of *The*

Animal World and turned the journal into an invented inventory of irreal animals which were not extinct but had entirely failed to exist: the cerulean shark, for example, and the paleozoic flea. Hašek's character Marek in *The Good Soldier Svejk* speaks of 'my bat from Iceland, the Faraway Bat, or of my domestic cat from the peak of Mount Kilimanjaro, called the Irritable Bazouky Stag-Puss.' Švejk was a master of the hybrid, and 'lived by selling dogs — ugly mongrel monstrosities whose pedigrees he forged.'

I am still deep in Ripellino's exquisite book, itself written in a hybrid form. According to the author, it is 'a capricious book, an agglomeration of wonders, anecdotes, eccentric acts, brief intermezzos and mad encores... I will fill these pages with scraps of pictures and daguerreotypes, old etchings and prints purloined from the bottoms of chests, reclames, illustrations out of old periodicals, horoscopes, passages from books on alchemy and travel books printed in Gothic script...'

All travel happens in hybrid time: in preparation for the future journey, in the present of the trip, and in the memory as it slips into the past. The experience of travel is a hybrid one, a collection of impressions — a taste, no more: glimpse, a snatch, a whiff, a brush. It is always a matter of how you see, and to catch different perspectives the observer stays light on their feet, moving until things come into alignment: anamorphosis. Travel uses hybrid tempos: a scamper and a skedaddle or a slow, deep draft, lost and absorbed. The best journeys involve a mixture of modes: a bus, a bike, a tram, a canoe, or a horse. Travel uses the hybrid mind, guided by curiosity, seeking desire-lines, open to serendipity, listening for correspondences, touched with alchemy — as above, so below — knowing there are patterns in all things and that meaning is made out of those patterns.

Travel depends on advance imagination that conjures where to go. Travel can be entirely imaginary, as in the Here-Be-Dragons journeys of Sir John Mandeville, who was accompanied by his imaginary friend, a praying mantis named Sir John Mandible. Travel can include the past: in a novel by Svatopluk Čech, the beer-drinking philistine Mr Brouček takes a fictitious trip to the fifteenth century. Or it could be a journey to the personal past, happy or sad. (In German, a gloomy or sinister voyage is *finstere Bootsfahrt*.)

In Prague, I visit an island in the Vlatava river. There is a magnolia tree. It is marked 'Magnolia Tree. Temporarily closed.' How can a tree be closed? Only asking.

There is a 'Freud sculpture hanging in mid-air' that is not temporarily closed. The figure hangs like a man on a gibbet, a dead man several storeys high, and there is a man-hole-cover directly beneath him, so if he slips, he will fall from the stars to the gutter, a literal Freudian slip. Nearby there is a 'Growjob Institute.' Go back. Read that sensibly. A restaurant on the corner sells 'best beer' in English, with a mural of Švejk.

Oh, I love Prague, I think aloud, the Dancing House, also called the Drunk House, the ancient underground alchemical laboratory with a tunnel to Rudolf's palace, the story of a street so narrow that a visiting tourist had to be lathered in soap and squeezed through like greasy piglet. Legend has it that Faust, alchemist and necromancer, was Czech, and emigrated to Germany taking the name Faust von Kuttenberg/Gutenberg, inventor of the printing press. Apothecaries were called 'materialist shops'and in Prague the shop sign for apothecaries was a brightly coloured angel with spread wings. She reminds me of Nemesis, swooping in with the correct measure or dosage of medicine.

I also see that you can go on a self-guided tour in a beer museum. I skip that, as I can take myself on a self-guided tour of beer in my own fridge any time I like. From there, I click on something and end up completely immured in an expensive boutique shoe shop with no way out. My dad wouldn't have been seen dead in a shop like this. He isn't to be seen at all.

*

One of my greatest wishes had been to go to Wenceslas Square. One of my greatest disappointments is seeing Wenceslas Square.

For a start, it is not even square, but rather the shape of a word I am allergic to. *Oblong.* (Other words I am allergic to include *doily* and *convenient.*) It is oblong and half a mile long. 'Only once,' wrote Nerval to Gautier, 'being imprudent, you spoilt your ideal of Spain by going to see it. But I have already lost, kingdom by kingdom, province by province, the most beautiful half of the universe and soon I shall not know any more where to seek a refuge for my dreams...'

Under a huge splat of a flat oblong sun, with a flat beer in a warm glass, I stare at the emptied shadowless places, bored as bins. Opposite the bookshop is a Duplex and a Debenhams and there is a KFC just down the road. The street-side ground floors of all the buildings are identically banal. Tourism has made Wenceslas Square into a monoculture of the damned, the shops managing to be both expensive and cheap at the same time. I wish I had not come here. Petr Brandl suddenly appears, drunk and gurning, showing me his painting of 'St Peter's Cock' on Wikipedia, and of course I click on it but St Peter has a set of keys and a reprimanding look on his face for my misreading the title.

The Academi bookshop is next to Marks and Spencer's. How horribly *convenient.* My father would remember that he could use an extra pair of socks. He likes to look after his feet as befits a tourist to Czechia, because the traveller, wayfarer, pilgrim, or vagabond is an archetype of Czech thought, peripheral but present, as witness. Josef Čapek's 1936 novel *The Limping Pilgrim* describes its hero pausing in ditches, finding that his path 'does not pass through places' but is 'simply a state.' I feel the same, immobile at my desk, Google Earth spinning seductively before my eyes.

On Easter Sunday in Wales (oestrous Easter, wobbly lambs, fluffy as chicks), I go on a virtual tour of St Vitus Cathedral. Spinning the cursor, the whole cathedral becomes a kaleidoscopic merry-go-round. Out to the Square of St George, I look right up into the sky. There is a hole in it. Quite a big one. A whale by any other name. I go to Golden Lane to a historic pub and visit a goldsmith's house with windows of honeycomb and a turquoise bird cage. I enter the house of a fortune teller with a skull sitting on a doily. I am shocked. Not by the skull, but by the doily.

I follow one detour after another, committed to detourism, taking the curly route, rococo and baroque and yet repeatedly finding myself at the wave's crest where hope and disillusion meet.

There is an ecotechnical museum in Prague, devoted to sewage disposal. My father would have loved it. In Jungmann Square near Wenceslas Square, I find a Cubist lamp-post dating from 1915 for dogs who do square poos. I click on a rooftop at random and it swoops to a sign on a closed door saying 'Avant garde Prague on the first floor.' Art at random appeals to me. Found poetry. It is actually a front for a travel agency. The Facade Gallery is not a front, but is an actual art gallery, and its front windows are painted by various artists.

There is an exhibition called SOMA SEMA at the Museum Kampa. Soma Sema means 'the body: the tomb,' referring to the idea of an unlimited soul trapped in a limited body. I suddenly feel giddy and realise that I want to go home.

I check on Rome2Rio to see if it knows the best way for me and Herbie to get from Prague to mid-Wales. It does not know. It will tell you the second best way and the third, but we are going to take a direct flight home, landing at Llandegley International, DVWP. Asterisk.

Between Cross Gates and Pen-y-Bont, deep in mid-Wales, is a sign saying that you are now two and a half miles away from Terminals 1 and 3 of Llandegley International. It specifies distance but, crucially, not direction. Two and a half miles north or south? West or east? Or even two and a half miles upwards?

There is no Terminal 2 on the sign. There is no Terminal 1 or 3 in actuality. But Terminal 2 is perplexing. Although the airport, being open for flights of fancy only, has no Terminals 1 or 3, Terminal 2, by dint of not even being signed, double-doesn't exist. Dada. My dad would have loved it. Its creator, Nicholas Whitehead, is reluctant to concede that Llandegley International isn't real. 'It's real in the sense that Wednesdays are real,' he says plaintively.

Asterisk. *Deus Volente Weather Permitting.*

Before we leave Prague, though, I will try, just one more time, to find my father. With pure serendipity and no foreknowledge of its existence, what comes up on the screen is a sign that announces boldly I AM PRAGUE. Fair enough, I think, you can self-identify as a capital city, why not? After all, Toyen, a leading Czech surrealist and partner of Štrysky, gave herself the name Toyen which can be translated as 'she's he.'

By the I AM PRAGUE sign, on Google Street View, there is one single unpartnered black boot detached from its human. I like this boot. 'Nothing is impossible,' says I AM PRAGUE, aka the Illusion Art Museum of Prague. However, it *is* impossible to enter because the museum is temporarily closed, but I go in anyway. And then, wonderfully, my trip is transformed.

There is a huge painting on the floor which, from one angle, looks like a giant hole in the floor, giving onto a view of a bar room and billiard table. This painting, 'The Hole' by Jan Jirovec, shows a bell with a Habsburg eagle that fell through the house. There is a collection of buttons and a typewriter, cogs, a clothes brush, cockroaches and a key which, seen from one spot only, gathers together to make sense and assembles itself into an anamorphic head of Franz Kafka: from only that one point of view does everything align. It is close to the NO EXIT sign in the museum.

St Wenceslas on horseback is charging forward, shattering the frame of the painting, and plunging right out into the room. There is a portrait of a man made out of 1,500 pieces of newspaper. There is a sculpture of a trashcan pouring out rubbish which, seen from one particular angle, reassembles itself into a *trompe l'oeil* of a Van Gogh painting. Ludic, illusory, the whole museum teases the eye and I know with absolute assurance that he is here, my father, turning the rudiments of actuality into humour, safely protected from the emotional content of art, taking an engineer's delight in what is both unexpected and explicable.

I have found my father.

The Age of the Trickster

The hour of noon — high noon — is the hour of power. The sun, ultimate source of all energy, is at its height. The blazing. The zenith. The noon sun marks a line, straight up and down, the time without shadows when shady characters are reproved by noon's straight sightlines. There is something Absolute about midday and midnight too; they are the strict centres of the day and night. Nemesis takes her place in these moments of power, limit, stricture and certainty. Straight down the line, her remit is the sharp truth.

One mythic character is not, traditionally, found at noon: the Trickster. He frequents the margins of the day, not the centre. The Trickster hour is the enigmatic time of twilight, with its shadows and uncertainties. Trickster delights in the sleight of hand that you can get away with when the lights are low: his remit is deception.

The Trickster is a universal archetype: he informs Bugs Bunny, Zorba the Greek, Eshu and Anansi. Krishna is Trickster in the Hindu pantheon and Hermes in the Greek. Nasruddin is the Sufi Trickster. There is Brer Rabbit, of African origin, and Karagöz in Turkey and the Monkey King in China. Pippi Longstocking, Matilda, Fantastic Mr Fox, that orange show-off addicted to admiration, is a Trickster, as is the Cat in the Hat, Don Coyote, Wile E Coyote's nickname for Don Quixote. Coyote is one of the Native American Tricksters and over the border in Mexico, where 'coyote' is *coyōtle* in Nahuatl, the ancient Mexican Trickster is called Huehuecoyōtle who gives good parties and is said to start wars just because he is bored. (And, with the attention span of a gnat on a cider-mission, Trickster is easily bored.) Loki is the Norse naughty-one, Azeban is the Trickster of the Abenaki people, and he is a raccoon, one of those mischievous neophiles, drawn to the novel and the new. Unruly raccoons take risks, outwit humans and are hard to catch, they are born looking as if they wear a harlequin mask: Harlequin is another Trickster.

Dafydd ap Gwilym, cocky, rude, charismatic and funny; a dazzling communicator who fascinated those who knew him, smacks of the Trickster. Many of the most attractive characters in culture, from Puss-in-Boots to Saul Goodman (*Better Call Saul*) and Malcolm Tucker (*The Thick of It*) are Tricksters.

Mischievous, lustful, hungry, Trickster is also curious and clever with contraptions and technologies. He is an attractive, charismatic character. Trickster plays tricks and sets traps for others that he is often caught in himself, he dupes and is duped. He crosses all the boundaries of ethics, he is neither good nor bad but is amoral. He is a change-maker, moving the story forward. He is a dicey character, and a petty thief siphoning a little off the top of a lot. Usually male, he is a debased and debasing character often associated with the bum: Bart Simpson's 'Eat my shorts,' and all the cartoon clowns who fall on their bouncy backsides. Trickster is rude and often a bit of a dick, unruly and unruled by grand ethics, instead he is ruled by his stiff little ruler in the underpants. He doesn't just rip up the rulebook, he uses it for bog roll. Trickster is the turbo-charged laxative for the constipation of boredom in the body-politic.

Slippery as an eel gone pickpocketing in a slimy fishmarket. Boastful as a raccoon snorting cocaine off a tycoon's bald patch. Double-duplicitous as a fake ferret on the filchy-filchy. Trickster glimmers in word-play and innuendo: *A woman walks into a bar and asks the bar-tender for a double-entendre so he gives her one.*

You see Trickster in *Borat*, duping people into revealing their misogyny, or anti-semitism, or racism. You see him in the *Yes Men*, who pretended to be Dow Chemicals and in that role apologised for Bhopal, robbing the rich of their lies to give truth to the poor. You see him in *Brass Eye*, and in *Private Eye*, tunnelling right under the feet of those in power and undermining them.

He bends the truth till your head hurts. He lies compulsively, often about food or sex. (The cookie-jar? Me? I didn't inhale the cookie.) He is a fabulator and counterfeiter. Legerdemain is at his fingertips, distracting the attention, pointing with one hand '*Look! Up there!*' while the other hand swaps the cups.

He disturbs the status quo, arse over tit, bouleversé. Crucially, the mythic Trickster is *never* in power. Rather he is on the edge, marginal, outside the tent pissing in. Because he doesn't have power, we are sympathetic to him, the challenger who will take on the establishment, the little fella, the brave new guy on the block ('new guy' is *novichok* in Russian, as they joked their way to poisonings.) The Pink Panther, that cartoon made of bubble-gum, stretching and lounging around on top of his cartoon titles is funny. Jacob Rees-Mogg, swaddled in power, doing his Pink Panther impression in Parliament lolling on the cushions of his entitlement, is not.

Boris Johnson and Nigel Farage are Trickster figures, charismatic for many, and (in)famous for persuading people to vote Brexit with a big fat lie on the back of a big fat bus. A change merchant, Trickster's role is to create chaos *and then skedaddle*. Farage did this after Brexit, as if he knew that any kind of real responsibility will out him as a twat, the drinking man's twat. But Johnson was a Trickster who got into power.

The Trickster character is always hungry, for money, sex and power. So Johnson's ambition for the role far outwitted his own ability to perform the job. Like a walking Peppa Pig, whose praises Johnson sang when he forgot the serious speech he was supposed to make to business leaders, Johnson is a portly man, a boozer, who was allegedly 'ambushed by cake' in a delicious Trickster phrase, both recalling the Trickster's ability to set traps and be caught in them, and the Trickster appetite. Early reports suggested that he would be ousted by fellow Tories, in the so-called Pork Pie Putsch, a meeting held in the office of the MP for Melton Mowbray. The Prime Minister outed for his telling of porky pies, by the MP for the town that is best known for its actual pork pies: this is why our satirists are unemployed.

The Trickster guides and misguides, leads and misleads, as Johnson led the country and misled both the populace and parliament. The Trickster is a liar, as Johnson was in his Tricksterish job as a journalist, where he lied for a living. (Bendy bananas. A Tricksterish slippery yellow line.)

When Partygate flooded the media, Johnson seemed to have met his Nemesis in several forms: the bendy liar on one side of the House of Commons, the straight lawyer in the form of Keir Starmer opposing him. Or perhaps Nemesis was coming in the form of the civil servant, Sue Grey/Gray, as strict, impartial, boring, rule-keeper. But the Trickster seemed a step ahead of her. The thin blue line of the Metropolitan police might perhaps have served as his Nemesis, but went oddly quiet. His abiding Nemesis was the Queen, in her unforgettable dignity and isolation, mourning alone at her husband's funeral while Boris Johnson had spent the previous night partying with friends.

Ours is the age of the Trickster. And not in a good way. It has placed the Trickster not where he belongs, on the edges of society, but at the epicentre of events. Contemporary culture has plucked him out of the gippy edges of time, and given him the power-hour of noon.

At a glance, it is repulsively funny. Trickster stalks abroad. Brandishing blue underpants and bog brushes in the purlieus of Basil the Blessed; blonde buffoons, all bums and bumptiousness; bawdiness and bodily-functions galore; a ballooning baby blimp of an adult in nappies.

Trickster is here in a flatulent tirade of tweets from someone called President Fart. He is there in Rudy Giuliani, that oily lawyer with fake hair-colouring dribbling down his cheek, the only man who adjusts his shirt by manipulating his dick. Bum-cheeks out, greasepaint tawdry, a rancid sexuality runs through it, call-girls peeing on presidents. To put a false colouring on something is a term for trickery as Trump paints on his fake orange skin. Make-up.

You can't make it up, this sort of stuff, a comedy slice of life staged in a car park between a bit of rumpy-pumpy and the mass grave of Covid, between a sex shop and a cemetery. You can't make it up, because they are making it up, for real. A bombastic *covfefe* mesmerises a world: the spirit of the Trickster is at large, and it is fascinating. Revolting, yes, but captivating, as comical as it is sinister.

Never, ever give the clown a gun. Once the clown is armed, he is terrifying. While the mythic Trickster has no power and must have no power, the contemporary Tricksters-in-power retain some of the characteristics but move into the realm of gangster, dictator, or tsar. Funny? Not funny.

In the 2019 film *Joker*, directed by Todd Phillips, Joker is a Trickster figure played in a minor key. Abandoned and abused as a child, he suffers mental ill-health, delusions and a laughing-tic. The city of Gothenburg is in decay, where Joker is picked on and bullied. In a society of underdogs, he is the under-clown. Cuts to social care means he no longer has medication, and his delusions create a mental chaos for him: without medicine, he cannot tell reality from fiction. Then a fellow-clown gives Joker a gun. That is the moment when he ceases to be a Trickster figure but becomes the dangerous psychopath who inspires a riot.

Trump portrayed himself as the plucky outsider taking on the establishment, using slippery Trickster speech he incited the lethal insurrection at the Capitol, in January 2021, on the back of his pants-on-fire lie that the election was stolen from him. Chaos? Not chaos. It was a planned and attempted assassination. They hoped to find Mike Pence and execute him by hanging. Representatives Alexandria Ocasio-Cortez and Nancy Pelosi would probably have been killed, if found. 'Murder the media' was scrawled on the walls. It was fatal and horrifying. It was also a Trickster's trick, a pseudo-coup, a *coup-de-théâtre*, a con-man's coup because Trump had not been able to get the army to give him the real deal, a military seizing of power.

The QAnon 'shaman' left a note for Pence, that read: 'It's only a matter of time, justice is coming.' Intended for Pence, it could be seen as addressed to himself or even Trump. Nemesis would come, eventually, though Trump's followers were upset when Nemesis arrived for them in the form of the FBI. 'I never thought leopards would eat MY face,' sobs woman who voted for the *Leopards Eating People's Faces* Party (— Adrian Bott on Twitter).

Nemesis showed up for Trump too, when he was impeached. His initial legal team quit just days before the trial began, although as historian Julian Zelizer remarked, the Republican Party would not allow the impeachment to be successful: 'Trump can go on the floor to read lines from the *Joker* movie — they would still vote to acquit.' During the impeachment, Trump's lawyers said the footage shown was 'tricks' and a 'hoax.' The QAnon 'shaman' on his arrest was quick to find the right word. He felt 'duped' he said, by Trump. He was. Boris Johnson ridiculed the impeachment trial as a 'kerfuffle,' a one-word, drive-by lie, intending to recall a hapless bombast with fat fingers rather than a dangerous fascist attempting a vicious assault on democracy.

Trickster is transactional, loves cutting deals and ensuring commerce, he is there in double-entry book-keeping, often using deceptive or fraudulent business practices, always needing money and near-constantly in debt. 'I do deals,' says Trump, mired in debt. He is a wheeler as well as a dealer, and prefers to be portrayed on the road, always on his way somewhere, often to rallies, Road-Runner whizzy. He never fully inhabited the White House: it is too dignified a dwelling for the Trickster. He didn't have the stature, though his bum was too big, notably when, in the rump of his presidency he was pictured 'working' at a child-sized desk. Trickster is never dignified and flouts the norms of behaviour, though few people would do it as audaciously as Trump strolling nonchalantly in front of Queenie.

Why did people vote for this clown? many people asked. Trump provided what the Trickster always offers: sheer bloody brilliant entertainment. People were dissatisfied and felt themselves scorned. They were bored. Trump saw it. He would give a humdinger of a party. The rally on January 6 would be 'wild.' He himself was, like all Tricksters, easily bored, and a communications addict, of TV, tweets, and attention. Like the Trickster, Trump was also a storyteller, something Michael Humphrey in *The Conversation* analyses. Trump's tale goes something like this. True America is being undermined. True Americans can see it. If you can't see it, you're either not a true American, or you're being fooled by fake news. Only Trump, the outsider, the new guy, the *novichok* on the block, can stop it. But the entire establishment is against him. So he needs your help. C'mon, help the little guy. He'll give you a good time if you do. That's the clincher: Trickster's lovely, lazy bribe.

Trump savvily aced Twitter and could hypnotise a crowd, like Jesus did. Like Hitler did too. Trump insulted, boasted, scapegoated, implied, creating a kerfuffle of language (and what an amazingly Tricksterish word that was to fluff up.) Sometimes, off-teleprompter, it became clear that, like any Trickster, he'd tricked himself and had lost control over his own speech bubble though he had retained control of the nuclear codes. Never give the clown a nuclear warhead.

Trump shored up his power with those who walked a rather bendy line. Steve Bannon was arrested for a classic Trickster offence: fraud. Roger Stone is the self-described political 'dirty trickster' who urged Trump to seize power if he lost the 2020 election. An early, though short-lived appointment was Anthony Scaramucci, 'the Mooch,' whose name rings the Trickster bells. In Italian, *scaramuccia* is literally the 'little skirmisher,' the *commedia dell'arte* masked clown, Scaramouche. Trump ally, the chair of the American Conservative Union is called Matt Schlapp (pure schlapp-shtick). Sean Spicer leapt onto the world stage with the first big lie of Trump's presidency, declaring Trump's inauguration crowds were the largest audience ever, thus inaugurating the era of 'alternative facts.' Shakespeare's most acute observation of the Trickster is Autolycus, (the 'lone wolf') who catches people in a snare on their way to a sheep-shearing and cheats them. He 'fleeces' them, they are 'shorn,' Sean the sheep, while his contribution is that he adds a little spice to life. Sean Spicer was a good Trickster name, but Trump trumped it, his name containing 'rump,' the bum so associated with clowns, the rump position of the little-guy Trickster while trump means to fart, and also to fabricate, so 'trumped-up' means fraudulent, as in 'making a trumped-up allegation of election fraud.' A trump card is played in card games, the casino ever a haunt of the Trickster, while to trump, to trumpet is to boast, as the Trickster always does. Trump is an accident of naming yes, but it is cantilevered by the outrageous turbofictions of our times into a role heavy with destiny in this mythic present.

Trump was fully aware of his wow-factor, that people wanted someone to cause a wild rumpus, to start fights and be entertaining. When he lost the election, he turned on Mitch McConnell and attacked him for being boring, describing McConnell's 'dedication to business as usual, status quo policies, together with his lack of... personality... Mitch is a dour, sullen, and unsmiling political hack.'

The Trickster walks a tightrope. He can fleece the sheep but not slaughter it. He swindles but does not bankrupt. He ambushes but does not execute. He flirts but does not grab women by the pussy. He might pinch bums but he does not crush a police officer between two doors at the Capitol, till his howls of pain ricochet around the world.

The difference is in the issue of power. The Trickster is peripheral, penniless and relatively powerless. He might shake things up power and disrupt the established order but if he actually assumes power, he immediately ceases to be a Trickster. The sinister clown causes a particular terror: that we might be duped to death.

The mythic Trickster both tricks and treats because his lies are fun. They are Bart Simpson-sized, little fibs, pickpocketty-sized swindles. When the Trickster is at the heart of power, everything changes. The lies are big as Charlottesville, the 'good' fascists, and the gaslighting of half a nation with the Election Lie. When the Trickster is in power, the lies are Auschwitz.

How did Hitler and Goebbels create the right conditions for the Holocaust? By lies, blaming Jewish people for Germany's hardship. One of the most obscene anti-Semitic lies is the mediaeval grotesquerie claiming that Jews took part in the ritual slaughter of Christian children, using their blood for the unleavened Passover bread. This is just so QAnon. When the Ku Klux Klan gave Trump their support, when the racist flag of the Confederates is billowing over a fatal insurrection at the Capitol, Voltaire (who knew a thing or two about anti-semitism) is on-point: 'Anyone who can make you believe absurdities can make you commit atrocities.'

Hannah Arendt wrote in *The Origins of Totalitarianism*, 'The ideal subject of totalitarian rule is not the convinced Nazi or the convinced communist, but people for whom the distinction between fact and fiction (i.e. the reality of experience) and the distinction between true and false (i.e. the standards of thought) no longer exist.'

Trump has a veritable hinterland of liars at his back: white supremacists, Holocaust deniers and anti-Indigenous historical revisionists create fake history. Climate denialists, Covid-deniers and creationists create fake science. When people are insufficiently educated in science, history and critical thinking, they are gullible and dupeable: a valuable political commodity for Tricksters in power.

Trump lies by accusing others of what he is doing himself, so the Democrats were, he said, 'colluding with Russia.' He called the media who wouldn't lie for him Fake News, Fraud News and Morning Joke. The Trickster vocabulary piled in: his political enemies were, in his words: *crooked, lying, shady, slippery, sneaky, corrupt, cheating, little, shifty, sloppy and fake.* Total Trickster vocab. His public lies were counted in the thousands: 30,573 lies during his time in office.

Metaphors morphed into reality. We are being infected by an actual virus. We are also being infected by the multiple viruses of misinformation on the loose. Misinformation about the vaccine and Covid itself ('exaggerated' and a 'hoax') flooded both pre-poisoned hate-groups and, paradoxically, the wellness community, people in organic and health food circles, yoga practitioners and so on. It went viral in groups who considered themselves left- as well as those who were right-wing. Meanwhile, his lips spiked with lies, the superspreader-in-chief was at the White House, laden with a literal viral load and loaded with the language of lies so when he spoke, his lies were both metaphorically and actually spraying poison.

Trump's lie that the election was stolen was as poisonous as Novichok to the body-politic. The twist in Trump's tale: he actually has a near-constant fear of being poisoned himself, which is why he orders food from large chains such as McDonald's and KFC, because it is pre-made and no one could know a President was about to come into contact with *that* nugget.

★

A key part of the Trickster shtick is this: he tricks others then is tricked. First the duper, then the dupe. Whose dupe is whose? If Trump is playing Trickster, who is tricking him? Putin.

Russia has a fine Trickster tradition, the great Basil the Blessed, shoplifter-saint, was a Holy Fool only too willing to speak truth to power, while the fictional con-man Ostap Bender famously 'knew four hundred relatively legal ways to make the population part with their money.' But in Russia as in the USA, the Trickster took power. Putin trumps Bender. He is weaponised. He is loaded too, gangland loaded, the peacock of the kleptocracy.

Putin loves lying. He lies with effrontery, he lies with aplomb, he smirks as he lies. He lies to seize power over others and he lies to speak power to truth. Compared to Putin, Trump's a loser. Basil the Blessed stole from the rich to give to the poor. Putin reverses it, robbing the poor to give to the rich.

The great liar of London, Boris Johnson, or Bojo to give him his professional clown-name, played his part in shoring up Putin's power by letting the Russian kleptocracy keep its wealth in London, using it as their beautiful launderette, washing blue money the colour of underpants. Journalist Craig Unger reports how Russia had been grooming Trump for years, not that Trump was the only one: Russia had its fingers in a lot of custard pies. The Trickster is often a bit of a dick, but when it came to Russia, Trump was a total tool.

Putin is the consummate Trickster-in-power. He is greedy without limits. Engorged on Russia's wealth, he builds himself a palace on an estate several times the size of Monaco, near the Black Sea, revealed in a documentary by the anti-corruption campaigner Alexei Navalny, Putin's personal nemesis. The palace cost over a billion dollars and the money was gained from backhanders and from skimming off the profits from many Russian industries. One source of cash came from the purchase of medical equipment: Putin profits from the sickness of others.

The palace is flamboyant and excessive. It is tricked out in the hideous curdled glamour of the kleptocracy. But his palace, in all its mightiness, is undermined by a tiny little fleck of a thing, a spore, no less. Fungus the Bogeyman. The mould, both snot-green and bilious black, snuck in because of a trick, through the little gap between appearance and reality. The palace was built with numerous fake walls, tricking the visitor into thinking them real. Plasterboard was put on top of the concrete, and the mould started growing between the two surfaces. The rot set in. And it stank. There was no fresh air, and the ventilation did not work and so the mould spread, in spite of the whole building being disinfected at least twice. The ceilings leaked: top down, it was corrupt. 'Fish begins to stink at the head, not the tail,' said Rumi: the rot of corruption starts at the top, with the chief.

Putin likes his toys. His entire palace is a play station. He has a colourful private life and at his dick-tation, a room in his palace is dedicated to pole-dancing. He has an aquadisco; an underground rink for ice hockey; a hookah bar, and a casino, illegal in the rest of Russia. Putin also has an entire room for a train set which performs 'amazing tricks' and runs rings round a model of which building? The cathedral of Basil the Blessed. Basil was canonised and then cathedralised in a jaunty and jesterish creation, all cupolas and exorbitant merriment, bulbous and turbanish striped like a beach ball, swirling like a helter-skelter. Meanwhile Putin is shown in a montage wearing a jester's hat made of dollars.

Putin spends the same amount tricking out one toilet with a bog roll and bog brush as an average Russian pensioner will get to live on for an entire year. Putin's bog roll holders cost over a thousand Euros and his bog brush sells at 700 Euros. (A royal flush? You were *had*, Vlad, they saw you coming.) The documentary reveals Putin ignominiously, trousers round his ankles, a tasteless playboy, a gnome guarding his gold underground. For all the power and might of the great dictator, it is the sheer littleness of Putin that Navalny aims for in his documentary. The small-mindedness of wealth. The literal embarrassment of riches. The contempt was infectious, and when crowds came out to protest Navalny's imprisonment, they carried bog brushes of painted gold, and blue underpants.

Navalny's greatest weapon is the truth. In himself, Navalny demonstrates what greatness looks like, the vision and courage of a more-than-life-size hero, with some stains, though: he has a nasty anti-immigrant streak of brown on his underpants. Putin has tried to portray Navalny as guilty of the Tricksterish crimes of 'fraud' and of 'dodging' bail (how mirrorish the accusations) and Navalny, in spite of the grim seriousness of his situation, and his legal diligence in evidence at every point, nevertheless nicked the Trickster clothes off Putin himself. From the dock, Navalny bestowed on Putin the moniker of Vladimir the Underpants Poisoner.

Putin's agents had smeared Navalny with lies, poisonously dishonest, but had literally smeared poison, Novichok, on Navalny's underpants. It was a low trick. But then, recovering, Navalny tricked the trickster. With sublime chutzpah, he (assisted by Bellingcat, a great nickname for our friend Nemesis) made a prank phone call, duping a Russian agent into revealing what he had done. Navalny himself (pretending to be an aide to a top FSB official) made the phone call to the FSB operative Konstantin Kudryavtsev. Samuel Beckett could have written the dialogue.

N: And on which piece of cloth was your focus on? Which garment had the highest risk factor?

K: The underpants.

N: The underpants.... Well, imagine some underpants in front of you, which part did you process?

K: The inner, where the groin is.

N: The groin?

K: Well, the crotch, as they call it. There is some sort of seams there, by the seams.

N: Wait, this is important. Who gave you the order to process the codpiece of the underpants?

★

Putin's greatest weapon is lies. For many years, Putin had an ideologue-in-chief, the aptly named Vladislav Surkov, who blended political spin and circus, theatre and politics. Surkov the ringmaster, Putin's deputy prime minister, postmodernised Russian politics. As the *Economist* said in 2013, Surkov 'engineered a system of make-believe that worked devilishly well in the real world. Russia was a land of imitation political parties, stage-managed media and fake social movements.'

Before the invasion, Putin was already calling a part of Ukraine *Novorossiya* (New Russia: how Trickster loves the new) and he bestowed on this entirely trumped-up country a history, a flag, a news agency and several Twitter feeds. Propaganda has been around since Herodotus but postmodern lying has a nasty twist. To be caught out in a lie has usually been a source of public shame, but now, with the insouciance of a practised psychopath, a lie is a matter of pride. Russian news broadcast a woman relating that a child had been crucified by Ukrainian nationalists. It was a complete lie, but when confronted with its falsity, Russia's deputy minister of communications simply remarked that ratings had doubled because their media strategy was *entertaining* the public. Hook 'em, spike 'em, dupe 'em. *Dezinformatsiya* is the word, pumped out through TV, and trolls and tweets.

Lies are poison, and truth is medicine, as the film *Joker* shows: without his medicine, he cannot see the truth of things. *Joker* shows urban rioters in a plethora of clown masks. Trickster adores the territory of masks, disguise, concealing and revealing. Trump's followers revealed their support for him by refusing to wear facemasks. Meanwhile Trump, Johnson and Putin united to cover up the fact of Russia's collusion in the 2016 Trump election, and in the Brexit referendum. By supporting Trump, Putin weakened

America. By supporting Brexit, Putin weakened Europe.

And then he struck.

In February 2022, when no one thought he would, Putin invaded Ukraine. He expected opposition. He did not, however, expect opposition from the man who was the voice of Paddington Bear in Ukrainian who also, in a comedy sketch, pretended to play the piano with his dick. The President of Ukraine.

Volodymyr Zelenskiy used to be a comic actor, and portrayed a fictional character who becomes president by accident. He became wildly popular, and then realised that what he'd done by fictional serendipity he could do in real life. In a New Years' Eve comedy show, he announced he would run for president, positioning himself as the Ordinary Man, the Little Guy.

Zelenskiy won the heart of the world in a week. He was a Trickster who got serious. A man who had spent his life playing for laughs was suddenly the voice of a nation under threat. But more, even, than this. He spoke to the conscience of the watching world: this is what heroism looks like. This is courage. This is the voice on the frontline, naming what is right and wrong. Putin, in his hubris, crossed a line.

Zelenskiy was a Trickster who became Nemesis.

★

In Paris in the nineteenth century, the Théâtre des Funambules was built for the juggling, clowning acrobats, and with the *funambules* (literally the 'funny-walkers') came a host of Tricksters, jokers and clowns, experts in sleight of hand and sleight of mind, bendy and fun. Gossip spread here, all kinds of news, both true and false were in the air. Les Funambules was regarded as populist entertainment by Le Grand Théâtre, the French tradition that performed the classics of grandeur. One was serious, the other silly. One broadsheet, the other tabloid. One had authority, the other had the shits and giggles. The boulevard des Funambules was also known as the boulevard of crime, and people might be fleeced, or tricked, or lied to: they might even be robbed but they would be entertained. With Le Grand Théâtre, they would get the solid classics and leave with their pants on, but they might be bored. They could choose. What happened? The public flocked to the Funambules, knowing what they were letting themselves in for. At the heart of Partygate, Johnson was defended by fellow Tories who said voters had known what they were voting for: he was no saint, for sure, but he was, they said, 'box office.'

It is simply human: we the public, strolling along the boulevard, will always prick up our ears at the sound of a tin whistle and thrill to the high wire act. We still do. The contemporary Tricksters in power are Funambules, grabbing attention with chicanery, eschewing sensible authorities.

The Trickster goes for entertainment over accuracy, and on the Internet, the boulevard of public life today, Trickster is in his element. This, an amoral no-man's land, is his terrain. In its range and speed it covers the world in a leap second, with its crazily-amazing networks in a dizzy parallel of the brain sizzling, synapses snapping, near-instantaneity. And at the same time, it invites its users to skim, to flick, to go shallow rather than deep, to be waylaid by gossip and the little picture rather than the big picture. In return for the coin of attention, it will offer pompoms and Picasso, prayers, pissed-up rows, protest and platitudes, puerility, porn, politics and profundity. And it won't guarantee your safety from its sinister violence, its masked anonymous attacks.

Online, each of us can be caught in a web of our own making, dopamine whizzing for faux-attention and delusory status and likes, photoshopping ourselves to become our own fake news channel. Everyone, Tricksterishly, may be caught in a phishing net, trapped in circles of complexity leading to constant anxiety. Trickster is associated with keys and locks, locking himself out just as often as he plans to lock others out. I need a *password* for an account to buy a pair of *knickers* and I can't *remember* it because *no one* should have to remember a *password* to buy *underpants*.

It unites us in our silos and divides us from other viewpoints, it fools us with bots and facilitates the most sinister Tricksters of our age, bombing us with fake news customised for our preconceptions and predilections.

We are being duped. But only sort-of.

We are choosing to stuff ourselves with totty and clickbait (to bait, to hook, are very Tricksterish acts) rather than serious journalism. Of course it is beguiling: I know it, being waylaid by a Tricksterish sprite: *just one more leedle clicketty click for something funny*: I don't want my mind to be a passive thing, a blank page for any passing player to piss on... *and yet... I click the bait.* We, like the mythical Trickster, are duping ourselves, collectively preferring salacious entertainment to responsibility. Accuracy is painstaking to create and demanding to read. Manipulation and misinformation is a lot more fun. We have collectively invited the charlatans in, colluding with conspiracies.

Plandemic released its viral load in 2020. It recalls the fictional film *V for Vendetta* (2006) which alleges that the British government deliberately created a biological attack as pretext for exerting vast control over the population. Those who believe this is happening now are not so much blurring the lines between fact and fiction but first crossing the lines and then double-crossing them. At the Capitol attack, many people wore a *V for Vendetta* mask. *Plandemic* was the Trickster in power, flitting across international boundaries, leaping over the (yawn-alert tedious) world of serious science and (yawn-alert sensible) actual facts with his far more entertaining lies. 'Free speech' is used to justify anti-vax lies, which have resulted in deaths, particularly among communities with a terrible history of being mistreated by the medical establishment. With Covid and supposed free speech, though, it is a toss up between the right to lie and the right to life.

A film called *Ask the Experts* released a viral load of top twaddle including pretending that Covid-19 was a 'scam' and 'the greatest hoax in history.' Conspiracy theories tell their believers that most people, the 'sheeple' as the contemptuous term has it, are the idiots being duped, shepherded into folds of lies in woolly stupidity, while those who support the conspiracies are the cunning clever wolves. No one wants to be the Trickster's dupe, the fall guy, the twat in the hat. And *that* is precisely the trap.

Trickster loathes the very idea of expertise. 'We've all had enough of experts,' as Michael Gove infamously declared. Experts and authorities are greater and grander and older than the Trickster, who is green with youthful ignorance. Nigel Farage and Boris Johnson, being rude, opinionated, cavalier and stupid, were far more exciting than some careful academic accurately detailing the damage of Brexit. The most grievous example is the climate crisis where the media, smugly promoting debate and edginess, sought ratings via verbal punch-ups rather than accurately report the situation. In the UK, TV's lowest moment was Channel Four commissioning *The Great Global Warming Swindle*, calling climate change a hoax. The Tricksterish media fell right into a Trickster trap, hoaxed by their own programme-makers, they swindled a world. Nemesis (in the person of climate scientists) was ready, standing patiently by to explain how the world has limits, why these limits matter but the spirit of Trickster-in-power out-shouted them all too often.

Trickster is shameless. The quiet, inner voice of conscience, or of honour has no place. Having no conscience and fearing no God, Trickster can live entirely in the amoral world. Indigenous cultures often consider the Dominant Culture to be the Younger Brother and something of a Trickster, noting its selfish immaturity, its appetite and greed, its technical cleverness but lack of wisdom, its short-termist refusal to take the long view. For Indigenous cultures, the Ancestors have ethical authority and the Descendants have ethical rights, so society must look ahead seven generations to guide any action taken today.

Trickster in myth is surrounded by the bigger, stronger and more powerful gods and goddesses who hold the line, lay down the law. For while Trickster bends the law, he doesn't deny it: it is by law and order that his disorder is defined and contained.

Trickster without any law surrounding him is terrifying. His little sexual peccadillos become acts of savage rape. His fingersmith approach to other people's money becomes a gargantuan robbery. His fibs and fabrications become the nauseous miasma of truth-sickness in the public mind.

The body-politic needs no more Kool-Aid laced with lies, but medicine from somewhere, some calmer, wiser, quieter, deeper medicine. Witch-hazel. A glass of fresh water. Air that is clear of smoke and mirrors. Values that the Trickster never possesses: Compassion, Respect, Courage, Wisdom, Humility, Honesty and Truth. The Trickster can only truly be himself when he stays in the margins, but when Trickster seizes power, he routs all those older, kinder virtues.

Nemesis, strict and dignified, is needed to lay down the laws and limits, to take the Trickster down a peg or two. Those opposed to Trump have tried to bring him down to size, in the baby blimp, and the viral meme of Trump as a toddler on a space hopper, refusing to leave the party of the presidency and throwing a toddler tantrum, but these have no more power than the workings of Nemesis in the comic world, where Trickster might get some cartoon-comeuppance, singeing his whiskers, for instance, or the Cat in the Hat being given a steely stare and a big telling-off by the goldfish. But Real Life needs Real Nemesis. It is in short supply, because collectively we have given power to the Trickster. When societies destroy nature, and make the gods optional, a power vacuum of belief is created: a pastiche-pantheism where everyone is a goddess, a princess, and anyone can have anything 'because you deserve it.' In a pantheon, the Trickster *can* step in. In a power-vacuum, the Trickster is *bound* to step in. And not in a good way.

Trickster favours those who speak from the margins, those with less status, anti-establishment, and that is why there are so few right-wing comedians. If you own power, you forfeit the funnies, sorry guys, that's just how the comedy-cookie crumbles. The comics and satirists and cartoonists, the piss-takers, shit-stirrers, the stand-up comedians with a bladder on a stick, poke fun at those in charge, taking pot-shots with a gun which fires bubbles along with its truth. (Bubbles. Not bullets. Only saying.)

Parodists, comedians and satirists deplore the fact that their craft is made redundant because the clowns are in power, because you can hardly exaggerate when the political world sways so giddily on such a lethal tightrope. In all the thefts of the Trickster-at-large today, bankrupting nations and stealing trust, here's another.

They have nicked the effing Trickster.

Give. Him. Back.

I want the Trickster-at-little. I want to be able to laugh at the daft lies and ingenuity of the 'little guy' rather than fearing the 'strong men.' I want the enigmatic figure of Trickster by twilight, the ambivalence and the intrigue. In a world of masks to reveal and conceal, masks to lie and masks to save: will the real Trickster please stand up?

I want Borat to pounce on Rudy Giuliani, with his hands down his pouch. ('She's fifteen! She's too young for you.') I want the satirists and jokers, Jonathan Pie, Charlie Brooker, Stewart Lee, Brass Eye, Banksy and Basil the Blessed. I want the spoof on the telly, the spice in the soup, the twist in the tale, the dice on the edge, the lucky penny, the wild card, the sorry-not-sorry, the four-leafed clover, the bells on the boots, the tassells on the cap, the blank in the Scrabble, the crack in the pavement, the fool's errandry and knight's errantry, the quixotic and the serendipitous, the spin in the serve, the hand-of-God, naughty Maradona, the frisson, the off-cuts. Win some, lose some, happy go lucky, I want Puss-in-Boots, the Cat in the Hat, Thing One and Thing Two. I want Zelenskiy alive and happy, playing the piano with his ... dreams.

Songlines —and a Hit List

It was midday. I was in my study. There was some iffy sunshine, some pointless clouds and I was idling, trying to get to the admin pile, but in that flat, dull moment, I wasn't concentrating. Some times of day call for your total attention. That one didn't. It was just ordinary. There was no music and no laughter in it. I had recently returned from a long trip to West Papua, and though the journey had been very hard, physically and emotionally, I missed it a lot. I missed the vitality, the spirit, the friends I had met. And then, plonk, right into the noon of nothing came the email.

I was sent a hit list. And one of my friends was named on it. My day was blown open, into something far, far bigger than me. I had to write about this, to do something. I would need to take people with me, in spirit.

What is it like, this land of West Papua? Wherever I walked in the highlands there, I was given hospitality. I was offered food, water, a place to sleep, and in return I was asked for news or for a song. It is an ancient aspect of sacred hospitality, that the wanderer may play minstrel to the place where they arrive, and that anyone coming from afar may bring news. I tried to bring news from recent places and people I had spoken to, but I was never good at singing. I would sing, though, if there was sufficient cover from other voices.

Out on a mountainside one night, myself and a small party of West Papuans were trying to dry our socks by the fire. Well, drying them was a little over-optimistic – making them a bit less wet is more like it. Leaning back against the walls of the makeshift hut, the men – my guides and friends – began singing, as they did every evening.

They sang of the sock-soaking rain, turning everything to mud. They sang of the rush of heady sunshine in these rainforest highlands. They tucked flowers into their hair and made up a new song that had them in fits of flirty giggles: 'We saw the girls in the grass skirts today, whe-hey.' Their laughter was infectious and 'whe-hey' needed no translation. And then they sang a part-song, with a basic melody held by one singer, the others extemporising around it, in a syncopated rhythm.

After a while, I shyly joined in the round-song that went round the circle of the fire, the ring of toes and wet socks propped up on sticks, until it resonated inside our chests, interrupted as one person would break away to relieve himself outside or cadge a cigarette or just laugh out loud for pleasure. Laughter is a lingua franca here. One of the guides, when he knew he was about to fall over laughing, carefully lay down first, then honked his laughter like an almighty anthem.

I had gone to West Papua to talk to those seeking independence from Indonesia. I was entranced by the music. In West Papua (half of the island of New Guinea, with Papua New Guinea a separate nation to the east, and Australia 150 miles south), songs and freedom are indivisible.

Scientists now believe our human ancestors sang before we spoke, music preceding language. Songs communicated emotion and developed social bonds. Singing with others is an unmediated, shared experience as each person feels the same music reverberating in their individual bodies. Singing is part of our humanity; it is embodied empathy; it is utterly, sweetly, audibly convivial.

In many traditions, the world was sung into being: Indigenous Australians believe their ancestors did so. In Hindu and Buddhist thought, *Om* was the seed-syllable that created the world. Here, in the West Papuan highlands, people call the soul *etai-eken*, which means the 'seed of singing.' It is the most beautiful definition of the soul I have ever heard.

Everywhere I walked in West Papua, the land was resonant with song. People yodel greetings from one mountainside to villages over the valley: *Aiieeeeeee* ('Put away your bows and arrows, we're friends,' it says). Playing mouth harps, drums and guitars, people sing village songs, tragic songs, love songs, flirting songs and songs of independence. Improvising long and funny songs in blank verse is a common skill. In Dominic Brown's brave and beautiful film of West Papua, *Forgotten Bird of Paradise*, the unselfconscious soundtrack is people singing of loss, anger, love and freedom.

Benny Wenda, a Lani man from the highlands, is the West Papuan independence leader now in exile in the UK, and a singer. There are songs for everything, he says: songs for climbing a mountain, songs for the fireside, songs for gardening. 'Since people are interconnected with the land, women will sing to the seed of the sweet potato as they plant it, so the earth will be happy.' Meanwhile, men will sing to the soil until it softens enough to dig.

West Papua is a land of contrasts: mountains in the clouds and fringes of coastlines; the gleeful chutzpah of the penis gourd (long or short, curly or straight, some topped with a plume of feathers, some used as a pocket for a wad of tobacco or a bit of cash) and the miserable degradation of human rights abuses by the Indonesian military. Mud and music. Guns and ukuleles.

While I was there, the guides sang the routes of paths in the mountains, music which mapped the land. I asked Wenda if this was a version of the Indigenous Australian songlines, in which the paths the ancestors took in the Dreamtime are memorised in songs, like musical maps. With them, people can travel across country they have never seen before. Wenda agreed, telling me of a specific song for his people's sacred mountain, Beam, their creation site and home of their ancestors, and how, as people climb that mountain, they sing that song.

It seems to me that there are versions of songlines all over the world, as in Sami *yoik* songs, too, where art evokes nature and enchants the land. It is possible that the idea dwells deep in the human psyche. 'We are the tongue on the body of the land,' says a Yolngu woman in Australia. Our eyes are alive to paths on the land: we are irresistibly drawn to them, following them as they tell their tales. The human brain, too, is threaded with tracks, neural pathways.

In West Papua, there are songs of respect for the land and songs of anger against its devastation. A Papuan band, Black Paradise, investigating human rights abuses around Grasberg (the Freeport gold and copper mine), has also collected protest songs from local Amungme people, who consider the Grasberg mountain sacred. Political music 'gives people strength,' says Wenda, 'and motivates them.'

I have been to the Grasberg mountain: sacred to Papuans, they call it a giant Mother and like other mountains it is associated with dreams and ancestors. I was told of dream-shrines on the mountain where you go to get a dream to guide you: a mountain that should be mined only for dreams. Now, for miles around, it is a lifeless, toxic wasteland.

The scene: my study back home. A long way from the giggling singers, sock-drying on the mountain.

I've been sent a hit list, forwarded to me by a friend in West Papua. Fifteen people are picked out for assassination, and one of the names—on a list which includes the head of the Baptist churches, youth leaders, legislators, students, and an anthropologist—is a friend of mine. All the targets are unarmed West Papuan leaders and thinkers. The hit list was compiled by Kopassus, the Indonesian military special forces responsible for massacres and human rights abuses in West Papua, where the world's most underreported genocide has taken place. Women and children have been raped and whole villages bombed, napalmed from the air. One person in ten has been murdered by the Indonesian military under its illegal occupation: at least 100,000 people, according to Amnesty International.

For almost half a century, ever since Indonesia invaded in 1962, the international community has been complicit in the killings. British and American companies have supplied much of the weaponry. The cultural genocide and mass murder is widely ignored by the international community. Papua is cursed with resources, and international corporations are making a killing. BP, for instance, has an £8 billion natural gas project there, and the palm oil industry is destroying the forests. In 2017, in an extraordinary act of collective courage, 1.8 million people

(70% of the Indigenous population) signed a petition to the United Nations asking it to respect West Papua's right to self-determination. The people did this in spite of being beaten and tortured for spreading or signing the petition. I've seen it: a gigantic block of a book, testament to bravery and hope, and also witness to the hurt of decades.

This is the nearest I get to losing faith in Nemesis. Nemesis hates invasions, is committed to stopping people overstepping the boundaries, punishes transgression, and yet successive Indonesian regimes have broken all the laws, the mythic, the human, the natural, and the international without any pushback. Nemesis is watching, aghast, but the international corporations have tied her hands behind her back and stuffed her mouth with dollars. International governments have refused to pay attention, racking up debts of conscience that can never be repaid. In spite of widespread peaceful protest, Papuans live and die in danger and without the due allotment of their own land for their own people.

How is it possible that such an atrocity continues unopposed? As I see it, there are three barriers to action: the ignorance barrier, the integrity barrier, and the innocence barrier. The ignorance barrier is created when an international media considers some lives too inconsequential to count and some nations beneath notice; the integrity barrier is created when the profit motive overrides principle. The innocence barrier comes into play when the electorate's own goodness prevents them believing what their governments do in their name.

The current horrors in West Papua originated when, in 1962, the withdrawing Dutch colonists put West Papua in the care of the United Nations, on the condition that Papuans would be permitted to vote on their own future no later than 1969. In the meantime, the U.S.-sponsored New York Agreement handed control to Indonesia, without the Papuans' consent. Indonesia invaded, led by General Suharto, who would later become president. Papuans didn't stand a chance: like the Na'vi of *Avatar* fame, they lived in a land of precious resources.

In November 1967, before any vote took place, President Suharto's representatives organised a meeting with banker David Rockefeller and other major corporate players to hand over West Papua's resources. Japan and France got the forests while the U.S. giant Freeport-McMoRan was given a mountain of copper and gold, the Grasberg mountain. In return, Indonesia got billions of dollars in corporate tax revenue.

The Papuan 'vote' was finally conducted in the form of the infamous 1969 Act of Free Choice, when 1,026 West Papuans were threatened and intimidated into mouthing statements in support of integration with Indonesia. Suharto's special envoy threatened to cut out their tongues or shoot them if they refused. The U.S., UK and Australian governments knew this to be a mockery of democracy, contravening UN law and the Universal Declaration of Human Rights. In masterful understatement, a British Foreign and Commonwealth Office briefing that year stated that 'the process of consultation did not allow a genuinely free choice to be made.' The American embassy in Jakarta in June 1969 knew what was in store for the Papuans: the act of free choice, according to the embassy, 'is unfolding like a Greek tragedy, the conclusion preordained.' In their ongoing silence these governments have colluded in genocide. Furthermore, the U.S. and Britain have lucrative arms deals with Indonesia, which uses the weaponry to crush Papuan democratic independence.

The Kopassus hit list, leaked to the investigative reporter Allan Nairn, names those who, with unfathomable courage, speak out for freedom and for democracy. For this 'prohibited speech' these unarmed civilians, including my friend, a church leader, are targets because they have 'reached the outside world' bearing witness to 'the issue of severe human rights violations in Papua.' These are the words of Kopassus itself.

Few people know about West Papua: it is unwitnessed and unreported. This is the ignorance barrier. In partial penetration of the ignorance barrier, in 2010, footage of Indonesian soldiers torturing Papuans was smuggled out; as it was widely broadcast, the world heard the screams, yelps and gulps of fear and pain. Then the websites hosting the footage were subject to cyber attacks. More usually, human rights groups repeatedly bring West Papua to the attention of the media who repeatedly ignore it: through their omissions, the press tacitly colludes in mass murder. In a form of lethal meekness, journalists say Indonesia refuses entry to the media. This is entirely correct and entirely spurious. It is not difficult to go there: buy a ticket, say you're a tourist, and get your notebook out, or your camera. That's all we did, that tiny handful of us from the UK who, over the last few years, have visited to report back.

One person who was not ignorant of the situation was Barack Obama. Ahead of his 2010 visit to Indonesia, fifty Congress members wrote to him concerning the 'slow-motion genocide,' and Congress held a (barely reported) hearing on Papuan human rights abuses. Rather than defend Papuan democracy and attempt to halt a genocide, Obama restarted funding to Kopassus (allegedly to fight terrorism)—a decision noted to breach the U.S. Leahy Law forbidding funding to military units that violate human rights. The Kopassus document showed their systematic targeting of civilians. Number five on their list was the president of the Papuan Presidium Council, whose predecessor, Theys Eluay, had his throat slit in 2001. There was international connivance in a genocide.

Beyond the ignorance barrier lies the integrity barrier, by which corporate gain is considered more important than ethical foreign policy. This attitude has been abetted by racism: John F. Kennedy's administration dismissed West Papua as 'a few thousand miles of cannibal land.' The British embassy in the 1960s refused to concern itself with human rights in West Papua because it was merely 'a matter of principle involving a relatively small number of very primitive people.' This racist language is still being applied: Mary Beard refers to indigenous people as primitive: BBC's presenters still, shockingly, following suit. It matters, this language. By describing people as primitive, you make them less human so they matter less. You set them up for slaughter.

I'd like you to meet one of these people. My friend is university educated like those who call him primitive, but he is wiser in his mind, kinder in his soul and braver in his spirit than they can ever hope to be. He is unnameable for obvious reasons. Like many Papuans, he is given to giggling. He is from the highlands, where life itself can seem an intoxicating song, where the beguiling mountain bird of paradise sings at dusk, and 250 languages are spoken.

In Ancient Greece, mountains were called *agrapha*, 'unwritten,' undescribed, and these West Papuan mountains, too, are ungraphed, unmapped, although sung everywhere with songs of independence, freedom, *merdeka*. Papuan society has never known either jail or slavery, because of a belief that freedom is essential for life itself. From every mountainside, the songs of freedom ring. With an almost superstitious recognition of its potency, Kopassus cannot say that word. In their report, freedom, *merdeka*, is written only as an initial: *M*. Freedom to them is an unspeakable word, unwritten as mountains, as they assassinate those who cry out for it.

Local people who oppose the Freeport mine face the military: I was told of villagers tortured and murdered, the soldiers sticking needles in people's eyes, axing people in the head, killing people with red-hot iron rods, 'as you would kill rabbits.' The songlines turn to screamlines.

Tougher than the ignorance barrier and the integrity barrier is the innocence barrier. Part of the self-image of both Britain and the U.S. includes an innocent belief that our governments will (for the most part) act ethically. So hard is it for innocence to accept that governments would connive in a genocide that the facts may be denied in order to preserve that innocence, the easy lie preferred to the difficult truth.

In 1978, a West Papuan anthropologist turned musician, Arnold Ap, formed a band called Mambesak (Shining Bird). He sang protest songs against mining, he recorded songs from the length and breadth of the land, and played the songs of his ancestors. He sang, above all, for freedom from Indonesia.

For Papuans, Ap was a hero. He was John Lennon and Bob Dylan rolled into one. People tenderly cherish almost worn-out cassettes of his music; women sell their sweet potatoes to buy batteries for doddery cassette players. Wildly popular, he fostered a renaissance of Papuan pride. Like Chile's Victor Jara, he was his country's icon of protest song. Like Jara, he was killed for singing. Arrested and tortured by Kopassus, the Indonesian special forces today being funded by the US, he was killed in 1984. Mambesak musician Eddie Mofu was killed with him, and other Papuan singers have died in mysterious poisoning attacks. While facing execution, Arnold Ap wrote his last song, The Mystery of Life, recording it on an old portable tape recorder; then he wrapped it up with a letter and sent it to his wife. 'The only thing I desire is freedom,' he sang, making it his personal and political epitaph.

So while we are fools for innocence, Indonesia annihilates a nation of singers, a sacred mountain is destroyed, Indonesia has created the opposite of songlines. Instead of the convivial song of life, mass murder. Instead of land evoked and beloved, an environment devastated and destroyed. But the spirit of Arnold Ap is still alive, says Wenda, in the cultural self-respect he nurtured. 'Music is our life. Indonesia oppresses us and kills us, but song brings the human spirit alive. It is an act of resistance. Never surrender.' The Indonesians may kill the singers but they cannot kill the song and freedom remains the unwriteable word for which Papuans die.

Sky-grandmothers Hurling Stars

Different qualities of light makes us see things differently. We see 'according to our own lights' but our minds are also affected by the times of the day and by the turning lights of the year. Noon light is about knowledge, seeing connections. The best of noon-thinking is great clarity, and an ability to see far horizons. I like thinking about thinking, and I especially like the ways in which different cultures think about thinking, how much education matters, and how important it is to ask precisely what good education actually is.

Take a human being. Lean it gently on the earth and let it listen awhile. Ask it then what are the good words and true. Ask what is the core curriculum for the human heart, the *coeur* values which children should learn. And, like a fundamental law of metaphysics, the answers seem to come back the same all over the world. Nature. Story. Ethics. Respect. Balance. Creativity. Spirit. Insight. Gift. The art of being human.

A few hundred people, mainly Totonac, a culture surviving from pre-Columbian times, cluster together in the centre's large candle-lit, flower-strewn courtyard. From tiny children to old people, everyone is dressed with care, the men wearing white cotton trousers and tunics, the women white dresses. All colours have meaning; white symbolises purity of thought.

Copal incense weaves the breeze. Banana-resin is used to paint shooting stars and flowers on the pottery which is, they say, a sacred work because it comes from Madre Tierra, the mothering Earth. 'Every object is charged with thousands of years of knowledge,' says Salomón Bazbaz Lapidus, the centre's director.

Laid out on the ground is a hand-tended and mind-attended mandala of what education could aspire to be. A path of huge, waxy banana leaves links exhibits of traditional medicine, storytelling, pre-Hispanic healing saunas, pottery, dance, painting, theatre, cotton-culture, carpentry and — candidly now — tourism. Looked at in the whole, it is a pathway, a *camino* of pedagogy: 'because we are following a long path not to be conquered.'

I had been invited here, to the Centre for Indigenous Arts in Papantla, in the Mexican state of Veracruz, 300km east of Mexico City. The centre was celebrating the anniversary of its founding (in 2006), and promoting indigenous education: decolonised schooling. Not by chance, it is October 12, the day when, in 1492, Columbus arrived in the so-called New World. Here, they come not to praise Colombus but to bury his legacy because — as an act of pointed protest — this date is now widely honoured as the day of indigenous resistance.

During the day, there are long blessings and speeches to confirm and celebrate the centre's work. The *camino* of pedagogy is walked *poco a poco*, they say: little by little, each step involving public consultation, soaked in dialogue and steeped in ceremony, each word crafted to articulate their *cosmovision* (their conception of life) without compromise. The *camino* is walked with an old slowness. 'Much listening to the grandfathers and grandmothers,' says Humberto García García, the pedagogist.

It took eight years to develop the ideas of education now symbolically spread at our feet. Everything has meaning: the green circle showing the natural world, the centre of everything; stars, representing a person's special gift. Well-rooted trees show how knowledge does not, must not, disappear; and circular designs illustrate how knowledge builds by people discussing things in circles. Seeds show the importance of putting concepts into practice: planting an idea so that it grows into its reality.

'The worst thing you can do is impose,' says Domingo Francisco Velasco, a traditional healer. 'This is the main problem with humanity.' The Spanish word *imponer* carries strong meanings and a harsh history. The cathedral's imposition symbolises it perfectly: the subjugation of a continent, the imposition of the Inquisition which tortured and slaughtered *curanderos* (indigenous healers) because their knowledge was forbidden; the imposition of what I call intellectual apartheid.

★

In Mexico City, the cathedral — this stentorian thug of a cathedral — is sinking. Built to crush the Indigenous temple beneath it while its decrees pulverised indigenous thinking, Mexico City Metropolitan Cathedral is sinking under the weight of its own brutal imposition.

Walking nearby once, I was captivated by music. Closer, now, and I came upon an indigenous pre-Hispanic ceremony being danced on the pavement hard by the cathedral. Copal tree resin was burning, marigolds were scattered like living coins, people in feather headdresses and jaguar masks danced to flutes, drums, rattles and shell-bells. While each cathedral column was a Columbus colonising the site, the ceremony seemed to say: *We're still here.*

A young man watched me awhile, as I was taking notes, then he approached me smiling.

'Do you understand Nahuatl?' he asked.

Head-shaking smile.

'Do you want me to explain?'

'*Yes!*'

And he spent an hour gently unfurling each word. He was abjectly poor: his worn-out shoes no longer even covered his feet and his clothes were rags but he shone with an inner wealth, a light that was his gift, to respect the connections of the world, between people, animals, plants and the elements. He spoke of the importance of not losing that part of ourselves which touches the heart of the Earth; of listening inwardly to the spirit within, and also outwardly to the natural world. Two teachers. No one has ever said it better.

'Your spirit is your *maestro interno* (your internal master). Your spirit brought you here. You have your gift and destiny to complete in this world. You have to align yourself in the right direction and carry on.' And he melted away leaving me with tears in my eyes as if I had heard a lodestar singing its own quiet truthsong.

★

Like my lodestar friend at the cathedral, Domingo Francisco Velasco at the Centre for Indigenous Art, indicates two places where knowledge comes from: the great within and the great without — the speaking earth will teach the listening mind if we are willing and wise. 'Knowledge is *here*,' he says, his hand across his heart, and his face glowing — at once shy and certain. 'You have to search deep inside to find it for much is known already in the head, hand and heart,' while the natural world, he says, is teacher and guide. He speaks a river language, clear, constant and clean. 'In nature there are places where you can find your moment and be revivified. Places to understand nature and be understood by it.'

This idea of education matters far beyond the (very great) importance of cultural respect for indigenous societies wanting to transmit their unique cultural heritage to future generations. It reaches further, into the heart of the relationship between humanity and the natural world, for the goal of this *camino* is to align people correctly with nature's laws, the principle of Nemesis. This is not about 'environmentalism' as an optional hobby but a matter of survival. Arguably, because of climate change, there has never been a more important moment for the Dominant Society (called the 'Younger Brothers' by many indigenous cultures) to learn from older cultures, to pay attention to their ethics, valuing the natural world above all, and to do this through wise education. You could say that it is Indigenous cultures who vouchsafe the truths of Nemesis most devotedly, in finding and following the laws of nature.

The expression of dissatisfaction with imposed imperialist education has a long history. In the early twentieth century, Rabindranath Tagore set up Santiniketan in Bengal, as a radical alternative to British colonialist schooling. Classes were held outdoors; the natural world was honoured as a teacher. Stories, music and art were integral to learning. Exams were not. Nor was the world of business. Generating art in everything, Tagore's aim was to regenerate the moment with noticed beauty to turn the meanly quotidian into a daily ceremony. Meanwhile, Krishnamurti's educational philosophy of Krishnamurti (1895-1986) began with a revulsion at the ways in which the typical education of his time served nationalism and economics, and he taught ethics: the goodness of the human being. These ideas of schooling have echoes today in Forest Schools, the Reggio Emilia system, and the multitude of fledgling radical schools that emphasise nature and art, and value moral, meaningful learning as much as academic work.

Radical education has often focused on similar themes: from Devon to the Sierra Nevada, from Bengal to Veracruz, people speak a common sense of mind and body learning in each other's service. Education must include the hands as well as the head, the heart, the soul, the feet, comments the pedagogist Humberto García. Appreciating the senses through which we apprehend the world is a thought which makes perfect — feeling — sense: a touching, sensitive knowing.

It is not just the overtly colonised indigenous cultures that know this, not just the nations that have suffered imperialism or slavery, but any human being who has felt the stress, cruelty, insufficiency or marginalisation of education. Anyone who deplores seeing education manacled to corporations. All who resent seeing children as colonised subjects in the empire of the school, or decry the kind of education which meanly markets children as earners, consumers and debtors-to-be. This *cri de coeur* can be heard wherever people, in exasperation, anger and bewilderment want to snatch their children away from a toxic ideology that damages nature, and human nature. The Dominant Society, say the Arhuaco people of Colombia with real bitterness, knows little of the natural world but much about how to destroy it. At the core of Arhuaco education is the sacred duty of maintaining the balance of life: the protection of nature.

If this is the cherished end of the *camino* of pedagogy, how might those steps be taken in relation to individual children? It is a matter of one's gift, say Totonac people: the seed that needs to be discovered and nurtured from childhood. In effect, they say, like some of the more gifted educators of the Dominant Society: do not ask *if* this child is gifted but ask *how* is this child gifted.

In a traditional Totonac story, the sky-grandmothers merrily hurl stars at young children and the ones that stick are their gifts. So important is this sense of gift that it is inherent in the name Totonac, which means 'three hearts.' They gloss it thus: we need three hearts — to ask to know one's gift, to receive it, and to give it in service to the world. Totonac language is scented with metaphor — 'our speech is full of flowers,' they say.

Gift is a lovely word: it has lightness and lift, it is an open-handed and open-hearted word. And it shines, this word, lighting your path, a lodestar for the *camino* of your life.

Humberto García García realised that his gift was for pedagogy itself. His first school, he says, was Totonac culture, including learning from the elders through ceremonies, pottery and medicine. He went on to university and to postgraduate study in formal pedagogy, and was invited back to help with this initiative to rethink education. He smiles, partly woefully, partly proudly: 'I had to unlearn what I learnt at university. All my academic qualifications were not enough to cope with what I had to do here.'

The healer Francisco starts to explain to me the Totonac calendar of sacred time but right then a bell rings: a call to Catholic prayer. To be polite, I ask if he wants to attend. Our questions cross in mid-air as he, equally politely, is asking me the same. We smile at the perfectly-timed interruption. 'This is it!' he exclaims. 'The Catholic religion has broken our knowledge of the natural calendar.' He is saddened by the Church's persistent separation of people from nature, for without that relationship people lose three things, he says: respect, humility and generosity.

It cuts them to the heart to confront all that colonialism has done. García talks of sadness, confusion and fear, but also how the collective pain became a journey of discovery, to open their truths to the world. Willing to let in the glinting words, he says softly: 'We are sharing something which is both reality and metaphor.'

Francisco, likewise, bows to the words which matter: 'It's a school of life. It makes meaning. What is important is not only what we see,' he says, emphasising a distinction between knowledge typified by sight, and poetic knowledge, an embrace of the significance of others, the participation of oneself with the world outside oneself, the mediaeval 'sympathy.' At our feet lie the visible signs: seeds, leaves, circles, pottery — each one in itself a sympathetic symbol for concepts in the imagination.

If beauty is in the eye of the beholder, meaning is in the mind of the bestower, filling the world with mystery and metaphor.

There can be few more dramatic examples of schooling in mystery than the education of the Tairona *mamos* (priests) of the Sierra Nevada in Colombia. The Kogi, Arhuaco, Wiwa and Kancuamo peoples are descendants of the Tairona civilisation and their *mamos* are educated for their role from very early childhood. The tiny apprentice is taken to live in a dark cave, waking only at dusk and forbidden from seeing the daylight or even the light of full moon. He is taught songs, myths, the ancient ritual language of the *mamos*. Nine years pass.

Then the deepening training begins — another nine years, still dwelling in darkness, learning the knowledge written in stones, forests, lakes and mountains, hearing about the Great Mother, studying divination, meditation and the sacred duty of maintaining the balance of the natural world. It is the development of insight at the price of sight. The gift of vision given in darkness. The inward eye intuiting the mysterious before seeing the material.

But the Arhuaco people realised their material world was being stolen as the mestizos repeatedly cheated them in transactions that resulted in the Arhuaco losing their land. In terms of the human mind, it is as if the strengths of the right hemisphere of the brain (including metaphor, intrinsic value, a sense of the divine, the sacredness of life and nature) were emphasised, but the strengths of the left hemisphere (including price, measurement, and maths) were not. They decided their education needed something extra. Training in business. Accounts. Purchases. Sales. So in 1915, the Arhuaco asked the Colombian government to send them teachers for maths and written Spanish.

The government infamously twisted the request, sending in Capuchin friars who prohibited indigenous language, called their cultural heritage 'devilish' and 'heathenish' and enclosed children in a school that was called 'the orphanage.' The friars fined the children for every word they spoke in their own language (the price was ten cents a word, in the 1930s) and, as if performing the truth of Oscar Wilde's cynic, taught the children, the Arhuaco said, 'nothing of value.' The Arhuaco rid themselves of the friars only in 1982, literally drumming them out, surrounding the mission buildings, singing and dancing with accordions and flutes so the priests couldn't get a wink of sleep. When the Capuchins left, the Arhuaco set about transforming their education systems.

What do you get if you decolonise education? The best of both hemispheres, it seems. One Arhuaco initiative, the Centro Educativo Indígena Simunurwa, set up in 2007, includes numeracy and literacy in its syllabus. They use mobile phones and radio stations to communicate with international human rights organisations. They use their own language, stories, art, rites of passage, spirituality, music and law. The input of the elders is vital, and rivers and fields are 'classrooms.' Indigenous cosmology is taught alongside Western philosophers while certain plants are considered teachers, as they are across the Amazon, in diagnosing sickness as well as treatment. Arhuaco *mamos* are griefstruck because certain plants have 'vanished without even leaving us traces of their knowledge, of their teachings, of their healing properties,' they say.

Back in Papantla in Mexico, Bazbaz sweeps his arm protectively around his centre — which has been awarded a UNESCO award for Best Practice in Safeguarding Intangible Cultural Heritage. The plaque itself is decorated with stems of vanilla, a plant revered for its healing qualities. 'Twenty years ago, this wouldn't have been possible,' he says. It was made possible by the Zapatistas who, in terms of indigenous cultural self-respect, 'gave an alert to Mexico and to the world.'

The Zapatista movement ('For Humanity: Against Neoliberalism'), a left-wing uprising to defend the rights of indigenous Mexicans armed with poetry, guitars and guns, found its most eloquent spokesperson in the storytelling Subcomandante Marcos. He is not indigenous by birth but has become so by listening: the opposite of the queasy quadroonerie of essentialism, imposing its fascism of blood. Love for land is absolutely not the same as nationalism or blood-lines. Through humility, through humanity, through humus, Earth itself speaks to the indigenous human mind.

Marcos tells a story called 'The Words That Walk Truths,' a story about creating something which can carry light within it. This 'something' is a star, composed of earth, water, fire, air, lightning, heart and word, 'the good word, the true one.' This story, he says, comes from the deep earth. 'Dark is the earth, and dark is the dwelling where the first word, the true word, rests.' It is darkness which carries light.

When the healer Francisco speaks of the best kind of education, he applies it widely: 'This wisdom is not just for indigenous people but it should be universal.' There is a reason why we live on Earth, says the pedagogist García, because each of us has a service to perform, 'a gift to develop in life, to reach the light and to give it as an offering. It is blessed.' True education mirrors qualities of life itself: generous, generative, diverse and creative.

Rabindranath Tagore's philosophy strongly influences Schumacher College in Devon in the UK, and visiting there recently I met Martin Shaw, its mythologist-in-residence. If I played Fantasy Cabinet, I would make Shaw my Education Secretary. He calls himself a storyteller, though I would call him a storydoctor, using myths to heal, by psychic surgery if necessary. 'Story is a sharp knife,' he says. Stories are revered as teachers of true stature all over the indigenous world; encoding ecological knowledge or ritual significance, they can caution and adroitly admonish, pricking someone's conscience without shaming and they can console.

He mentions the Gaelic tradition where educational stories were called the 'swan feather cloak,' and 'every moment of your life should have you clothed in story.' Without that, children feel unsupported and isolated. 'What I see around me is children with colonised imaginations. They don't suffer a deficit of attention,' says Shaw, 'but a deficit of images that arrest the soul. Once you provide them, you are in the business of real education — to lead out.'

Name me something, I ask, which is important for children to learn.

'Manners.'

I smile, leaving a broad pause.

'They need to learn to be gallant. The kind of education I want results in affecting their relationship, as adults, with the Earth, so that in time we move from a society of taking to a culture of giving, in a society of relatedness. I want them to believe that if they don't say an inventive prayer, the Moon may not come out. To know that they themselves are a little part of the ecosystem that for a few years glimpses itself through human eyes. Inventiveness is so innate in children: it is not hard to provoke a courting culture, to speak Firebird language.'

I hear it. I know it. I honour it.

The furious tenderness of Romanticism is here, with its fierce kneeling in the presence of the natural world, not a rose-tinted moment of cultural history but a perennial and necessary aspect of the human psyche — and children are the great Romantics.

'Romanticism is activism,' says Shaw. 'And in children it is essential, it is not an indulgence. This kind of education is so basic it's like re-finding fire.'

Meanwhile, in the Sierra Nevada, after eighteen years of creating a world in the darkness of the imagination alone, one morning dawns like no other as the young *mamo* is led out to see his first sunrise on the astonished mountain.

The image he had painted in his mind, no matter how shining, will be dim by contrast. The world of his thought, no matter how generous, will be meanly bleak in comparison. The picture he had made will be shabby and poor beside the spiralling, splendour-swept world, its transcendence finally and truly beheld. The shock of rapture. Dazed by beauty and amazed by light. This is a sight whose resplendence leaves him awestruck for life: to see the radiance of the divine Earth and to know it holy.

Evening

Hearth: A Thesaurus of Home

There is one quality of evening that seems almost universal. The day's travels are over and the journey home begins. There is a sense of everyone turning towards home as the sun casts its shadows longer. Home-time. Dinner. Fireside. Little children needing tucking in. Chickens in their coops. The sheep in their folds. I say 'almost' universal, for there are those on the peripheries, teenagers on the periphery of adulthood, for example, and others for whom evening is a call in the reverse direction. Get out, get yowling, cats on the evening prowl... But for most of us, evening means turning back towards whatever — or whoever — constitutes the hearth of our lives.

I love the word hearth. Hearth is a nest-word. It holds within its nest many other words. Hearth, h-e-a-r-t-h, contains 'heat,' h-e-a-t, and 'earth,' 'art,' 'eat,' 'hear,' as well as 'he,' 'her,' 'are' and 'tea' (thankfully. We'll be coming back to tea.) And it holds, too ,the word 'heart.' The hearth is where the heart is earthed. Earth is the hearth, the quintessential home.

For me, in terms of language, the word 'hearth' is a thesaurus of home. But the home, the actual home, is a thesaurus of itself. A thousand things in your home or mine each speak the word 'home.' Two decades apart, two different people have carved wooden spoons for me. These spoons say 'home' to me, as does my house-key, long, large and simple. It is truly a key: a code-breaking word for home. One of the few things I have from my grandparents is a sage green mug, Denby stoneware, which my grandmother used in her life-long addiction to tea and Scrabble. Its quotidian quality has been treasured down the generations. If I hold that mug in my hand it spells 'hearth' to me and scores everything on the board.

My household holds many people including several artist friends whose work speaks of them. Each book in my house is a nest sheltering its author and possibly also the person who gave it to me. My bed, which I hand-painted with ivy up the bed legs and a magic tree whose branches hold glasses of wine, pineapples, chocolate and, yes, cups of tea, is home. Home is two cupped hands making a nest or a shelter — a *llan* in Welsh, now usually used to mean a church, but originally an enclosed and protective place, a shielded shelter. A garden can be the living breath of a home, where one can cultivate an 'I-thou' relationship of friendship in the view of the landscape architect Masuno Shunmyo, in contact with everything, including rocks and plants. The garden teaches that 'one is not alone, but always in relationship.'

Someone else can be, in themselves, a home: one's tell-first, the person who you tell your news and thoughts to, the person whose physical nearness makes you feel complete at the end of the day, psychologically at home. Boethius considered that there were three branches of music: the actual music of singers and players, and then the famous music of the spheres, and a third kind: *musica humana*, the internal music of the human body, in tune with itself as someone may be 'at home in their own skin,' that quality as modest as it is attractive, comfortably at ease in themselves, evincing a kind of inner harmony.

'This really brought it home to me,' we say, when we are intimately affected by something. 'Speaking home' means to penetrate or strike close. These phrases imply that the self exists on a cusp of vulnerability and defendedness, and suggest a relationship between home and honesty: 'telling some home-truths.' 'To come home to oneself,' we say, meaning a regaining of prior — and true — selfhood after an intermission.

Related to the word 'home' you find the Old Norse *heimr*, dwelling, village, both home and world. And in a sense one's home is a world. It contains the world writ small: the elements are there, with fire in a hearth or a candle, air in the windows, water in the bathroom, earth in a garden or window box or indoor plants. The related terms, Old Frisian *hem* and Lithuanian *kaims*, both mean home and village and, in a sense, a home *is* a small village. The bathroom cabinet, with first aid and pills, is a cottage hospital. A windowbox full of herbs is a cottage apothecary shop. In hospitality, every home can be a cottage inn, a cottage pub; a bookshelf is a cottage library; with the mantelpiece a cottage shrine; a littling world, but a whole one. And if each home can be a microcosm of the world, so the Earth has to be seen as a macrocosm of home: loved as such, tended as such.

A household is handmade, which is why interior-designered homes, machine-made, never feel homely. The homescape is homeshaped, turned by hand like slow carpentry, joinery enjoining person to place. It is crafted, rubbed by hand, in cleaning and making; it has the tactile texture of wood, paper and earth. Hewn from the world, it is selved into uniqueness. Delving through my novels to lend the right ones to a friend in want of books; delving out weeds in the garden, I am hewing my own being-at-home. Home language has this handmade quality — family nicknames for people and pets, or for the wheelbarrow, the shed, a favourite jug. Snug language, made to the measure of this home. Singular.

Our homes are so singular and intimate they smell of us. The warm smell of sleep on the pillowcase; the mint-scented soap in the bathroom steam. When I was a child, I loved sniffing other people's houses — puppy-like, I'd check out the one that smelt of pepper and so made me think of the Cook in *Alice in Wonderland*; the house that smelt of sandalwood and made me think of the Beatles. One of catpee. One of cakes. One of stale smoke and one of lavender. When I was a teenager I did a paper round on Sunday mornings and took the opportunity to feed my curiosity. One day, I rolled up a thick copy of the *News of the World*, shoved it like a lever in a letterbox and stared in, until stentorian voice from the garden behind me thundered: 'Can I Help You, Young Lady?' Awkward.

Our homes are confidantes of our rituals, wishes, secrets and hopes. They are as intimate, informal, and as singular as thou and thee; the intimate, informal and singular version of 'you.'

Home expresses thee: it is thou, distilled.

Thy innerness is outered.

Thy interior self is exteriorised.

Every home is, as it were, inside out, which is why it really is okay to talk to yourself at home, expressing in the outer air your inner mind.

It is familiar to you, where you know and are known. Home is an abode, where you bide (possibly with a 'bidie-in' as that lovely Scottish term has it; a cohabitant, a partner.) And to abide, to live with, connotes love, as language suggests more strongly in the converse: 'I cannot *abide* so-and-so, or such-and-such.' I loathe, and cannot live with them.

Something odd happens on the way in to someone's home. Look from the outside and each home is ordinary-sized, but step through the door and enter within, and it grows into a heroic portrait of that person, the patron, the Master or Mistress of Ceremonies. A mantelpiece or special shelf or the particular bit-by-the-kettle may be a shrine, privileging what (or who) is most important: the photos of the grandchildren, the mordant cartoon, the special whiskey, the talisman, the flowers. Your home is your castle. You can be at odds with the world, here, because your taste is the gold standard. One person's style is not another's — the grotesque kitsch of one person's knick-knacks another person cannot abide — and yet and yet and yet — each home-tender, tending their home, is making it a considered place, giving to it their attention, their thought.

For me, the language of home is Old English, its artist is Beuys, its material is wax and felt; its poet is Neruda and its philosopher Gaston Bachelard. In my kitchen there is a little bench by the windowsill where guests often sit, and I always hope they will look upwards because if they do (and only if they do) they will see my favourite quote from Bachelard: 'The house shelters day-dreaming, the house protects the dreamer, the house allows one to dream in peace.'

Bachelard writes of an ideal of home, as I do here. Ideal but also utterly common; the precious ordinary.

Salt. Candle. Seed. Shelf. Loaf. Mug. The quotidian things which are used every day, turning in the hands through the years of our lives and passed on, perhaps, down the years, grandparent to grandchild. Let me take you on a brief journey a moment, away from Wales to Calle Valencia, the street of potters in Úbeda, Spain. Here, Tito was born, lived and worked in this one street, under one sky, by one horizon. So long has this street been the home to potters that the subsoil under it contains remnants of pottery from Mediaeval and Renaissance times. His son, Paco Tito, also became a potter, as did his son in turn, Pablo Tito. The father hands over to son, who hands over to son, these hands which give and receive, which make homes every day, proudly serving the quotidian in forming the lips of a jug, tending to the edges of a cup. Historically, pottery was used in every part of life and in Úbeda, until 1955, there was no running water so people transported water in pitchers. A baby's first contact was with earthenware, as birthing chairs were made of pottery so as the child came out of the womb, it was contained within a pot; earth its first home.

Paco Tito has made twenty-five miniature sculptures in tribute to Cervantes' Don Quixote, and gently refers to 'My son, my squire' who we see in a photograph as a small child, held in the hands of his father. The hands which stroke a child, shaping circles of pottery in the eternity of generations, makes soul-houses with his hands. Start with earth, it made me think, and never forget that you need fire to make lasting art.

I visited their pottery with a friend, and bought a green mug. Back home, this mug is a touchstone of memory: it cost about ten euros and is priceless. The home is the place of your treasures, for those things which are favoured — chairs, rugs, coats. Our 'stuff' in that lovely, humble word. We feel we belong among our belongings. But with caution. For possessions can take possession, possessing us. 'You can't have everything,' someone once said. 'You can't have everything. Where would you put it?'

The hoarding of unwantable stuff, the ceaseless buying of more, suffocates a house and its inhabitants. William Morris spoke so precisely and wisely to that issue: 'Have nothing in your houses that you do not know to be useful, or believe to be beautiful.'

Hoarding makes you stumble as you walk through your home; it catches your ankles — this thing needs fixing, that needs washing, that needs to be hung up. Stuff, hoarded, stops you in your tracks, it is a stagnant sump where there should be flow, for part of what makes home comfortable is fluency — the flow of movement and the flow of fluent thought and speech where you don't feel silenced and stopped.

If I ruled the world, by the way, I would ban coasters. They stop the flow. The real flow. All those years of requiring yourself, your family, your bidie-in, your guests, to make half a million awkward gestures, to interrupt half a million anecdotes, to fluff the punchline of half a million jokes, to foul up free easefulness — for that? For a tabletop? Let it go. Something beautiful will happen inside you — a generosity of hearth more valuable than the world's most expensive table.

Because that is how a home is made — by usage — the rounded edges, the worn-down carpet, the kitchen table softened and moulded by years of elbows, plates and movements; the signature of use. This is what it means to be cosy, that lovely onomatopoeic word, that is how a house hugs you gently, the softest *hygge*.

Home is also a place of freedom, where you do not need permission, where you can feel unselfconscious. It is a place of freedom within the bounds set by the arithmetic of those who share it with you. Home is a place for one's companions (etymologically, *com*, with, and *panis*, bread: those who eat bread with you) and whether shared with friends or family, cats, dogs or books.

The home is a foundation, where your life is founded, and where you are to be found, unlost — seen, revealed and known. Here, one belongs. Home is where our tales are brought back to; what happened at school, at work, out in the world. Home is a core audience. Here is where we tell things first and where they may be most precisely heard. Here is certainty, assurance and reassurance. Home — Old English *ham* — is related to the

Sanskrit word *ksema*, which has been translated as 'the place your soul calls home.' The meanings of *ksema* include: dwelling, habitable place, ease and safety. The refuge, in other words. The home is the unsunderable place, which is why, after a burglary, victims often feel most keenly not the value of things lost, but the violation of their refuge.

And this is part of the reason why domestic abuse (and not just between couples) is so peculiarly vicious, because it breaks the spell of safety, splits apart the idea of refuge, poisons cosiness, jars all sense of ease and uses intimacy as a weapon. And when you dread going home — for the lightning striking gash of danger you fear there, then you are, in your soul, homeless. This is why the Covid-19 pandemic, swapping shelter for imprisonment, had such terrible effects for those unhappy or scared at home. Domestic abuse crushes who you are.

Dwelling is intrinsic to being human. Heidegger was fascinated by manifestations of dwelling (including the way that, as we saw earlier, poetry can be a dwelling) and he delved into language to show that the root of the German word 'to be' is cognate with 'to dwell,' declaring: 'To be a human being... means to dwell.' Housing is even more than a human right — a human having — it is part of what it means to be a human being. I have experienced years of home-lacking, and the knowledge leaves me quick to see how the lack of decent and affordable housing is an act of psychic cruelty, suffered by thousands upon thousands of people, and inflicted deliberately by successive governments.

★

Some years ago, I was returning home after being abroad for many months. I can't say I missed England, but I missed English. On my homeward journey, I heard English spoken — as a mother tongue — with relief and gratitude. I was home in words. Sometimes I find that if I say — or hear — the precise word for something, my psyche feels as if it has been welcomed: the word is offering my mind hospitality and I can feel at home. At other times, a particular word comes into view, unsought-for, but glowing like embers, inviting me in, to stay a while, have a drink with it. In the course of any day, words can be flitting-tents on a desert journey or quick shelters on a stumblepath.

Mother tongue. Native language. Word world. Language and land combined, like Langland peerlessly ploughing the earth for a harvest of eloquence.

Rose Auslander was a Jewish poet whose name became her destiny. Auslander means outlander; foreigner or alien, and she became a foreigner in her own land, a fugitive to escape the Holocaust. She hid in cellars fleeing from place to place: 'And while we waited for death, some of us lived in dream-words, our traumatised home in the homelessness.' After the Holocaust, she refused for some eight years to write in German, and instead wrote in English. In her 1978 poem 'Mutterland,' she writes:

'My Fatherland is dead.
They buried it
in fire.
I live
in my Motherland —
Word.'

Language is home. Words make shelters, they fluff out nests for themselves. They dig into the earth of their derivations, find their roots, at home in the families of language, at ease in their connotations with neighbours, the little neologisms skittering around their heels like puppies yapping for the attention they need if they are to survive. (I give you one such: chillax. A word that should have been strangled at birth.)

To dwell well is to be who we truly are and will become: to have a shelter from which to see the future with tranquillity, and permanence is one of the most important aspects of home. The home houses time. It shelters yesterday, today and tomorrow. It is where you have lived and will live. It retells your past; it treasures your present; it consoles your future. It holds time, precious and warm, close in its hands. It presses time and the juice of it — the wine of time — steeps each room. An intimate history, an enfolded present, an entrusted future.

Home is made in layers; a personal geology; strata laid by fifteen Christmases, layers of summer afternoons gardening. Overlays of splashes — a wide-flung glass of wine dancing *L'chaim* (To Life!) stains my wall, happily. Home is witness.

Home is the site of time turning and returning, the eternal return of the turning year, a sweet, specific calendar of snowdrop to daffodil to rose, of bird nesting and fledgling flights, of the sunslant in June and the hoarfrost in January.

Habits themselves create a sense of home: people say they feel at home when they are in their daily routine. Habits can house your hours, your life. A habit is both time (as in rhythm tapped out) and also a home, as in to inhabit, having a habitat. (A rabbit has a habit of habitat-tapping.)

You inhabit the home through habits, repeated actions, the heft of again and again, as time turns around the clock of you. Home is the place of returning, where you return and your friends return: where your road starts from and where it leads back to, each of us a Ulysses, weeping with love on seeing our Ithaca.

And where is Ithaca? Whose is it? There is truly not one Ithaca but rather a myriad of Ithacas, each one intimate, informal and singular: my Ithaca and thy Ithaca, and thine and thine and thine and thine and thine.

Writing this makes me feel a bitter fury, though, as if I have been forced to write a lie. All this — Ithaca of mine and thine — is what ordinary *should* look like. Having a wall to put pictures on, having the space for bookshelves, having somewhere for an unofficial shrine: all this is a human right, simply our due, and one defended in principle by Nemesis. But an ordinary, everyday kind of home has become extraordinary and the basic, sweet right to housing has been stolen. The absolutely commonplace has become a luxury that so many, particularly the young, are denied. The following chapter takes us there.

A Beggarly Account of Empty Boxes

Once there was a sheepdog who lived near me in mid-Wales. Bred to work, trained to work, work was his vocation, his calling, his joy. One day, a farmer from Southern England visited the local livestock market and was so impressed by this dog's working skills that he bought the dog on the instant and took him away. In his new home, the dog refused to work. Doggedly refused. He lost heart. He seemed sick. He pined.

A year passed. The farmer, frustrated, brought the dog back to the little Welsh town. This dog was rubbish, he said. He'd paid good money but the dog was absolutely useless. The original owners took the dog back. In the hills he knew, the dog sniffed the air. His ears pricked up. His eyes brightened. He shook himself and rolled with the elastic ecstasy of a young and happy dog. His glossy coat rippled in the breeze like long grass streaming in the wind. And at the first whistle he was off; he had forgotten no commands, was keen as mustard again, working as gladly and well as he ever had.

To be on the safe side, though, the owners popped him in the back of the trailer and drove him to the local vets for a check-up. There was no sign of mistreatment, no disease, absolutely nothing wrong: why had the dog been brought in? The owners explained the dog's baffling refusal to work for a year. His sickness, said the vets, was real — but not physical. The only conclusion they could draw was that this dog had been suffering from acute homesickness.

There is a Welsh word untranslatable into any single English word: *hiraeth*. It is homesickness, nostalgia, and longing, all together. An equivalent is the Portuguese term *saudade*, a word from a minor key, the melancholy dream-desire for what was. Kant remarked that people were not so much homesick for a place as for a time, the time of their youth, which Proust expressed so well in the smell of a madeleine. It makes me wonder about the five senses of nostalgia. For me, they would include the smell of lavender in my grandmother's walled garden on a hot summer day. The sound of wood pigeons in the trees at dawn. The touch of a purring cat. The taste of McVitie's digestive biscuits. The sight of my childhood blanket, a deep corngold colour.

Homesickness can feel as incontrovertible as the pull of a magnet, as irresistible as the force of gravity. Homesickness is an example of the heart's laws of physics. The centripetal tug drawing you ineluctably towards the centre, the focus, the hearth of your world.

A Swiss doctor, Johannes Hofer, invented the word 'nostalgia' an 'ache for home,' in 1668, and its symptoms included melancholy, incessant thoughts of home, heart palpitations and fever. From about 1680 it was understood as a potentially lethal illness, and its diagnosis spread around the world. When soldiers in the American Civil War were admitted to the first military hospital for the insane in 1863, the most common diagnosis was nostalgia. By World War II, soldiers were still being treated for it, though the term used was homesickness.

This word was created in 1756 as a direct translation of *heimweh*, a Swiss-German dialectal term from *Heim* meaning home and *Weh* meaning woe or pain. *Heimweh* was particularly associated with Swiss mercenaries fighting abroad in the seventeenth century. Famous for bravery, they were vulnerable to homesickness, longing for the mountains of their home. It was considered a serious disease and could lead to desertions, illness and even death. They were banned from singing traditional songs because of the nostalgic pain these songs created. Scottish mercenaries, hearing bagpipes, were thought to suffer the same.

The homesick are, in a sense, the lucky ones, because they have a home. We are, all of us, vulnerable things, like the pink at the base of the nail, the quick of it, so easily hurt without the tough nail to protect it from a shriek of pain. Each of us desperately needs the shelter of a home, because otherwise the exposure — of both body and mind — is vicious.

In London's Piccadilly, one evening, I watched a young couple sleeping. They looked sweet, curled together, almost happy. So intimate it was, I felt I shouldn't be looking. They were cuddled up on a thick red blanket, a sleeping bag spread over them both, on a freezing pavement in January. *A fucking freezing pavement in January.* On Charing Cross Road I stopped to talk to a young man whose home was the set of steps outside one of London's most famous theatres. From his stage, he spoke of his life, abuse and alcoholism and friendship. Home lost and found and lost.

Raynor Winn writes of her and her husband's experience of becoming homeless, and walking the South West Coast Path, owning nothing more than they could carry. She comments on the cruelty of people along the way who, if they considered them homeless tramps, condemned and disdained them, but who would find the couple inspirational if they thought they had sold their house to walk the path.

There is the absolute homelessness of street sleepers, but there is also relative homelessness; someone sleeping on a friend's sofa for months, or young people forced to live with their parents till they're in their thirties, simply because they cannot afford a home. Short-term lets and insecure tenancies are also forms of relative homelessness. Too many people know the flotsam homelessness of sofa-surfing, the 'beggarly account of empty boxes' as Shakespeare writes of the impoverished apothecary. Rents and house prices going up and up like rising sea levels, and so many people drowning. Meanwhile, high house prices tie people into debts of crippling interest payments, and the media, amazingly, informs us repeatedly that this indebtedness is good news as house prices rise. It is not good news for anyone suffering the effects of indebtedness. It is not good news for the younger generation who may never be able to afford a home.

Temporary housing is a slow-acting caustic, corroding vitality. For nearly twenty years, it fragmented my work, made it impossible to make plans, and put a terrible strain on relationships. I felt exiled from any sense of my own future: I was permanently temporary, living in waiting rooms, my life on hold. Each move felt like it took a year off my life, in stress and wasted time. The precious water of my life was spilling, pouring away without a cup to contain it. I felt spilled. I lost all my possessions twice over, including years of gifts and presents. I couldn't keep anything because I had nowhere to put them. To those who hath, more shall be given. To those who hath not a hathing-place, the little they hath shall be taken away.

Of course my experience is nowhere near the worst nor is it rare. It is a horribly common curse, this, of precarious housing, being underhomed, homeneeding, homelacking, homehungry. If nostalgia is an ache related to the past — being far from a home which did exist but no longer does, and if homesickness is an ache related to the present — being away from a home which does exist, then this homehunger is an ache for the future, for something which doesn't yet exist but whose need is felt bitterly now.

Insecure housing damages both physical and mental health. The staccato of temporary housing gives the melody of life no pause, no rest or serenity. Homehunger saps your energies, dislocates your attention; books are not properly read, food not properly digested, as if you are always leaning against a splintered prow-rail between a slippery deck and a fathomless sea, envying Odysseus for he at least had a home to be sick for. The homehungry hear the siren inside them, the slanted, maddening note of injustice. They feel the oceans around them, as they are jetsam on the waters, driftwood of a para-life.

There are, of course, things people can do to remedy their housing situation. Adult cuddles. Friends with Benefits. If you are willing to offer a landlord these, you may live with reduced rent, as the classified advert site Craigslist infamously demonstrated, hosting adverts by house-owners who wanted rent paid in a different coin. Young women, especially, are targeted by this, and some have felt had no option but to take up these offers. As Shelter's policy officer John Bibby remarked, this 'reflects the desperate measures people are forced to take as a result of the housing crisis.' In the Covid pandemic, Shelter reported that these offers of accommodation for sex had increased, often targeting young women already bruised by the effects of lockdown.

And, while so many people have nowhere to live, others buy houses as if they were playing Monopoly. A house in a village near mine was bought as a second home 'investment,' and at the time of writing it has been unused for eight years. Not one person has slept once in any of its many bedrooms. Not one dream has been dreamt there, not one joke told nor glass of wine drunk nor book read.

In the countryside, you can often tell which are the second homes. They are formidably neat, done up usually with fastidious consonance to the materials and design of the locality. But for all this, the second homes strike a dissonant note in the landscape. The owners doubtless think they own the place. I don't. Nothing is owned by buying. You own things by dwelling with them, knowing and tending things.

But there is really no such thing as a second home. There are homes and there are denyings of homes to others. As one more house is bought as a plaything — one in ten adults in Britain owns a second home — so one more family is exiled, in these cruel if bloodless clearances: exiled by toys. Hestia, the Greek goddess of the hearth, will only dwell in one home for a hearth is not an object but a result: the result of dwelling. Second homes are hearthless. Nemesis hates them. According to her laws, each person would have a place of their own, the allotment of home.

I don't blame individuals: I understand that people cherish their second homes as best they can, and that they often get profound joy and health from their time out of city-life. I just wish government policy made it a priority that everyone should have one home before anyone else had two. And I wish that second home owners could step back and see their role in the diminishment of convivial community. In the traumatic time of the Covid-19 outbreak, people were begged not to visit their second homes because the local health services were simply unable to cope with caring for people not registered in the area. The visitors would collectively bring disease and would undermine health and the healthcare system. Second homes spell death to community. A friend of mine is a Dorset maid, born and bred. She has worked most of her life doing public health work in poor communities around the world. Pregnant, she wanted to return home, to where her parents and all her grandparents had always lived. She was unable to afford to buy or even rent anywhere, as the majority of houses in her village were second homes, almost entirely unused, dead for fifty weeks of the year. She gave birth in a cow shed at the bottom of her mother's garden. I have always wanted those who own a second home to know this almost biblical story.

These second homes disenchant the land, blocking the literal footpaths and the metaphoric songlines. Houses and farms, when dwelled in, are small melodies of livelinesses across the hills: the windows are eyes, the doors are mouths. In the second homes, the windows are blinded, the doors are dumb and the chimney pots deaf to the wind. Eyeless. Rigid. A little *rigor mortis* in the mortice. The second homes have the tidied perfection of a grave. Tidy as the drains of Strata Florida. The second home owners have bleached the bluebells of their colour, siphoned off the stream and made twilight an investment opportunity as the intruder lights shine like corpse candles into the emptied night. What is finished is perfect and dead: these perfect cottage corpses. Dafydd ap Gwilym's grave has more life in it, more dwelling.

*

Homehunger speaks the obstacled language of im- ob- in- un-. The homehungry are unphrased, impeded, obstructed, incoherent, obliterated. Those without a voice are ignored and neglected. The imposition of the bedroom tax caused a massive rise in rent arrears and evictions. Almost two thirds of all the tenants who would be affected by the tax had a disability; many of them were disabled children.

The housing crisis, which twists so many lives out of true, is still too often perceived as a private grief, a personal difficulty. It isn't.

It's a politically-driven violation of human rights. The Universal Declaration of Human Rights states that everyone has a right to housing adequate for their health and well-being. U.N. member states — including the UK — are pledged to observe this.

In the UK, total homelessness rose by 26% between 2011 and 2013. In 2019, one person in every 200 was homeless, and every eight minutes a child became homeless. In 2021, in London, one person in 53 was homeless. Must *Cathy Come Home* be filmed every new decade for every new decade to forget? When will the greed of private landlords be seen as a cause of shame rather than admiration? At what point, when people buy second homes as toys while others lack first homes as necessity, does a lack of imagination become criminal? Danny Dorling, professor of geography at Oxford University, demonstrates that unaffordable housing is a result of widening inequality in wealth. 'The great housing insecurity of our times has been brought about by a minority becoming the hoarders of property, and this hoarding has been facilitated by successive governments,' he writes, advocating rent controls as the obvious first step.

Human skin is too thin a shelter against a cutting wind, for street sleepers whose only home is the 'bone house' as Anglo Saxon terms the human body. The human mind is also too thin-skinned, too sensitive for such rough living. Without the intimate nest of home, the psyche has two choices. It can stand on guard, on the ropes, jumping at the edge of itself, hyper-alert, readied, vigilant and brittle or else it retreats, withdraws, as the self seeks shelter ever deeper within itself to escape the pitiless exposure of an unhoused life.

Where exile or unhomedness is a choice, there can be power and vitality in the decision to leave: an exodus for an adventure; an exile for a divinity; a wanderer for a song. But circumstances force unfree choices.

I met a wandering minstrel in Berlin last year, a latterday troubadour, walking out one midsummer morning. A performer, dancer and actor, Lars would, he told me, prefer to have a home, but it is too expensive, this human right, unless he gives up who he is. Artists find it hard to be artists these days — there are no garrets for them to starve in. So, making a virtue of necessity, he is a nomad like so many young people. He has a small caravan in France where he keeps his books, but for the rest, he carries his *lares* and *penates* on his back. His household is just that: quite literally what he can hold. He also holds dear his hours, and his metaphors, making a hedge-hearth wherever he can, pared down like a mendicant's begging bowl and two cupped hands, and finding a home within himself, staying grounded, he says, and true to himself. Lars spent an afternoon once in the *Jardin des Plantes* in Paris where an Indian man asked him about his life.

'Ah, I see,' said the Indian at last, 'you're a saddhu.'

'How did that make you feel?' I asked.

'Recognised,' said Lars, instantly.

Spiritual traditions understand sacred homelessness, living in the present moment so fully that monks and mendicants who have no literal home, can find a home everywhere, spiritually. Mindfulness makes each moment a shelter. 'It is a virtue to travel through life without a home,' says the *Dhammapada*, the sayings of the Buddha. Lars and others are trying to make necessity into just such a virtue.

The price of a home is unjustly high. The price of losing a settled life is also unjustly high: it costs Lars relationships and the possibility of having children. The soft animal body wants a burrow but more than physical shelter, the self needs a place of sheltering, a self-scape shaped uniquely to you, where you can see yourself at the heart of your own life. The present is diminished without witness of walls. The past has no audience. The future is an alibi. Always elsewhere, out of reach, heard like an echo of silence, mute, uneasy, unjust and oddly lonely, the self without a sense of itself.

The hearth, as an earlier chapter explored, is the heart of the home. Put another way, the fireplace is the focus of a room — (quite literally in etymology, the word 'focus' is the Latin for fireside, and think *fuego*, fire in Spanish, or *fuoco* in Italian). There is a wider analogy: the *home* is the focus of the *self*. The house tends the flame of the individual. Each person needs a home so their flame doesn't go out. Thus the habits of our inhabitation are self-reflexive. Fire lights you. The bed makes you. Laundry washes you. Books read you. Wine drinks you. The garden weeds you. The roof mends you. The walls decorate you. Cats stroke you to sleep. The home builds you. The house holds you.

Since 2010, there has been a 165% rise in rough sleeping in the UK, and the homeless die on average thirty years younger than those with homes.

'Please respect this space!' says a notice handwritten on cardboard, on the edge of a chalked-out rectangle just in front of the National Gallery in Trafalgar Square. 'In memory of our fallen homeless brothers and sisters.' It is moving, the sense of camaraderie and the gentle defiance of taking back one symbolic and tiny plot of land. I speak to Mick who tells me about the launch of the Homeless Party, to draw attention to the situation. There are now 6,000 people sleeping on the streets and many of these are ex-army, which is why 'the fallen' is such a pertinent term. The trigger for homelessness is, for so many people, not necessarily unemployment or drug-use but splitting up with a partner. Following that emotional catastrophe, problems with housing, then work, then (possibly) alcohol and drugs ensue. It is a terrible truth that a personal relationship breaking down begins the process, and a social relationship breakdown cements it.

During the Covid-19 outbreak, the homeless faced new vulnerabilities: sick on the streets, many with pre-existing respiratory problems, they were badly affected. Ill, they had no warm bed to sleep in, no home to shelter them as they self-isolated. One of the few silver linings in the clouds of the outbreak was that some of London's homeless were housed: in the hotels emptied of tourists. And why, I cannot help ask, is their raw hurt not cared for in so-called normal times, by requisitioning the use of second homes? Everyone matters.

In the pandemic, the work of medics was newly cherished, people who, often without sufficient protective equipment themselves, were putting their lives at risk to help others. Treasured, that is, by most but not all. There were reports of doctors and paramedics and nurses, in the UK and India, who found themselves rewarded for their work by being evicted from their homes by landlords and landladies fearing they might get infected.

Sometimes it is out of the harshest situations that the most profound homes are hewn. A while ago, I had been speaking in the extravagantly elegant city of Cartagena in Colombia, as part of a tour when I had been the Hay Festival's International Fellow. I heard about a place they call the City of Women situated in El Pozón, a huge slum area of Turbaco. I wanted to go. It is built by women: they physically build the houses, brick by brick. It is built by and *for* women, a cruel proportion of whom are victims of sexual violence, all of whom have been made homeless — displaced — by the civil war raging in Colombia for a generation. 'Displaced' sounds so hygienic, as casual as a misplaced pair of glasses, an unfreighted, unsad, almost unsaid word. The realities, though, are heart-heavy.

They laugh a lot, these women from the League of Displaced Women — they laugh carefree as white sails on a summer sea, they laugh mischievous as cubs in spring, they laugh warm as cast-iron stoves in winter. In spite of everything.

I ask them about being displaced and their laughter evaporates. 'To be homeless! To have nothing — !' They cannot complete the sentence, just raise their eyes and touch their hearts with the palms of their hands.

Here are the figures behind which are the nightmares, the sense of shame forced on them, the feeling of filth which can never be washed away, the lives slashed apart, the horror: 32% of women report being displaced while heavily pregnant; 26% are victims of injury by the armed forces while pregnant, and in four cases such treatment resulted in miscarriage; 16% are victims of threat or attempted rape; 10% are victims of rape and 5% victims of sexual slavery.

Meanwhile, on the streets outside, graffiti reads: *El Cuerpo Es Mio y Yo Decido*. ('This is my body, and I decide.') Trees and plants line the street, kids swerve around on bikes past houses painted blue and pink, one painted bright azul and many with decorative tilings and greenery. There is a rocking chair in a little courtyard area, and mango and palm trees tickle the bright sky behind the houses.

'We were determined to have greenery outside,' they say fervently. 'We want less concrete, somewhere tranquil. We want green trees and nature because there hasn't been so much joy for us and these are a help.' Pots and ferns promote the growth of green thoughts in a green shade.

They show me a tree planted and a plaque for Patricia Guerrero (her name means warrior), a penal lawyer who founded the League. She was herself displaced and had been threatened and been given state protection, ('for what it is worth,' say the women.) Two hundred women came together, displaced from all corners of Colombia, not knowing each other but sharing a history of having to flee — often widowed, as their husbands had been killed in the conflict, often with children, sharing an experience of the kind of obliteration that comes from this combination of attack and displacement and, at the beginning, the feeling that they had no rights.

The League has so far built 105 houses plus an office. 'We dream,' they say, 'of a dignified home.' The women I speak to choose their words carefully; they know what it is like to have no words, no voice, and they say that this is a crucial part of the League, that it has given them the courage, strength and confidence to stand up and say with conviction 'I'm a woman and I've got rights.'

I make the mistake of asking if there are other examples of women building their own townships in these circumstances in Colombia. Other models? They shake their heads. 'Only us. This barrio is unique. We are the model for others.'

What is a home? I ask. 'A place which protects you and makes you secure, it is about love, and unity. Of course more than anything it is a house.'

Lubis Cardenas is now coordinator of the League. 'When I remember each woman first moving into her home,' she says, 'I get a lump in my throat.' Each time someone moves in, there is a fiesta, a party, I am told, but even when houses are finished, some people are afraid of taking a house because of what it might bring.

For further cruelty has followed them: they are targeted by the paramilitaries. Three years ago, a member of the League, Kayla Berrio Almanza, no more than thirty, was sent death threats. Then she was raped and assassinated. She was very active in human rights, they say, 'a strong character and a strong voice.'

The partner of one of the League was assassinated, the community centre was burnt down and youngsters have been disappeared. Why, I ask, when you've already lost your land, do they still come after you? 'Simply because we are trying to defend human rights and for that we are threatened,' they say. 'It's about power.' The government of this area is right-wing and associated with the paramilitaries and they don't want these women who are, in effect, human rights defenders. In Colombia, being 'accused' of being a human rights defender is tantamount to a death sentence.

As they show me details of the house: a sink, the toilet, breeze blocks, they add that one man helping the women was killed just for making breeze blocks. In the courtyard, one of the women semi-automatically picks up a broom and sweeps up leaves. That house-proud sense. And after the humiliation of rape, pride is a beautiful thing.

'We are doing this *contra viento y marea*, against the wind and the tide, against all odds,' says Lubis. 'We've been able to build dreams.'

It has been as important to rebuild identity as it has been to rebuild houses, they say, and point out how people who have lost their smallholdings, their local culture, their traditions, find that their identity feels precarious in a shanty town. The material side of losing a house is very tough, they say, but you can put the material stuff back together. The psycho-social fallout of displacement is very hard to manage. Hard — but they do it, constructing houses and reconstructing psyches. What are they like, these women? They are strong as an act of will, they are defiant, funny, hurt, spirited, vulnerable, tough, political, charismatic and kind. Arms around them.

Artifice and Pastoral

There is an evening in every year, just as there is an evening in every day. Autumn is the year's evening, forgetting summer but not yet fully aware of winter. I went to the Arctic, some time ago, arriving as the oceans were just beginning to freeze over, and the light was becoming shorter and more severe.

Autumn, here, is a delicate moment between the two poles of time. At midsummer, dazzling with light, the mind can be noonstruck by midnight's brilliance. Midwinter dark is potentially lethal and the mind needs stories and beliefs to survive it. The autumn is trickier than either, though, because the strictness of time at the poles is less predictable.

I was there when the polar bears were prowling, in this, the hungriest season of the bear year. For the Inuit in the high Arctic, it was one of the last whale-hunting days of the season, and the seas were colder by the day, with bear-paw ice and ice plates forming. The implacable ice, imprisoning waves.

If I imagine Nemesis as a place, I picture the Arctic. It is a place of strict limit by virtue of the laws of nature. The limits of summer ice and of winter sea ice dictate where people can travel, how they can travel, and if they can travel. The limits of temperature are the limits of life.

If I hear the tone of voice of Nemesis, I hear the way Inuit people speak. Strict with facts: rigorously honest. Facts, comments the anthropologist Hugh Brody, are the basis of crucial decisions so 'life can hang on accuracy and anything less than accuracy is reprehensible.' This, he comments was the case with Inuit people and indeed all the hunter-gatherer people he has lived with.

In the Arctic, I could hear this commitment to truth-telling in the tone of people's speech, slow, careful, exact. There was no sense of artifice. It was as if my very body could feel that their speech was authentic. Their tone of voice is the opposite of tricksterish contemporary politics, so full of slippery artifice, fake news, political posturing and outright lies.

And yet when I stayed in various Inuit communities for several weeks, I felt conscious of a terrible conflict between concepts: artifice versus reality. Reality was, always, the land and the laws of ice. Artifice came up from the south, melting ice, melting language, melting meaning. It was the evening of an entire culture.

In the home where I stayed, the small son spent hours every day engrossed in a computer game, its main character called Spyro. Part of the game included an old man offering to tell Spyro stories. 'Stories? Aw, no thanks,' says Spyro, scornfully. 'Stories, aw, no thanks,' imitated the child aloud. His grandfather, one of the community's elders, was a fund of tales: of foxes and men, bears and ice, stories with truths deep within them.

'This is a flight simulator,' enthused one man, showing me the virtual-reality program on his computer.' You can fly over this exact place.' You can, in other words, pretend to be where you already are.

For those younger than about forty, hunting was a lost skill. These generations were forced to go to White (*Qallunaat*) school, so had no childhood apprenticeship in hunting. Not knowing how to survive on the land, they were dependent on jobs and housing fixed up by the government from way down south, and on store-bought food.

One young man, with no money and no knowledge of the land, tried to go hunting to feed his family. He took his son with him and they never came back. The bodies were found eventually, the son's face eaten by ravens. This is a stark result of the strange artifice of their lives. Younger people become effectively imprisoned in these tiny, claustrophobic communities, and Pink Floyd's *The Wall* is popular ('We don't need no education'). The rates of suicide, violence, alcoholism and drug use have rocketed.

I asked one Inuit woman how she felt about the land. 'I remember it was beautiful,' she said wistfully. The land was still there, a few yards from her door, thousands of miles of land as wide and beautiful as it ever had been but she was weirdly — artificially — alienated from it. Not so the elders, traveling by boat, Ski-doo or dog-teams. They knew how to hunt, they knew the language of the land, those dozens of distinct words for snow and ice, on which your life may depend. They cherished the freedom of the land, that non-negotiable authenticity.

The elders are less confident of their knowledge now, because of climate change; I was told of an elder who went through the ice and drowned in a place where it never would have happened before. We're north of everywhere, they say, and the first to feel these changes. 'I'm the last man standing, so be careful with me,' says one, in elliptical vulnerability.

This is the reality of climate change, in a time when artifice, spin and outright lies have dominated the debate: the Politics of Artifice. Perverse and cruel, it is an ideology that commits itself to the primacy of the fake and declares war on all that is natural.

Conceptually, one could say that a series of artifices has caused climate collapse. Artificial, unsustainable energy use. The artificial present that takes no account of its effects on the seventh generation. The artificial humanism that insists that human activities are supremely valuable while other creatures and habitats have no intrinsic value. The world's richest nations and individuals have adopted a high-risk credit strategy, over-borrowing from the Earth, taking the wealth of fossil fuels, heedlessly racking up the toxic debts of CO_2 in the atmosphere, and addressing the bill to future generations, to the nation of Tuvalu or to the Inuit. We have borrowed from our children more than carbon: we have borrowed sky, serenity and life, and we are barely bothering to apologise for defaulting so grossly on the loan.

The financial market is index-linked to its own artifice, and having created synthetic wealth for a few, it has demanded that ordinary people should pay in real terms. While hundreds of billions of dollars were poured in to rescue the financial market (that peculiar and greedy artifice of credit, futures trading, short-selling, hedge funds, and gambling), the question remains why there is not a similar, immediate amount of money put toward the rescue of the climate, that radiant, generous, and delicate reality.

The Arctic has its chiaroscuro effects; the black feather on snow, the red whale blood on a white frozen shore. Perhaps because the Arctic is a place of such stark realities (death and the raven, or the midnight sun), somehow artifice seems yet more artificial by contrast: television's simulacrum and the virtual world, that über-artifice, seem to jar against the human senses more here than anywhere.

Staring at the screen of the flight simulator, you are in actuality screened off from where you are. Being anywhere in the virtual world, you are nowhere in the real one. Facebook is here, of course, being everywhere.

The small boy playing Spyro was stupefied and spaced out, his senses dulled by the anaesthetic of artifice. The human spirit needs authenticity for its vitality and intelligence to flourish; we know the world bodily and we are intelligent not only with our minds but through our senses. Another term for stupidity is non-sense.

Out on the land, in the Arctic, intelligent hunting uses all the senses, not just the usual five, but a sense of duration in time, a sense of direction in space, a sense of weather, a sense of being watched. In the world of artifice, though, I am exiled from all my own senses, alienated even from myself, existing as a screened-off simulacrum of myself.

I can't kiss you with an emoticon. I am alone, I am pale, I am chilly, I am tired, listless under the lifeless glow of my computer, keeping in touch with you on Facebook. I cannot. For in what e-twilight can my hand find yours?

As humans, we are endlessly, delightfully enchantable. Our enchantability has led us to love the moon and ice, the spirits of the land, prairies, dogs and dragonflies. Our enchantability has given us song, dream, fiction, fascination, enthrallment and the iridescent quality of art's illusions.

But this enchantability is also our vulnerability — making us prey to simulacrum, artifice and con tricks. Gullible, we can be snared by falsity. There are two kinds of fiction: fiction that is a dream and fiction that is a lie. There are two kinds of enthralling, too: one, the enthralled rapture of a theatre audience, the other, being in thrall, being literally in slavery, to the giddy, mesmerising world of marketing and advertising, spin, PR and political deceit. The age of oil, with its slick pretence of permanence, has tricked us badly. Modernity, seeking artifice with such avidity, demanding deception for entertainment, has fostered its own credulity, so the lies and deceits of the media, were eagerly swallowed not because they were such good liars but because our society is fascinated by the fake.

'Beauty is truth, truth beauty,' wrote Keats in a line of crystallised genius suggesting to me how authenticity is always beautiful but artifice has an ugliness at its core. While art sensitises its audience, artifice desensitises its consumers, brutalising the soul.

Let me tell you a true story about artifice. One morning (it was a scruffy morning, lapsang souchong tea, watching last night's dirty dishes for any sign of its becoming a self-organising system) I had the radio on, and it was covering the story of an unhappy lad, only seventeen, who climbed up a multi-storey car park and for some three hours he delayed, agonising about his life and wondering whether to jump, a strange, sad Hamlet of suicide. The story was cruelly extraordinary in the very ordinariness of my morning. A crowd of some 700 people gathered, and people in the crowd began jeering, cruelly goading him to jump. 'Jump, you ****, jump,' it was reported, the expletives deleted. How could anyone be so unfeeling? The reason — as other onlookers were the first to say — was that people were not reacting to the reality of what they were seeing, but were instead responding as if they were watching a film or computer image; living too much in the artificial worlds of TV and computer games, they were as if numbed, said a bystander, so that they were desensitised to the reality of the man's pain and the possible ending of his life. He jumped to his death. People in the crowd shoved forward to take pictures of his dead and mangled body, and the local chief constable reported that people in the crowd posted pictures of the scene on the internet after the event.

Something similar is happening in wider society. The grand artifice of the online world, with its compulsive screen-addiction leads to a kind of myopia of insight and accretions of cruelty.

We are exiled from our home in nature, whether it is the ice, the deserts, the plains, the mountains or the woodlands. In the artifice of space travel, our emissaries into outer space looked back at Earth with a new comprehension of how it is our priceless, irreplaceable, peerless home.

Ask an astronaut. In the Arctic, I met a sculptor, Looty Pijamini, who told me about a previous visitor, Neil Armstrong. Pijamini had taken the astronaut out to sea, and asked him about the moon. Was Armstrong ever frightened or lonely? Yes, Armstrong answered. When they'd finished orbiting the Earth and were about to fly out of Earth's orbit, he felt both lonely and afraid.

In literature, that sense of homesickness for nature has best been expressed in the pastoral, from Virgil onwards. Virgil had his lands confiscated and wrote the *Eclogues* in exile and longing. The pastoral spoke of nature as home, our most essential belonging.

From the moon to the potting shed: consider how deeply people love their gardens, how people moving house feel a wrench when they leave their gardens as if they had themselves been uprooted. In pastoral, the psyche can come home to the colour that knows it. And it's perhaps unsurprising that there is a homesickness for pastoral in this age which, through so many varieties of artifice, creates such pervasive exile. 'I remember it was beautiful,' said the Inuit woman, nostalgic for something that was still there but from which she was exiled by a conglomeration of artifices.

Time is the right size in pastoral. Generous in presence and languorous as summer, time is measured by sleep, wine and love. The hour of the pastoral is evening, when the exile feels the keenest nostalgia, when the day is yearning serenity. The pastoral is human-sized. The human body is as present in pastoral as it is absent in artifice. No voice can speak louder than this valley, so there is no false proximity of a faked-up news story telling me lies about elections or climate. In the pastoral, there are textures of the body's belonging: felt, wool, wood, leaf, fur, wax.

In the pastoral, the world is familiar: the squeaky gate, the cottage garden, the snug joining of things, each acre and each person known; no globalised financial meltdown, no statistics, no hyper-powers or media moguls. There is democracy, here, freedom, and the commons. In the pastoral, one person's lambs can be as funny as anyone else's; no one is compelled by artificial media to compare their own lambs with some celebrity shepherd's.

Wordsworth, in the great pastoralism of the Romantic movement, famously wrote of the 'host of golden daffodils' at his home in the Lake District. But now, instead of real daffodils, thousands of artificial ones have been planted. ('Plant,' of course, has two meanings, one a green reality and the other a ruse, a deceitful artifice.) They have been planted for the tourists coming at Easter because, owing to climate chaos, the real ones are blooming too early and wilting before their time. Time is gone awry in an artificial world.

But whisper the word 'pastoral' and you can feel the scorn, you can almost see the lip curling in metropolitan sneer. If you speak positively of pastoral or indigenous philosophy, of mountains, metaphor, and meaning, you will be told that 'you're not living in the real world,' by which is usually meant the 'reality' of mortgages, credit, loans, debts and share prices. The artifices of the financial system and profit are accorded more 'reality' than the true realities of climate and the natural world of rivers and mountains. You may say that pastoral is idealised nature and therefore not realistic. Of course. But while the whole purpose of artifice is to deny the real, the whole purpose of pastoral's idealisation is to augment the real, as dreams and art augment the everyday with deeper truths. The Inuit boy playing Spyro was being denied all realities while his grandfather's stories offered enhanced realities, the Arctic fox chasing the horizon in a story which yielded more meanings with each telling.

Speak positively of the pastoral, and you will be told that you can't put the clock back. There is a past in pastoral — the reason for its nostalgic character. Alexander Pope wrote of pastoral that 'its idea should be taken from the manners of the golden age.' This past, though, operates like the past in the Indigenous Australian Dreamtime; a past that is also present and future, a deep time surrounding the now. It is not a time behind us but around us and, beautifully, within us.

You will be told, too, that pastoral is a kind of romanticism, as if that means a fey and falsifying version of things. This scorn comes from the culturally illiterate who forget that the Romantics were revolutionaries for equality and diversity, who sought direct witness of the real world, yes, the rivers and mountains, and who were not tricked by the artifices of the Industrial Revolution.

Mostly, these remarks are made by the ideologically deaf, who have never troubled to listen when Indigenous people and the world's poor point out that the material progress of the West, from Columbus onward, has been at the expense of their lands and lives. 'We are being killed for this thing called progress,' said one Papuan man to me, bluntly. As sea levels rise, the peoples of Kiribati and Tuvalu will be drowned for it.

Most profoundly, the scorn for pastoral comes out of the long history of the Politics of Artifice. The poet Gary Snyder once remarked that about 400 years ago, Western society came to a fork in the trail — and we took the wrong path. It was a path away from the natural world, away from our intrinsic dependence on it. Almost all indigenous societies have honoured this relationship, the deep home where we belong.

Indigenous societies typically honour the concept of reciprocity, the sense of balance, the acceptance of cause and consequence, and the understanding that for everything taken, something must be given. The balance, essentially, at the heart of indigenous thought is this: that there is always a price to be paid, by the hunter as well as the hunted, by the healer and the healed, by the shaman and the society. There are always consequences, and wisdom lies in recognition and respect for that principle: Nemesis again, friend to all who would befriend all.

But about 400 years ago, in the West, a new era began, heavily influenced by Francis Bacon, promoting the age of human supremacy, arguing for artifice and a politics of cruelty against nature.

Francis Bacon was a nasty piece of work. His utopian novel, *The New Atlantis*, published in 1627, is a eulogy to artifice and control. It is set on an island of engineers who honour a statue of Columbus. They live surrounded by the wildness of the ocean, and they hate those seas. Nature, self-willed, unpredictable and glorious, is Public Enemy Number One for Bacon and the engineers. She must be 'bound into service'; she is something to 'conquer and subdue.' Passages of *The New Atlantis* are eerily prescient — and approving — of novel technologies including genetic engineering and types of weaponry much like napalm or, indeed, Agent Orange.

Bacon sought 'a blessed race of heroes and supermen' to dominate nature and society, and these supermen translated perfectly into Nietzsche's *Übermensch*. When you know that Nietzsche influenced the Nazi movement, and Nazi eugenics can be seen as rooted in Bacon's philosophy, you see a tainted genealogy of ideas. At the heart of fascism is a love of the fake, engineered world and a hatred of diversity; this is its persistence — not only in those who overtly call themselves fascists but in deep, covert philosophies.

The key exemplar of the politics of artifice is the 'Technological Singularity' often referred to simply as the Singularity. The Singularity is understood as a point when technological progress becomes so rapid and complex that the human experience will be surpassed: we will live in a post-human age. The concept was popularised in 1993 by Vernor Vinge, in *The Coming Technological Singularity*. Futurists such as Ray Kurzweil have embraced it and have begun working for the coming so-called Intellectual Revolution — a term intended to invoke the massive societal changes of the Industrial Revolution. As a movement, the Singularity (like hard-right Libertarianism) supports genetic engineering and nanotechnology as well as Artificial Intelligence and so-called transhuman intelligence, speaking of machine minds evolving beyond human perspectives and emotional traits, looking for human-surpassing advances which recalls Nietzsche's Zarathustra contending that 'man is something which ought to be overcome.' The Singularity is obsessed with acceleration; *Accelerating Times* is the newsletter of the Acceleration Studies Foundation, and there is an organisation called Accelerating Change, for whom the past is worth nothing more than a quick glance in the rearview mirror. Contrast this with the deft and subtle nature of both past and future in the Dreamtime which knits an authentic eternity into the present.

There is a conceptual hyperlink between the transhumans of the Artificers' dreams, the Singularity, a hatred of nature, the crushing of indigenous cultures, the lies about the climate crisis and the severity of climate collapse as a piece of geo-engineering at first hapless but now deliberate. This is the Politics of Artifice.

What stands against this? The Politics of Pastoral. It always has. Just as Bacon's cruel theoretical attacks on nature were in the ascendant, that great metaphysical poet Andrew Marvell came to nature's defence, and used the pastoral to do so. Just as the Industrial Revolution brought its own onslaught against nature, the Romantics defiantly stepped forward on behalf of wild nature and the Politics of Pastoral. Today, just as nature is under threat in reality and conceptually from all aspects of artifice, so now there are those who relish being modern Romantics (*Subcomandante Marcos. Poet. Revolutionary. Romantic,*) those who speak in support of the people of the land, those who would defend the pastoral as our home.

In the Arctic, language is melting with each elder's death, every one a word-artist of a melting world. The younger generations know fewer and fewer terms and when the words for ice and snow melt away, so the knowledge they contain melts too. (And indeed there is more: the land itself, the ice to which those words referred is melting and vanishing in the early effects of climate change.)

Proponents of the Singularity cherish Artificial Intelligence and its technological language, that sere, barren communication of a plastic world. I already know I cannot live there. The human spirit needs language, shimmering and liquid. The virtual world, the antinatural world, kills metaphor. I couldn't call language 'shimmering' without knowledge of the natural world, light on water. I couldn't call metaphor 'metaphor' where there is no carrying and no border to cross. Language is 'fossil poetry,' but if you've never found a fossil, held it in your real hand, given it to your real friend, you cannot treasure Emerson's remark. We are animated by the tutelary genius of language.

While artifice refuses metaphor, pastoral delights in the radical generosity of similes. I go back to the daisy, that metaphor, the day's eye, that gives to any garden dozens of humble suns. Pastoral swells with meanings, allusions, conjectures, modalities, connotations, it is washed with emotional colour, it is myriad-minded, allegorical, comic, symbolic, seasonal, sad, crescent with meanings and the reckless grace notes of plurality.

This meaning and no other, says artifice. No pluralities, no connotations, no similes, no puns. Meaning, at its most totalitarian. One meaning. One Fake One. Like plastic, it will yield nothing to the touch of the mind. And suddenly then how bleak the world, how untextured, how singular and how unminded.

The meanness of meaning in artifice has a pernicious political counterpoint: the rise of The One State, in effect. One Singularity. One culture. Consider Peter Thiel, Facebook board member and early investor, who describes himself as 'way libertarian.' He is heavily involved in The Singularity, and co-wrote a book called *The Diversity Myth*, an attack on multiculturalism. For The Singularity loathes diversity.

In the politics of the Artificers, there could be no Inuit sculptor talking about Whitey on the moon. There would be no Tukano woman entranced by the magnificence of meanings of the jacaranda, no Dani men with their superb and curly penis gourds and that Papuan ability to extemporise poems of their lands, no Navajo, no Sámi, no Maori, no Mayan people of the Zapatista Rebel Army, just one enormous statue of Columbus at the Northwest Passage.

The worst scenarios of climate collapse evoke a world wasted, what biologist E. O. Wilson called the Eremozoic Era, the Age of Loneliness, when, as a result of the extinctions brought about by human activities, the Earth will be barren of almost any life. Postapocalyptic, it is horribly posthuman. This is a nightmare for most of us, but an ambition for The Singularity.

The Singularity longs for transhumanism, as a time when humanity will become posthumanity. It is cruel and it is unkind. It's also un-kind, not recognising the kinnned-ness of the human to the natural world. It is a pitiless vision, and a blinded one, for all true vision, as Marvell knew, depends on pity. ('These weeping eyes, those seeing tears.') In the oceans of the human heart, oceans of saltwater and grace, it is pity which unrolls worlds.

The pastoral vision is as kind and necessary as water; the waters within the human body, in about the same proportion as the oceans are to dry land, the liquidity of all metaphor making like things of the same kind. (These gentle puns of liking which no artificial intelligence could ever know.) The kinship of the human to the kind and wild world.

> The mind, that ocean where each kind
> Does straight its own resemblance find
> Yet it creates, transcending these,
> Far other worlds, and other seas,
> Annihilating all that's made
> To a green thought in a green shade.'
>
> Andrew Marvell, 'The Garden'

The mind has oceans and no artifice can copy its comprehension of this entire and laughing world, rude, splendid, ferocious, wild, tender and true. The mind has its strictures of ice, too, knowing it is the laws of nature that must be obeyed, those laws nowhere spelled out as clearly as in the black and white strictness of the lands of ice.

Twilight and Otter

It is twilight and at the waking edge of night, a crescent otter breaks the surface of the water, looping up from its dive, in its mouth a crescent fish shines silver, a little late moon. I'm in Scotland by a river I have just come to, with an otter I have just met. Otters make me gasp, ridiculous with childhood. I am laughing on the inside as if I was drunk on fresh water. One scampers up on to a rock to eat its silver fish and I lick my lips, tasting the prize. It slides back into the water and I am streaming with glee.

Night chases day like one otter cub chasing another. Otter *Ludens*, they are creatures of play, on the margins of day, and they fathom both air and water, influent in the element that becomes them. Every otter is a play on words, a one-word pun, for the word 'otter' is related to the word 'water.'

My kitten's name, Otter, is apt. He is ludic from nose to paws. He often sleeps like an otter at rest, on his back with his paws neatly meeting over his tummy. He has diurnal spurts of joyful playfulness, one at dawn and the other at dusk when he mews imperiously at me until I join him in playing with a toy mouse, and then he hurls himself in curly crazy circles around anything. He is also black and white, sporting the livery of twilight.

In the woodlands at dusk, a pine marten runs a quicksilver streak through the trees, mercury in motion. It freezes even faster than it flows and is gone. 'The sky is darkening,' wrote a Neapolitan of the seventeenth century, 'darkening to the colour of a wolf's snout.'

I hear a badger, grunting, shoving stones aside: he means business. Then I see him, touched by two-light, day-streaked and night-stroked, a piano keyboard playing a twilight sonata in a minor key for the maligned creatures of twilight, the badgers themselves, the wolf, the hare and the bat – flittermouse in flights of arpeggios to catch moths. And owls.

From nowhere — and in utter silence — a barn owl slips between the trees, as if there is barely a feather between this world and other. Only one sense registers it, not hearing nor scent nor touch — only sight. The eye struggles to see, tries harder than it does in the easy light of day. This is the difficult, bewildering light, where a tree stump with its black fingers of roots looks like a badger, and the eye must tug objects back into their proper outlines as the wind ruffles leaves into faces. This is the tricky hour — when the eye plays tricks on you, foxing you with a deer shadow. 'In the night, every cat is a leopard,' as the Italian proverb says. Sight, ruler of the senses during daytime, and untrickable at noon, is now, at dusk, losing power to the insurrection of the other senses.

At twilight, I find myself breathing in deeply, as if unconsciously I lean towards scent, drawn towards the fragrance of some flowers and plants, so strong at dusk, including evening primrose, night-scented stock, jasmine, angel's trumpet, wisteria and honeysuckle. I find myself smelling things at dusk as if they had simply more to say at that hour. Pub smells. Woodsmoke. Food. The smell of leaves on a wet pavement. I am intrigued by the very air, asking more questions of it. I want to know things in the air as if I too am a bit more of my animal self, and my sense of smell is coming into its own.

Reliance on hearing increases. The body stills itself to feel more, quiets itself to hear more. The word 'listen' is an anagram of 'silent.' In the willing silence the tentative senses are attentive. If there is a dawn chorus, I would suggest there is also a dusk chorus, a westward flow of quiet, a whisperous Hesperus rolling across all the world, slowly, continuously, punctuated by a hare drumming, a coyote howl, or owl hoot at owl-leet, owl-light, which is one term for twilight. Other terms include the 'dimpsy' and 'crow-time,' as crows roosted and 'cock-shut' as well as the gloaming or the 'shutting-in,' the time to bring the animals in and bolt the doors. There is 'smokefall' and in Greek dusk is *lykóphos*, wolf-light. The only word for twilight which I hate is 'crepuscular,' an exoskeletal word, one of the very few words in the English language which is (to my ears) not onomatopoeic.

Night seems to come up from the earth, from the chthonic, if you are out in it. The trees seem to grip the earth with their knuckles now, fingering the black soil. Darkness doesn't fall, it rises from the roots. From indoors, looking out, it does fall, perhaps, in a cadence of sun fall and the autumn, the fall season, is when twilight is most meaningful. Accidents — a nasty fall — happen more often at this hour. Luck, though, too, is associated with twilight — the moment of chance and hazard, how fate befalls, how 'it fell out,' they say in fairy tales. The mischief hour. Because twilight resists duality, it doesn't say lucky or unlucky, it says both chance and mischance, in the hour which is neither night nor day as time swings on its hinges: is night half open or day half closed?

The sky holds a little last handful of light cupped in its west left hand. It is a west-side story. Twilight is the between-light, after sunset and before night when the sun's light is still present in the sky even after the sun is gone. Twilight invites the penumbra-mind, seeking the dusky nuance of shades of grey. It is 'tranquillity shot through with sorrow,' according to Victor Hugo. Different modalities of light evoke different modalities of mind, and twilight wonders and questions things, unsure. Twilight is an enigmatic reflection, that other word for thinking. Something is in the air, electric and inter-intelligent, in this hour of ambiguity, of paradox, opaquely suggestive. As the reflection of psyche and light are both elliptical, certainty is bewildered: it is a moment when mind is half open to night and star-guided. Only one hour in twelve is a twilight hour, dusk or dawn, and twilight is the trickster in the pack of hours, as Hermes is the trickster of the twelve Olympian gods, on the edge of divinity, the least of them, in the pantheon of Proper Gods.

Something shifts its weight from one foot to the other. Trickster is abroad. Duels are fought. Messengers are heard — or shot. Poems are hunted. Traps are set.

It is the uneasy hour, when predator may become prey, and prey may become predator, because everything which rises must also fall, and everything forced to fall will rise in fury. The English language refers (unkindly) to 'an unkindness of ravens' and to a 'murder of crows' as our society murders the creatures of the twilight. Badgers have their claws torn out, their teeth smashed and then, tied to a tree, or in a pit, have dogs set on them, to the death. Badgers are also gassed and shot, slaughtered in thousands upon thousands, in a sanctioned killing to attempt to stop cattle from getting bovine TB. It didn't work, studies showed, and studies were ignored. Bats, sweetly sensitive listeners to acoustics to which we are deaf, are treated as loathly pests.

By twilight, preparations were made for smuggling and owling — the illegal export of wool. 'The landlord robs us all day: we'll rob him all night,' is the nocturnal vow of poachers — predators of animals, prey of gamekeepers. Normal laws of daylight did not — could not — apply. In a famous Welsh tradition if, between twilight and dawn, someone could build a turf cottage on waste or common land, it was theirs forever.

Teenagers belong in twilight; their body clock urging them out, to the 'nocturnal, beastly roaming about,' according to an observer in Paris, 1651. All over Europe, history records how twilight was the hour of 'Lewde youthes,' as reported in Coventry in 1605, running amok in riots and obscenity, German youths yodelling, Danish youths chasing the dark, hell for leather, with horns, bells and trumpets.

The social clock changes. The alteration at dawn from asleep to awake is, if we sleepers allow ourselves, a misty hour, slow and dreamily self-estranged, where the psyche can feel as easily lost as a walker in fog. It is an enormous shift but mostly private. On the streets at dusk, though, the publicly-lived life is transformed from the sensible sober world of daytime work to the happy-hour glee of release, the lid-off bubbling over, people spilling out of bars, beer spilling out of glasses, conversation spilling out of mouths. Day has ended but night has not yet begun. There is a human instinct to gather; we are starlings now in a human murmuration.

I feel tugged by something ancient within me, to meet people, to stroll. The longing for a *passeggiata* seems to me to be a universal human yearning, to see and be seen at evening. At dusk, society steps away from the day's curt command to obey Captain Clock. Time itself is on the loose. Hours are as easily and sweetly lost at dusk as they could be at dawn.

Twilight upsets the day, subverting its settled order. The establishment Middle C of daytime rises to an F sharp at dusk, the eerie augmented fourth, the tense, alluring, weird interval, called, famously, the Devil's Interval, used in the opening of West Side Story, and also in Wagner's *Twilight of the Gods*. It is a loophole, a *loup* hole, a hole for the wolf (*loup* in French) to pass through. If it is played after Middle C, this is the one of all the twelve notes on a piano keyboard which make the hairs stand up on the back of your neck. This interval was suppressed by the church of the Middle Ages for creating a space that let the devil in. But this gap, this interval, is necessary to let the trickster in.

At twilight you must mind the gap, the interval, the rift, the opening. Twilight may trouble the day or console it, may pacify or perturb, may treat you or trick you. What is peripheral becomes paramount and for humans our peripheral vision is actually better now than by daylight: this is literally and metaphorically true.

The youngest of Hinduism's gods, the trickster in the Hindu pantheon, is the child Krishna. His skin is the blue of the sky at dusk, and he goes thieving at twilight and dawn, stealing milk and butter, upsetting the householders: a mischievous, naughty, mercurial divinity.

Trickster is the least of the gods, and his appearance is only possible within a pantheon of gods, because the Trickster resists duality, being neither good nor eveil. When monotheism turns up, the Trickster disappears, because the One God assumes all goodness, and then libels the Trickster, calling him devilish and expelling him into the pitch black night, tarred and crow-feathered. Hermes is also called Mercury and the raven represents him: indeed many of the creatures of twilight have something of

Mercury about them, pine marten quicksilver in the woods, and the mercurial 'harebrained' hare.

Hermes-Mercury is god of no man's land, as twilight is no man's hour. Margin-dweller and double-dealer, an unpredictable god, he promises neither border control nor safe passage. The security guards are asleep and otters have swum into their dreams. Passport controllers are drunk in charge of a pack of cards, and the joker is playing them. Customs officers have emigrated, twilighting as impressionist painters.

Trickster is reliably unreliable, the riddler, the fiddler, he'll fiddle you: he plays Paganini when Jupiter plays Purcell. Trickster is the riff, he plays you extemporised brilliance in the cadenza, then throws a wolf note to trip you up. He deals in luck, good and bad, but never pays his debts or gives you your due. Trickster will swipe your wages, then give you a windfall. Trickster will light the lantern to let you find your way and then, in a gust of wind, will snuff it out. Trickster is the will o' the wisp, played by Puck, the night flitter and by Robin Goodfellow leading the wanderer astray at night through bogs and forests, laughing as he does.

Trickster is as playful as an otter but, I've known fishermen say, otters 'steal' their fish. Prometheus and Loki, tricksters both, steal fire. Raven steals fire too, and food — he is ravenous — and sun, stars and moon. Trickster is a thief, the wrong-footing, fly-by-night, tall-tale-teller, latch-lifter, fence-breaker, lock-picker: he is light-footed, with feathers at his ankles, and light-fingered. At twilight Loki is abroad, look to your picked-pocket, my friend, it happens in the interval, the tenner is now a plucked note, now a plucked note, the pizzicato fingers in the glissando of your smooth pocket.

If Trickster is one part of the body, it is the funny-bone. But Trickster is never only one thing: he is the ankle, wrist, hip, knuckle — all the joints of the body as he is god of the joints (the junctions) of the day at twilights. 'Articulus' is a joint in the body and a joint, a turning point, in the year — as the All Souls' Night, May Day, solstices and equinoxes are the ankles, wrists and elbows in articulating the body of the year. It is all an articulate pun. Trickster articulates (Hermes-Mercury is the messenger and the god of writers.) And all these words link, of course, to art and to the artist, trickster in the pantheon of Proper Jobs.

Jacob is the extraordinary trickster of the Old Testament, the name Jacob means trickster, deceiver, heel-grabber — and, yes, Trickster can cheat and lie — he's a bit of a heel. When he has been wrestling with the Angel all night, at the twilight of dawn, the junction point, the joint of night, the Angel admits he cannot defeat Jacob, so touches the hollow of his hip, he goes for the joint. In blessing, the Angel says, 'now you will be called Israel because you have contended with god and won.'

Names and their meanings. Words and the roots of words. Signs and the interpretation of signs: all these are the domain of the Trickster, so Hermes-Mercury, god of signposts, is god of translators. As the divinity of speech, writing and eloquence, 'Hermes' gives his name to hermeneutics, the art of interpretation. Part of his paradox is that his own signs are hard to read; he made himself shoes of branches to hide his footsteps; his messages may be hidden but are treasured when found. Hermes means 'he of the stone-heap' — the cairns of rocks by which a hidden path is revealed, the cairns which protect the traveller from being lost. He is god of what is hidden, or missing.

In terms of metallurgy, hidden gold is found by mercury, for as mercury only adheres to precious metals, so mercury leads the way to mined gold. So Shakespeare's trickster, Touchstone, is named after the stone that is used to reveal the purest gold. In myth, it is Hermes who fetches Persephone from the underworld, so the golden harvests can once more fill the cornfields. The spirit of Hermes travels between ordinary daylight and the deep subconscious of dream, instinct, metaphor, and poetry, coming back with the mind gold. He goes by twilight, the hidden hour, the cairn hour, when the cairn is most important to travellers, the hour of lost time.

Every day at twilight, I lose my way. My path through the day usually seems clear. I can walk fine. Until dusk. Then I sink. I stumble. I feel changed. I can work hard in the day, whether it is writing or housework or generally fixing things. Come dusk, though, something happens. I flag. But this is not exactly tiredness or hunger. I feel that I have lost my path. I need to look around, check where I am and what is happening. I am not anxious, but alert in a very different way to that of my daytime self. I am stilled inside, but sensitive to the world. I may be both predator and prey. I feel a quivering kind of electricity. But the strongest feeling is that of being temporarily lost.

I need to look for my bearings. I want a cairn, some sign of significance, quick, feathered, fleet, lively. I want to catch the news which most enjoys the dawn and dusk, for Mercury is god of the best of the media, and Mercury, of course, was once a common name for newspapers. Or I want a fire, for the twilight hours, and the fire's presence will create a certainty of both place and time. I want to know the social news, or get a message or hear a story; something of Hermes.

In his book *Last of the Light*, Peter Davidson notes how the 'blue hour' is 'beloved of nineteenth-century French writers and painters,' and he quotes Ruskin's response to the twilight sadness in Turner's painting *The Fighting Téméraire* as 'a blue, deep, desolate hollow of darkness.' For some, twilight is the hour of whispered vespers. For others, the hour of hesitant tryst, hesperous and suggestive. For others yet, the hour of the quiet swindle, the twilight robbery of the conman. It is the hour of the voice whether news-telling, at prayer, at question, at deception, at promise, the hour of the voice at story — not any particular story, but the story of story, to see things otherwise, neither black nor white but open to interpretation. People gathered, traditionally, at twilight, for knitting or spinning evenings, and told stories, spinning tales, twilight inside twilight, the ever-curious mind trying to see in the dark: what happened next?

Perhaps it is twilight when we are our most animal selves, when I become otter, when we all feel our wings. Jennifer Ackerman, in *The Genius of Birds*, writes, 'Twilight is a rich source of information for navigating animals of all types. It's the only period in the day when birds and other animals can combine light-polarization patterns, stars, and magnetic cues.'

By twilight, the mind may want to offer the silence into which other voices may speak. Or the oceanic feeling into which a dream can swim. The uncurtaining, the rift, the torn veil, the mind open to the presence of what is usually ignored.

At twilight, the innerness of things is outered. Twilight has an inside. You can climb into its cocoon, curl up there, hear a tale take you anywhere as vastness becomes intimate and the intimate vast. In this interior hour, the daytime's team-spirit solidarity melts into the thinner air: it is the hour of the solitaries, now, alone, together, an encounter of different kinds of solitudes. I have spent hours at twilight, solitary, waiting for the other solitaries — badger, hare, pine marten, owl — and here I find the paradox of solitudes. Alone and never alone, I am part of the twitching, whiskered, sniffing, alert, listening world.

Twilight is a state of mind. Thought flits silent between trees, a feather for your thoughts? I am owling the night.

Language too easily equates light with knowledge — it came to light that; she lit on an idea; in the logic of Enlightenment. Noon has an exactness of light and thought. Light sits flat on things at midday, leaves nothing to the imagination, no penumbra, no uncertainty. Is noon the least-prayed hour? I love the brightness of sunshine at noon, but it is not the only way to see. There can be a kind of light pollution applied to the mind. Noon-thinking, at its worst, is simple binary: shade versus sun in a black-or-white argument. Clever thoughts have clarity while those less so are 'dim.' We praise the 'brilliance' and 'lucidity' of ideas and disdain 'foggy' or 'hazy' thinking or a 'lack-lustre' (literally light-lacking) spirit. But it was not ever thus: 'The owl of Minerva begins to fly only at dusk,' wrote Hegel: wisdom comes at the end of the day with the enigmatic and suggestive time of evening, estranged from the solar certainty of noon.

Light is how we think. Sunrise lifts the human spirit, in a peerless daybright melody glinting like sun on water as Peer Gynt is in the sunrise of his life, in the aspiration of sky, the happy-go-lucky folktale hero setting out into his own dawn. Rainbows, for Paul Cézanne, represented the luminous sense of losing oneself in art: 'We live in a chaos of rainbows,' he wrote, although the poignancy of a rainbow to me is that they are made out of tears. Sunset is, in Old English, *sunnansetlgong*, suggesting the going down of the sun which settles itself into evening. The day breathes out. The sunset also settles birds, colours, children and flowers; sunset can elicit a depth-charge of soul-values, the cadence of evening harmonies, a softening decrescendo, a quieted credo of tranquillity.

Logos sets its fixed ratios with the rational sun, but in its setting, Mythos stirs and rises, cannier than we can know at noon. Twilight, twolight, reminds us every day that the psyche is a twice-dweller, fluent in other languages intuited by night. 'Evening words are not like to morning,' as the traditional English proverb says. When day shuts up its shout, the twilit mind asks dusk to usher in its utterances.

We say 'it dawns on me' but not 'it dusks on me.' Yet that way of knowing is a deft vision as the mind, free of daylight jesses, is ownerless as an owl and deeper than it appears on the surface. I have sunk my fingers to the second knuckle deep down in the feathers of a tawny owl before I have touched its tiny body.

The mind in its own twilight wonders, questions, interprets, prays and wishes. Every modality is twilit — maybe-minded — it might be, could be, would be, it longs to reach out, stretch this elastic hour for its mystery and meaning. For now there is moonrise in the mind and the poet is listening, thinking the world by twolight, the actual and metaphoric. There are no horizons to the mind, now, no limit to its insight.

The mind is remembering its roots. There is a tangled, knotty, subterranean, word-root in Indo-European: *men*. Words that derive from this include the English 'mind' and 'remember.' In Old Norse, *muninn* means 'memory or mind,' and is the name of one of Wotan's (Odin's) ravens sent out at dawn, to gather information and to return at twilight with the news. Its companion raven is

Huginn, from the Old Norse word 'thought.' There is wisdom that comes by twilight, the story says.

But the shouty and powerful gods of modernity threaten the creatures of twilight, hating the wild minds of teenagers, loathing the raven and crow and planning to exterminate the badgers with a cruelty only matched by its stupidity. Ours is an age of gods engineering our own twilight, banging the seasons together and buckling the year until harvests so willing, Demeter, Ceres, so serially willing, cancel their yields, the cornfields are not golden but ashen, and Hermes can no longer recover Persephone.

The twilight of the gods was brought about when the laws of the gods were broken, the World Ash Tree cut down. These are the bone stories, told in the marrow, created from a species-unease at what we feared we could do, a society playing for real its own Endgame, where instead of 'All that rising corn! And there ! Look! The sails of the herring fleet!' all we can see is ashes. 'What dreams!' writes Beckett, 'Those forests.'

Dreams, says George Steiner, 'can be the last refuge of freedom and the hearth of resistance.' In ancient times, dreams were not considered to be personal but were messages from the gods, the dreamer the messenger. Every dreamer is Hermes by night.

Back from Scotland, at home and with my kitten asleep in bed, I dreamt. And this was my dream. It was a dream to break my heart, to crack my mind like a twisted rubik cube. It was lightning in the noon of night; it split my sleep apart like an axe splits a log. A hot sleep, reeking midnight and I woke on the stroke of twelve, my head aching, on a night when all that's left is the truth.

It was a dream of the fury of the beasts, a living lightning shaking the world to speech until in its ferocity it shrieks a dream from the subsoil. The animals came as witnesses called by Nemesis bringing a case against humans for breaching the wise limits. Everything is breakable. Everything wounded beyond forgiveness. With a collective refusal to think by twilight, modernity has wrenched a world out of true and something — a kind of universal patience — has snapped. Crow has got the searchlights out, coldly turning human movement to carrion. Mole is hammering nails through the gamekeeper's wrists and knees, hanging him upside down on a gibbet as a warning to others. Bat scribbles slogans on his face. There was a loophole in my night and the wolf leapt in, cracking a mobile phone in her knucklebones, radio-tracking a herd of men and women to coordinate our fleeings. Hare has raced the pilots to the planes and won, he has picked up the knack of the opposable digit and is flying drones against us: harebrained no longer, he pilots the sun into cornfields to strafe them with fire. The quicksilver pine marten is laying exquisite traps of mercury to poison us with our own trick. Badger, perhaps angrier than any, has taken the spade from every garden shed and sharpened the edge to silver and is digging upwards, slicing up into our ankles like you'd strike at a hated rootwad of brambles and, as he does, he strikes sparks off the flints in my ankle bones, while I sleep.

We kill the badger and libel the wolf, speak evil of the owl-leet and turn the flittermouse to comics. We hate them, the twilight ones, and now their loathing comes back at us. Bruised by my dream and my ankles screaming, I say: 'But I'm on your side, I am part of the Resistance, I've been on your side all my life. I am a Partisan.' 'Then this is a message,' came the terse, furious reply.

I am jolted awake by an electricity of mind, I am cattle-prodded, flung, still dreaming, into a kind of wakefulness, a twilight state of mind. And I lay unable to sleep, unable to wake, dreamwrecked till three.

And Otter? What of him? He is there in the potent penumbra. Now waking, now sleeping, playing the edges, riffing on the shores, Otter Ludens, like my mind half on the dry land of being surely awake, and half in waters of sleep. My Otter, meanwhile, kitten of the half-and-half, of dawn and dusk, is now lying on his back, wrapped in the kelp of deep sleep and dreaming our better dreams.

Night

Skate Fever

This was the best night of my life. It was winter, some years ago, and the temperature had been below freezing for days. With a group of friends, we chose a clear night, planned which lake we would go to, and cleaned our skates. Then someone said, 'Let's do it in costume,' and we did. A party of us wore full evening dress plundered from charity shops; feathers, fascinators and fake furs. We took musical instruments and wine and food, walked to the lake after dark and skated by moon- and starlight, lanterns scattered around the edge of the lake like fireflies. The hills were bright, the ice was silver, my heart was singing. Wrapped up and amazed, the small children and puppies stayed at the edge, near the soup and the woodfire on the lakeshore. However, the ecstasy — in its root 'standing apart' — comes from skating out to the lake's centre and farther to its far and silent shores. Another time, when the best skating was to be had on a field which had been flooded then had frozen, we timed it for the full moon. 'A calendar! Look in the almanac. Find out moonshine, find out moonshine!'

Mid-Wales has been my home for decades. Walking, mountain biking, running, canoeing or borrowing a friend's horses, I have come to love this land. The best thing ever, for me, is skating out on the lakes in winter.

I suffer from a seasonal illness that was once very common in Britain but is now rare. It still afflicts the Dutch, though, in their thousands. It strikes me like delirium, when the lakes nearby freeze over and the ice issues an imperative: *Carpe diem*! Get Your Skates On! When I skate, I feel that I am flying and my heart soars with exhilaration: I have never felt more alive, quick to the quick. Romance, yawns and suicides, they say, are all infectious. So is play, and skate fever is a highly contagious form — beware!

In these Welsh hills, years can pass without the waters freezing, and the gaps between skating winters are getting longer. This, too, is a result of climate change. But this deep cold has brought a few precious days of frost and rapture. If *joie de vivre* could be distilled to one image alone, it would be a skating party sliding down the hill to wake the lake.

This kind of joy contains the deep meaning of revelry and play, as the historian Johan Huizinga wrote in his masterpiece *Homo Ludens: Mankind at Play* — culture itself 'arises in the form of play.' 'Play cannot be denied. You can deny, if you like, nearly all abstractions: justice, beauty, truth, goodness, mind, God. You can deny seriousness, but not play.' Flemish paintings of ice-merriment depict lovers and children and horse-drawn sleighs; the Dutch still hold carnivals on ice. In homage to *Homo Ludens*, we played, interludic in the intercalendrical between Christmas and New Year, honouring the play ethic rather than the work, the ludic revolution rather than the industrial, racing one another and improvising a new form of hockey with a skinny, squeaking rubber chicken. A local farmer came on skis; someone else tried to fly a kite; puppies slipped comically on the ice and children slid and pushed each other over.

Skating oscillates between the twin arts of conviviality and of solitude: you can join up with the carnivaliers for hot chocolate laced with brandy, then swing away on a trajectory of glorious freedom, a world apart, ('all, alone, together' wrote e.e.cummings in his poem 'skating'). One skating day, I was circling the centre of a lake and found my movement mirrored in the sky as a bird of prey, similarly alone, circled curiously overhead.

Real skating, wild skating — as opposed to rink skating — always suggests this twofoldness: the vivacity of a party and the exhilaration of solitude; the water which freezes and thaws; the crisp breath in and the steamy breath out; life above in air and death below the ice. You swing a long arc out to the left and a curve back to the centre; a long arc out to the right and a curve back to the centre, each skate leaving slender S's, cut into the ice like cold calligraphy. The twofoldness is an image of balance, the balance which — as every skater knows — comes best from movement.

Skating, diving and dreaming are all forms of flying. 'When to his feet the skater binds his wings…' wrote the aptly-named poet Robert Snow, not to be confused with Robert Frost ('style is the mind skating circles around itself as it moves') or indeed with Samuel Taylor Coleridge ('The frost performs its secret ministry, / Unhelped by any wind.') Another Robert, Robert Walker, meanwhile, is more famous for skating than walking, for he was painted as *The Skating Minister*, in a work attributed to Henry Raeburn, the childlike glee of his activity contrasting with the buttoned-up dignity of his ministry. (Walker spent his childhood in Rotterdam, so would have skated on the canals of the Netherlands in winter.)

The god Mercury was, according to Coleridge, the first maker of skates, and every skater has wings at their feet. The flight is compelling to watch; huge numbers of spectators turn out for ice races in Holland, and millions of people watch figure-skating championships in the Winter Olympics – not so much for the element of competition but for the momentary quality of flight, of sheer grace. Out skating, the birds (accustomed to watching us trudge) hover and gaze at skaters as we humans fly across the evanescent ice.

In the Dutch painter Bruegel's *Winter Landscape with a Bird Trap* the sense of swift movement in the skaters is such that, 450 years later, they look as if they're moving. My eye jumps from figure to figure, each caught in a slightly different pose, the effect like the early animation thumb cinema, the flip-books which rely on the eye's persistence of vision to give the impression of speed. Peasant Bruegel, as he was known, paints the equality of ice-games: this is an open carnival of the commons where even poverty cannot stifle the zest of play which steams through the boisterous carnivaliers with such immediacy you can almost hear them laughing.

People have been skating for perhaps five thousand years, maybe longer. The oldest known skates in the world, made from the leg bones of animals and found in a Swiss lake, are thought to date from 3000 BCE. Similar finds have been made in Russia, Scandinavia, Germany and Britain, where the first written record of skating occurs, in a work by the twelfth-century monk William Fitzstephen, who describes the children of London skating with cattle shinbones under their feet and tied to their ankles: 'They fly across the ice like birds… then attack each other until one falls down.' Some things never change.

It is the Dutch, though, who have the fullest known history of skating. First, ice-skates were fashioned from cow ribs, which were drilled so they could be tied to boots, and then, beginning in the fourteenth century, skates were made of iron runners fixed to wooden platforms, and skaters used poles to push themselves across the ice. Around one hundred years later, the Dutch invented the sharpened double-edged blade and threw away the poles; by 1600, they had fashioned curled wooden skates with steel blades. The patron saint of ice skating, Saint Lidwina, is Dutch, while old ballads, describing the great frost and ice fair on the Thames in 1684, speak of:

> The Rotterdam Dutchman, with fleet-cutting scates
> To pleasure the crowd shows his tricks and his feats
> Who, like a rope dance (for his sharp steels),
> His brains and activity lies in his heels.

It is a playful history. A 1904 travel book, *Holland*, records Dutch winter traditions when 'all the world is out on skates, on business or pleasure bent,' people pulling sleighs made from packing cases and 'a freight of laughing babies.' Skating competitions 'form the chief amusement of the winter.' And, as it appeared in Bruegel's painting, ice-skating was an inclusive sport, enjoyed by all classes, unlike the tendency elsewhere in Europe for it to be reserved for aristocracy.

About skating they were never wrong, the old Dutch masters. In Rembrandt's *Winter Landscape*, for instance, a figure in the foreground puts on a pair of skates—which do look like cow's ribs—and all the figures are wrapped in the warmth of Rembrandt's kindness, so that they look as if they will never be cold again. For all the sheer fun in Bruegel's *Winter Landscape with a Bird Trap*, there is a deeper hint that the birds are perhaps included for their traditional symbolic meaning, representing the human soul and suggesting that there is brevity in the revelry of ice and of life. Skating is as flitting as the flight of a bird. For bird or human, existence is as short as daylight in midwinter.

The first Dutch artist to specialise in depicting winter ice-revels was Hendrick Avercamp, working in the seventeenth century, and his paintings (with eel-angling, games and skaters falling on ice) hum with the playfulness that the Dutch, culturally, associate with ice. It is entirely fitting that Huizinga, author of *Homo Ludens*, was also Dutch.

The most festive of competitions is the Dutch skating race, the *Elfstedentocht*, the Eleven-Towns Race. It was first held in January 1909, and has been held only intermittently over the past century, because the 200-km track along canals and rivers will only freeze in the severest winters. The lower the temperatures remain, the higher the pitch of fever, as the excitement grows as to whether or not the race will happen. There is even a word in Dutch specifically for this fever: *Elfstedenkoorts*, Eleven-Towns Race Fever, a near-frenzy in any year, peaking when '*It giet oan!*' 'It is on!' is announced. One in eight of the population—around 2 million people—turns out to cheer on the 16,000 skaters, and there are stalls selling hot chocolate and pea soup along the route. (The New York City Marathon attracts a similar number with usually more than double the number of racers.) The evening before the race there is an enormous street-party in Leeuwarden, where the race begins and ends, sometimes referred to as the Eleven-Bars Tour, an evening of booze and bets and boasts.

Camaraderie overrides the competitive element: something funny happened on the way to the finish line in 1956. Five people completed the race in tandem ('all, alone, together'), and the judges withheld the prize. Why so? Because in 1933 and 1940, there had been joint winners when the race leaders chose not to compete but rather to hold hands, as they finished the race. The organisers formally forbade the practice after 1940, but the 1956 winners gloriously flouted the ruling and were disqualified. There are photographs of the five at the finishing line – faces of exhilaration and jubilation – skating for skating's sake. This is the best advice from the masters of skating: skate generously, for mean-mindedness cuts no ice out here.

Their defiance embodied the egalitarian history of Dutch skating. It hinted at the essential freedom of playfulness unbound by rules, and it resounded with the spirit of generosity, to share the pleasure. It is that spirit which prompts me to share not only the delight of real skating, but to sketch out a beginner's guide.

First find some skates. You need stiff boots, the blades sharp. Near me, some twenty years ago, the winter skating began when a local doctor collected a motley assortment of skates, among them a dainty Victorian pair and one pair of army training boots with blades screwed (slightly askew, it has to be said) to the soles — which is great for doing the involuntary splits but rubbish for doing straight lines. With another pair of tough farm boots, loads of children's skates from charity shops and car boot sales, and a pair of Dutch speed-skating skates, the good doctor induced a local outbreak of skate fever.

Next, find a place to skate. Rivers are a terrible idea, obviously, because ice freezes too unpredictably. Canals are also to be treated with very great caution — the overflow from drains makes the ice undependable. Fields that have flooded and then frozen are great, and there is no need to test the depth of the ice. Lakes are lovely. Coleridge took to the ice in the Lake District with Wordsworth who was a 'crack skater,' according to his sister Dorothy. (I don't think she meant it as a pun.)

So how do you test the depth of ice on lakes? Take a hammer and chisel, or a battery-operated drill or, if you'll be lighting a fire, take a poker to heat up and make a hole in the ice. When you've drilled a hole, stick your finger in, and the ice should be three or four inches deep, a fingerlength. This means it should be skateable, but let me at this point introduce a basic rule of skating; be both bold and reckful. If in doubt, stay close to the edge. Don't skate on snow unless you're sure of the ice underneath.

Take a safety rope. If anyone goes through the ice there'll be a chance of hauling them out. Take other rope for playing with children, puppies or sledges, and don't let them use the safety rope. Bring lanterns — tea lights tucked into white baker's paper bags glow like creamy magnolia flowers — and warm clothes, extra socks and 'second skin' blister patches, not ordinary plasters. Take a broom, too: if there has been a light snowfall, you can brush snow away while you go and, more importantly, a broom is good for novice skaters who can lean on it for support and (unlike a stick or a well-intentioned friend) a broom will not slip on the ice. Take food and drink and musical instruments. Tell kids not to throw stones or snowballs on the ice; it's fun but it trips skaters. For the same reason, tell puppies not to crap on the ice.

Like most things in life, skating is best done open-hearted. Trust each foot in turn, let your attention and your weight glide long on each leg. Lean forward into it all. Trust your wings. Trust the ice, too, but stay observant of its moves and cracks, try to read its history of thawing and refreezing and buckling. This is when skaters yearn for more precise language, for the distinct words for ice in Inuktitut, the Inuit language, because the words discriminate between how ice is formed which in turn tells you how it will — or should — behave. And, for Inuit hunters out on the ice, how the ice behaves is that upon which your life depends.

When I was in Igloolik, in the Canadian Arctic, I asked people about words for ice; I stopped writing by the time I'd noted thirty-three, accompanied by full descriptions. When I asked an elder for different words for snow, he reeled off fifteen hardly pausing for breath. These are entirely distinct words (not, as some overweening Europeans pretended, simply one word, extended by different prefixes and suffixes). There are many traditional games in Inuit culture, and sports that are also ways of travelling — dog-sled racing, for example — but the harsh realities of climate demand that ice is taken seriously and identified precisely.

The year has two generosities: that of harvest, as August augments into autumn, ripening and swelling; the other of white beginnings and open futures where all is possibility, wide as a frozen lake when you can no longer see the limit of it. A clean sheet of paper speaks of the same generosity where nothing is pre-scripted and anything can begin. A wide-open day, too, when time stretches untrapped by schedule, and offers opportunity, so spontaneity uncurls and basks in the extravagance of the open moment.

This is the generosity which *Homo Ludens* knows so well. The generosity at the heart of play: the spirit of excess, the sense of abundance, the figurative harvest of pleasure after work, the brimming possibilities of the extra and the gleefully unnecessary. The grace notes of life which arise in play.

Ice sharpens your thoughts and, out here, everything is sharp: skate blades, frost, sunlight in your eyes; even the contrast between day and night is sharpened by cold. Summer has an incoherent lushness, warm and lolling, rolling over everything else, slurred, heady with cider. Winter has a cold coherence, exact and electric, compact as skates laced tight, with blades sharp to the clean ice. Sharp with alacrity too, skating is a fleet and fleeting pleasure, swift to do and swiftly gone.

The silence is simple, coming from the stillness of ice and an immense and quiet sky. The ice is literally simple — the root of the word 'simple' means having only a single fold — and it uncreases your mind. In an unsimple world, the iced lakes give clarity, make thoughts glide easy as skate blades. It is a simplicity I envy: I wish I had the simplicity of ice. I wish I knew the cold serenity of snow by which no flake is ever twisted out of true. Here, close to the clear heart of things, ice is a good teacher.

It teaches respect for the limits, the depth of ice, the rules of safety. Nemesis is strict, and demands attention: consequences come quickly out on the ice. You have seconds or minutes at the most to avoid dying of hypothermia if you go through the ice.

And Nemesis is on your side with protective strictness, with her measuring rod and bridle: measure the ice and rein yourself in if it isn't thick enough. Nemesis is watching, though, with certain severity as collectively the wider rules and limits of ice have been so flagrantly breached. The ice is melting. Inuit people have drowned. Polar bears will likely become extinct because of it. The climate is changing unpredictably and frighteningly, leaving people of the ice depressed, anguished and anxious, being at the brink of the end of things.

★

One year, out skating, I saw sunlight, iridescent as it glanced the ice, dazzling and perfect. I saw moonlight, pale and gold, as the evening star rose. Sometimes the ice is black, so you can see the water, darkly dangerous below, and other times the surface is frosted white, with crystals all across the ice like strewn flowers.

In the air, I heard all the chatter and sounds of warm red life. Under the lake ice, though, the water boomed an eerie hollow moan, creaking below, an oboe of ice, then a cello string, low and sad. Always the reminder of twofoldness; life above, death below. And that was when Adrian Mitchell died, as the earth was cold as iron, a poet's midwinter.

It seemed so wrong that he of all people could have the warmth wrung out of him. He was so warm and I associate him with warmth of all kinds: warm wine, warm jokes, warm hearth and warm-heartedness above all. He was always warm and heart-ice repelled him, the cold, the mean-minded. I could never associate him with any ice except this kind – this kind ice for puppies to slip on, for kids to slide over. I was skate-happy that winter, but always underneath I heard a long, sad song for him, under those two weeks the grief-water rang so my soul-ice sobbed.

He was not someone who let scar tissue form, shining like glass, too many scars to sing. He was the opposite, refusing scars and welcoming song. I last saw him singing train songs. Pissed, gloriously choo-chooful, rosy with wine and friendship. They were trains with big engines, huge furnaces of heat. Big-hearted trains, big songs.

Big man.

Big as a lake, big as all sunset, big — that good old Anglo Saxon word — big as a champion, big as a balloon, big as Blake, big man, friend. I loved him. The 'big man,' in many traditional societies, is the one who gives the most away. He did this, giving young poets the courage, giving children the chance, giving words the whistle, giving poems the extra breath of jazz. I wish I'd gone skating with him.

The local doctor, now in his seventies but still the best and fastest skater around, was skating with me on a winter afternoon that had shifted into inexorable twilight. He fell heavily, landing badly on his shoulder; shaken but not deterred. There was one more hour before the light was completely gone, and he wouldn't leave the lake, not knowing when the ice-exhilaration would be his again. His shoulder stiffening, so that he was almost unable to take his skates off without help, he skated on, on, far into the dusk of the other side of the lake. It wasn't just the night he was fending off.

Of all my friends who skate, he is the one who knows better than any that life is short and skating days are precious. All things rare and lovely must be seized on the instant — in a lifetime there are so few skating days and each must be caught with glee. Skate while you may.

Skating is effervescent and evanescent. Vanishing at a point of joy, fleet as the sparrow which Bede described, flitting into the mead-hall for a brief, warm moment, then out again into the cold and dark, those birds symbolise the life of the soul.

I may have skated for the last time, for the lakes have not frozen in a decade and, because of the climate crisis, may never freeze again. I skate in my dreams sometimes. And waking, I sometimes think that I will never be able to skate again, except in my dreams.

Midwinter Dream with Saxophone

Winter nights bring the heaviest slumber of the year. Its tog-value is deepest snug, every duvet and blanket weighted with hibernation, every hour thick with night and deep with dream, every part of the body lulled and falling further into that good dark bedness. The winter solstice is also known as the *hibernal* solstice and that feeling of wanting to sleep like a dormouse — more, like an entire dormitory of dormice — folds itself around me, with gravity of irresistible force. How not? We are mammals and made corroborate with matter. French philosopher Jean-Luc Nancy says on falling asleep 'I coincide with the world.' In the wintersleep, I feel I have coincided with the season.

Nemesis is in league with the seasons, apportioning winter as much as summer, emphasising darkness as much as light. I, like many, don't like winter and I could say in a superficial way that winter is my enemy. But I have learned, or perhaps better *am* learning, how to look at the beauty of the rules of Nemesis. The darkness of midwinter is not our enemy but our friend: I believe this passionately, even though I am a midsummer child, solar-powered, and my favourite weather is pure sunshine. Correction. I believe passionately that midwinter darkness is our friend precisely *because* I naturally prefer summer and light.

One thing makes it easier to welcome winter and that is my love for good sleep, and hence my appreciation for the darkness in which the seeds of deep sleep may be planted. At the winter solstice, daylight is at its narrowest, the tightened, anxious and shortest of days. While winter lightlessness affects moods negatively in Seasonal Affective Disorder, there is also a polar opposite in the richness of a different kind of thinking in the dark months, the time of the year's dreams: a necessary dark. All the rivers of the world are flowing beneath you as you sleep and they rise into your dreams. In the deep turning time, dreams create light that emanates from within, the invisible but ungainsayable light that breaks into the dawn of significance. Inlit with insight, Theodore Roethke writes: 'In a dark time, the eye begins to see.' So the mind's light is crescent, first learning from a lucent world then shadowing it faithfully.

As Mike Parker comments, no one says of the summer solstice that it is time to celebrate the return of darkness, but many say of the winter solstice that it is the festival of light and the return of light. First must come a recognition of the dark and its inherent value. This isn't about the absence of light but the presence of dark. In good darkness, you know black not to be the colour of despair but the colour of potential — of possibility. Dark is necessary for the germination of ideas and insight. Dark is necessary for the kindling of seedlings and plans: it is easier to change your mind in the dark.

Antonio Machado writes of 'a heart made mature/by darkness and art,' and Rumi says, 'Let darkness be your candle.' In 1796, writes Craig Koslofsky in *Evening's Empire: A History of the Night,* Christian missionaries from England travelled to the South Pacific to call the heathens from the dark into the light. But for peoples of Hawaii and Tahiti, daylight was profane and ordinary whereas the night was sacred, and darkness represented a sacral connection between creation, death and the ancestors. Some seventy-five years later, a missionary to an island near Samoa was told 'We love darkness. To us, darkness is good, light is bad.'

In befriending the necessity of winter and the long dark nights, it also helps me that I adore Christmas. In the days before Christmas one year, I was decorating the tree with my kitten, Otter, 'helping.' I looked at the calendar and saw with glee that it was the Day of the Truffle. The previous day had been the Day of the Cork according to the French Revolutionary Calendar.

One of the finest creations of the French Republic was this new calendar that refused to honour the establishment church and the dynasties of empire but instead paid its respects to a pagan, countryside calendar, the turning world of nature's months, the nomadic year walking through its seasons. It is a paean to Nemesis and her way of allotting to each its due, giving every day its import, and holding precious the tiniest herbs and the most ordinary of minerals. It honours the seasonal and agricultural world around Paris, and the months were named for snow, rain and wind, turning in spring through the seasons of sprouting and flowering, by summer becoming meadow and harvest, then the days of heat, fruit and vintage until the seasons of mist and frost return the snows again. It was used by the government from 1793 to 1805 as well as briefly in 1871, when the Paris Commune reinstated it for eighteen days.

Vendémiaire began in late September, followed by *Brumaire*, then *Frimaire, Nivôse, Pluviôse, Ventôse, Germinal, Floréal, Prairial, Messidor, Thermidor, Fructidor*. The English comically translated these as Wheezy, Sneezy and Freezy; Slippy, Drippy and Nippy; Showery, Flowery and Bowery; Hoppy, Croppy and Poppy. Less well known is that each day was renamed as well, to honour a specific plant or minerals or animals and, on some days, simple tools. There is a day of Slate, one of Ash, and the day of the Wheelbarrow. April 18 is the day of the Blueberry, followed by days dedicated to Knife, Rose, Oak, Fern and Hawthorn. It is as if the calendar asks one to live convivially with the earth and its seasons, its especial livelinesses of Snowdrop or Lettuce, rather than living with the remote artifice of empires and abstract gods. And you can see the turning world in this vivid calendar, so while June has days of Clover and Artichoke, Cornflower, Chamomile and Honeysuckle, the harshness of this month of December is etched in Bitumen. This calendar is ecocratic: it doesn't put the emperor above the commoner, it doesn't exalt only the apex species or the charismatic megafauna.

This calendar, hospitable to each day's totem, explains why my kitten is called Otter; because he arrived in my house on the Day of the Otter. He is so playful he practically makes the word 'otter' a verb — to otter, to play with an earnest joy, ottering around in the gladness of his days.

At the winter solstice, the French Revolutionary Calendar nominates December 21st as the day of Peat, moving into December 22nd as the day of Coal. It is a matchless observation for the darkest of days and the wisdom they bring for peat and coal represent the night of earth, and both contain within them a ferocious potential: peat is the dark earth from which things will grow, and coal is the blackest of things from which the brightest of fires will burn.

The solstice means, etymologically, 'the sun standing,' almost still, and it is hard to be unaffected by this sense of time slowed right down: the daylight traffic of the ordinary is in abeyance. With the slowness comes the quiet — even silence — of midwinter, which is for me never more noticeable than in that moment when, into the tingling hush of dusk at three o'clock on Christmas Eve, a boy soprano sings that pure and sweet note of the carol, *Once in Royal David's City.*

Ssshhh, listen, that hush says. It is a time not just for sleeping and dreams but a time for listening and reading. This is the storyteller's season, a winter's tale by firelight, a time of stories. I read a fair bit, but every year, as darkness gathers towards midwinter I get hungry for reading, a starveling for stories, nothing, but nothing sates this except a feast of gluttonous reading. I'll read fast, I'll read slowly, I'll read anything and everything. As long as there is enough darkness, I will read and the whole entire world, myriad-minded and undying will light my thoughts. History comes alive. And wolves. I am still as a stone on the outside but on the inside alive, avid, pouncing with curiosity.

And I know I am not alone. It isn't a personal thing: rather, it is a widespread human phenomenon. For many cultures, midwinter is for stories. Ojibwe people say that midwinter is the time for telling stories partly because people are not busy out on the land, and partly because it is dark and cold, but there is more. Many Ojibwe stories are about animals and, with a tender politeness, Ojibwe people say that in the deep night of the year, a lot of animals are sleeping or hibernating, and so, out of respect, people can tell stories at that time of the year so the animals won't hear themselves being talked about.

If it is the very darkness of winter that lights up the world of the imagination, the smoky djinns, the folktales, the wonder tales, so it is also true that the darkness of midwinter deepens my gratitude for actual light. Sunlight in winter is an exact treasure, diadem light when, in the brief brilliance of the sun, frost jewels the land.

I love walking the valleys and hills of Wales in winter. The valley where I live is a place of rainbows, elusive, eldritch hints. It used to be known for *dweomercræft*; the craft of healers, magicians, those who know spells, those who know the sourcery of words. Of course. It is a land where all the streams are young: unmemoried water which carries no past of courses gone by. Of course they laugh, of course they heal, the sources of Wye and Severn and Clywedog. As I walk these hills, I've tried to familiarise myself with all the river names. Nant Cynnydd, 'stream of growth, increase' (with overtones of that lovely Anglo Saxon word cunt, to English ears). Nant Gwyllt, 'wild stream.' Nant y Bradnant, 'stream of the treacherous valley.' It *is* treacherously steep, but *brad* means treachery or conspiracy and conspiracy recalls co-inspiring; a word with many harmonies. So 'the stream of co-inspiring' is my loose translation, for my own use. It seems appropriate to learn a little language from rivers. Rivers and languages are similar, after all, they spring from sources deep underground. They are both living, moving things and you never step into the same language twice. In Welsh, the word *tarddiad* is used for the source of a river and for the etymology, the source, of a word.

One winter, I walked hundreds of miles in these hills, with a friend who was very ill. His lips were grey, his skin was blue-grey and yellow. When this illness first hit him, he couldn't breathe, his chest hurt, and he had thought he was dying. He refused to see a doctor. (I did persuade a friend, a retired doctor, to come and talk to him, but they found a bottle of brandy and got drunk together, leaving me with this precise prognosis: 'He will either die or he won't.') I was beside myself. You can't die, I told him: it's *rude.* At least you can't die without doing your utmost to avoid it. So we walked every day, through every weather, for hours and hours. There is medicine in these hills, and we found it, tramping for weeks in dogged pursuit of health. Several times, I have to admit, he looked as if he was going to sit down and die in the snow. I was terrified.

Because, along with disliking darkness and winter, I have to admit I am scared of death. This, too, is part of my wish to befriend Nemesis, for it is a matter of accepting the rules of the game. We can try to be well but we must die. There is a limit to life, and death has a strict kindness. You cannot have day without night, or summer without winter, or death without life, and our allotment of life is within the boundaries of death. Death, in the Nemesian sense, is not the opposite of life but rather the exacting stricture which gives it form and frame, the constraints of the rules of art within which the liveliest spirit can sing the most. Hal Ashby created one of the most vivid explorations of this philosophy in 'Harold and Maude,' where the young man who is obsessed with death falls in love with the 80-year-old Maude who relishes it precisely because by setting a term to living, death shows life more bright, and the colourful Maude, sucking the marrow out of life, is vivaciousness incarnate.

On Christmas Day of that year, we climbed a hill with another friend, a saxophonist. All of us had some deeply scorched paths of memory. All of us knew a loss of hope, for lover, child and dream. Between us we had lost to death two parents and a partner and two beloved friends gone. All of us knew how life could mess us up badly. And how we could mess up in turn. All of us knew the sound of the heart breaking. But all of us also knew the heart-mending on hillsides and at the hearth-sides of friends. We lit a candle and tucked it behind stones and moss. We flew a kite in high, cold sky. We drank homemade damson gin. Earth, air, fire and water: the elements of the heart.

The year was turning — very old and very young. As Christmas dusked, New Year was lighting the way ahead. This is a land both very old and very young. Geologically, it is one of the oldest places in Britain as the rocks here are older than almost any. But the rivers are so young and they scamper like children in wellies, splashing across a bog, springs welling up in the land like the laughter welling up in the child.

In walking, a great metamorphosis can happen — walking can prevent the sclerosis of emotional cages, walking can break you free of the confines of hurt and anger. There is reported to be a custom among the Inuit whereby a person, seized with anger, may walk out their rage, striding out in a straight line until their anger dissolves, at which point a stick may be left to mark the distance, a testimony to the intensity of their fury. Walking in nature is a treatment for depression, and walking, as pilgrimage, is part of many spiritual disciplines. Every walk teaches that in the turning world, 'this too will pass.'

There is a Tibetan tradition, the *Lung-gom-pa*, or 'wind meditation,' a practice of running by which the lamas seemed to fly, to run by trance-light. They could cover perhaps two hundred miles in a day, and could keep running for two days solid. There was a strong emphasis on breath-control and visualisation, as the lamas would imagine themselves being as light as a feather in the winds. Another and telling aspect of their training was to learn to keep their eyes fixed on a single star. They were often messengers, too, a word of both social and spiritual freight, for, as journeyers, relying on alms or gifts, they brought their own gifts in turn, of news or messages.

Through walking, there is slow, deep metamorphosis by which landscape is inwritten into the human being. The walker enters the world and the world the walker.

You are where you have walked. Walking, the wind becomes your breath. Walking inscribes itself into the whole body of the walker. Paths, once walked, create the sinews. Streams, drunk, enter the veins. Rocks, climbed, form the callouses of hands. Twisted tree roots curl up the body in muscle. Packed earth, tramped, becomes compacted vigour. The eyes? What of the eyes? They hold the skies, all the skies they have ever seen.

This is the ultimate reciprocal breath, in and out, as light as air, as free as wind, as clear as water, a gift-exchange as easy as light through glass, where what is finally achieved is transparency. Reckless, lovely transparency, where everything passes and the *passeur* and the pass are translucent to each other, a transparency as perfect and as simple as water and air and wind.

At New Year's Eve, we climbed the same hill, the same two friends and I. This time, we climbed at midnight, following a path we knew well. We saw two hares boxing at the bottom of the hill, and at the top we flew ribbons of prayer flags and drank two tiny bottles of fizzy wine. We threw six bright stones to the winds, 'for absent friends and lost friends' said the poet whose voice cracked with the weight of six past tenses. And the saxophonist played a deep blue solo to the darkness of the night until the midnight of the day and of the year chimed with a madeleine of all rivermusic; a stream of bells was ringing, almost inaudible from three miles away, the bells of a nearby church, which rose with the saxophone and the prayer flags and the love of auld acquaintance, old friends and old land, into air and memory.

Around the world, there is a widespread concurrence of ritual surrounding midwinter, and it seems an age-old human perception that it is a time for ceremony, reflection and renewal, with the play of dark and light at the heart of it. Newgrange in Ireland faces the winter solstice sunrise while Stonehenge faces the winter solstice sunset. For many cultures, the midwinter festival is a light festival: with candles, fire and lanterns. Not just with ubiquitous Christmas but almost everywhere, the winter solstice festival centres around family and feasting, including in China where the *yin yang* concept has lustrous validity: that in the moment of maximum darkness there is a seed of light. In Iranian culture, the winter solstice is celebrated on Yalda (Yule) night and includes a family feast, with pomegranates and watermelons because of the red colour, symbolising both the crimson of dawn and the life force. It also includes poetry, particularly Hafez.

Yule, from Jólner (another name for Odin), is associated with wisdom, healing, death, war and poetry. Midwinter also (in the

European tradition) honours the ambiguous figure of Janus, Roman god of doorways, looking both backwards and forwards and god of new year, still honoured in the naming of the month of January. New Year's Eve celebrates the passage of Time itself and the level gaze into the eye of Time takes courage, for Time is a concept as ambivalent as Janus to the human mind. New Year's Eve is a time after an end and before a beginning. It is a junction, a threshold — Time's strange pause in the doorway between the posts of two years.

In modernity's psychodynamic liturgy, a new year's resolution offers a release from learned responses and habitual behaviour patterns, and a chance for self-forgiveness. In all three cases, the seeking of forgiveness is only worthwhile if a new beginning is allowed, if the threshold of a new year is a place of release from the past. To make a resolution is to turn over a new leaf. Custom and nature intertwine here. The festival at the turning point of the year encourages both metaphoric new leaves and nature's literal new leaves: look back to step forward more strongly.

In the dead of winter, nature's energy is stored but unreleased, and the festival of new year can be understood in part as an ancient memory of sympathetic magic; the energy stored in the champagne bottle is uncorked, the frothy spurt of bubbles releases the seminal energy of spring. Paganism persists, pentimento.

The midwinter festival has always been characterised by release; audacious indignity flaunting itself uncorked. When, tipsy and garrulous, the Christmas reveller dons a paper crown, each of us becomes a Lord of Misrule where, in the upending of normal social rules, everyone is king or queen for a day, following the Mediaeval and Tudor Lords of Misrule whose presence released society from everyday restraints for the twelve days of Christmas. During the new year Saturnalia, Romans were released from duty in public affairs, law courts and schools, servants were released from servitude in a fizzing carnival freedom, and the statue of Saturn, bound all through the year, had his bands untied in symbolic yearly liberation.

'A year and a day' was traditionally the moment of release from several obligations, the binding time of a pagan wedding, the hiring period of labourers, the time during which a murder charge could be brought, and the time limit of a curse. There is something humane in an annual limit; 'forever' can be cruel, and endings can bring release and a quality of mercy, unrestrained.

In a spiritual context, release means the cancelling of old sins, and the mercy of forgiveness. Jews are required to seek the forgiveness of others at the Jewish new year. Catholics stress the importance of asking the forgiveness of God before the end of the calendar year.

But symbolically, the place of release is simultaneously the place of risk. A junction is the location of both maximum freedom and maximum anxiety, ambivalent as the crossroad was to the Romans — a place of opportunity, but also the burial place of suicides and criminals, a place of both chance and mischance.

It is a nowhere place, between departure and return, a halt between two roads. There is a boomerang relation between beginnings and ends. A beginning departure contains a returning end within it. But there is no similar energy in an end. The end does not entail a new beginning with any such inevitable tendency. Arguably, therefore, the end of the year provokes an unconscious anxiety over whether Time itself will continue, and the annual wake for the death of the old year is an apprehensive wakefulness to watch whether the fragile phoenix of the future will arise from the ashes of the past.

It is a gap in time that can make the human psyche awed and lonely. The tradition of holding hands is a clutch at comfort. It is also perhaps another instance of sympathetic magic, an attempt to encourage the new year to join hands with the old, to take Time by the hand and pull it in, through the doorway of Janus.

Doorways, of course, are highly ritualised places, and never more important than at New Year when what is at issue is more than the arrivals and departures of guests, but the arrival and departure of life and, indeed, time: it is the time of the exit of the past and the entrance of the future, where two-faced (and therefore untrustworthy) Janus rules. He survives in an unconscious heritage; his two faces, one looking forward and one looking backwards, is reflected in two new year customs: singing *Auld Lang Syne* looks back at the past, while new year resolutions look forward to the future.

The first-footing figure, standing in the doorway at New Year's Eve, is by custom a dark stranger, coming in silence. It is a neat personification of future time; the unknowable, inaudible arrival, a figure of elastic ambivalence, who might be your betrayer or defender, your hangman, confuser or friend. Riddled with ambiguity, the only certainty is that it will bring change. And how it is welcomed is a form of soul-hospitality.

Sacred Hospitality

My friend Jan, out gardening on her allotment one day, noticed a particular robin. It dipped, flitted and blinked, watching her in turn, its boldness endearing in such a tiny creature. Too high up in a tree, though, it was too far from the worms. Too low on the ground and even a brave robin's heart beats a nervous tempo. *Is-that-a-cat? Is-that-a-cat? Is-that-a-cat?*

It was late winter, and Jan worked to keep herself warm, digging over the soil. The robin watched, fluffing itself up against the cold. She found the handle of a broken garden fork, thinking *I know who might like this.* She stuck the wooden shaft into the ground and the robin flew to the handle, perfect to its perch. From then on, its breast the colour of embers, a little emblem of the fire at the heart of all life, the robin has enlivened the allotment with song.

My friend and the robin, 'the gardener's friend,' have shared the allotment for years now, as companion species. It is a relationship based on gifts: she gives it worms, it gives her song. There is a contract of sacred hospitality here, for nothing is too ordinary to be offered a hospitality of the heart. The quick of things, that vital essence, must be welcomed and cherished wherever it is found, not just because it is precious but because it is also vulnerable. A fork, then, for a robin, because the bird, no matter its exuberance, needs a flitting post above the cat's paw. Because birdsong is the first blessing of the day. And because any bird may be, in its own way, a kind of angel in disguise.

The very concept of allotments sits happily with Nemesis, goddess of due allotment, friendly and fair. In 1908, the Smallholding and Allotments Act made it a duty for local authorities to provide people with an allotment, to grow food and flowers. A little plot of land, a square of earth that is theirs. If you want an allotment of earth, but you don't use it, you have to give it up to someone who will take care of it.

Being a fair-minded goddess, Nemesis supports the ideas of due allotment, giving each of us an allotment of hours in life. Each of us a host in our little allotted lives and homes. Each of us a guest elsewhere. She suggests every scrap of life has a right to its place, its plot, its home, its life. She is the justice behind ancient laws of sacred hospitality.

Traditions of welcome agree on the importance of hospitality, knowing that all that is alive — every insect, every animal, every kind of plant — needs protection and deserves shelter. Nothing and no one should be without a home.

I have been the stranger at the door, hungry, thirsty and exhausted. I was walking across Spain at the time, on the pilgrim route, the Camino of Santiago, and on this particular day, I had reached a church hostel. Just. Reached. A hostel.

The door was open. I called out to the *hospitaleros* — the hostel-keepers, the hosts. They told me later that I went as white as a ghost and collapsed. What happened next was simply biblical. They gave me water to drink. One of the hospitaleros knelt down in front of me. She undid my laces and took off my boots. She peeled off my socks. And she washed my feet. Touched to the quick, I cried at the tender intimacy of this hospitality, sacred hospitality, offered to a stranger.

I was ill as well as exhausted, and they looked after me in the oldest tradition of hospitality — a hedge hospital along the pilgrim path. One of the earliest European examples of the hospital tradition were the Knights Hospitallers, whose lodges cared for those on pilgrimage or on crusade to the Holy Lands. But informally, of course, healing has always been part of hosting.

Hospitality today usually means the private hospitality offered to invited guests, or the commercial practice of the so-called hospitality industry, but there is a universal and ancient code of sacred hospitality, extending to strangers, travellers and wayfarers as a public duty, kindling conviviality.

'Come when you like, take what you see,/and once you have come, stay for as long as you like,' thus Dafydd Bach ap Madog Wladaidd, fourteenth-century Welsh poet, summed up how open-hearted hospitality speaks.

In Scotland, killing someone was homicide, but a host killing their guest — someone staying under trust — was so much more offensive that it was considered treason, in the concept of 'murder under trust' in Scottish law from 1587. Macbeth says of Duncan, his king and his guest, 'He's here in double trust: First as I am his kinsman and his subject... then as his host, who should against his murderer shut the door, not bear the knife myself.' Punchdrunk's *Sleep No More*, a production of *Macbeth* in New York, was set in a huge disused warehouse made to look like a hotel. The audience were referred to as 'guests' throughout, and as each of us wandered alone around the sinister space, we experienced the essential vulnerability of all guests, this vulnerability which demands a protective code.

The law of sacred hospitality governs the guest as well as the host, and the Massacre of Glen Coe in 1692 broke this code when the Campbells, billetted as guests, were given ten days hospitality by the MacDonalds. The English ordered that all MacDonalds under seventy should be killed, and the massacre was led by a Campbell. In popular memory, the fact that the Campbells slaughtered their hosts has meant they have never been forgiven.

I heard of an extraordinary breach of guestpitality recently, when friends living in mid-Wales told me they had heard a knock at the door one evening, and had opened it to find a stranger there, who was walking from Liverpool down to the coast at Cardigan Bay. He needed food, he said, and a bed for the night. They are kind people, and provided both, but were very disconcerted when the man criticised their food, and tried to pick a quarrel with them over the way they did their washing-up. Later, they heard that further on his journey, the man had stayed with an old couple and accused them of giving him watered-down milk, presumably semi-skimmed. So offensive was he as a guest that in the end he'd successfully picked a fight with one of his hosts, and was jailed for GBH.

Native American legends disdain hosts who are stingy; the mean and tight-fisted get their comeuppance in the coin of mockery. The stories also illustrate the rewards of warm and generous hosting. The Passamaquoddy people (First Nations of northeastern North America) have a myth which tells a story about a young girl who lives with her brothers and looks after the household while the brothers go out hunting. She is alone at home one day when a Chenoo arrives — a cruel, brutal, giant cannibal from the far north, with a heart of ice. He comes seeking shelter. She welcomes him and offers food and rest. The warmth of her kindness and her hospitality melts his frozen heart: she turns an ice monster human.

The Japanese tea ceremony, *Chadō*, the 'Way of Tea,' is about the hospitality of the heart. It is a way of communicating 'from heart and mind to heart and mind, soul to soul, depth to depth, thou to thou,' writes Robert E. Carter in *The Japanese Arts and Self-Cultivation*. This way of being with others, says Tea Grandmaster Dr. Sen Genshitsu XV, 'is contagious, for as the host attends meticulously to the feelings of his guests, then everyone else begins to attend to the feelings of the other guests.... an intense level of kindness prevails.' It is an attitude of tenderness to everything, human and more-than-human, animate and inanimate. It is thanks to tenderness, says Polish writer Olga Tokarczuk, 'that a teapot starts to talk.'

When Europeans invaded the lands of Brazilian Indigenous people, they were given hospitality. It is thought to be particularly because of the innocence of this hospitality that the idea of the 'noble savage' arose, according to John Hemming in *Red Gold: The Conquest of the Brazilian Indians*. Many Native Americans have had reason to rue the fact that they practised a tradition of sacred hospitality rather than a draconian immigration policy. 'Welcome' was the first word British settlers heard — in English — on March 17, 1621, when, by a quirk of fate, one of the first Native Americans they met, Samoset, had been to Britain and spoke a little English. 'Welcome... have you got any beer?' is the fuller version of Samoset's dialogue. Meanwhile, in 2016, the Standing Rock Sioux Tribe led a protest against the Dakota Access Pipeline, and tepees and tents were erected for people to dwell in to protect the land, for the pipeline, said Native Americans, would desecrate sacred sites, including the sacred stones which were like oracles which people could visit and read. It was the biggest Sioux gathering since 1876 and the Battle of Little Bighorn. People flocked to join them. Everyone, a spokeswoman said, was welcome, provided they came to protect the earth. They would offer hospitality to anyone who came knowing, in effect, the laws of guestpitality which govern humankind.

There is an Indo European word-root *ghos-ti* for a person to whom the law of hospitality applies, and it is the source of the words 'guest,' 'host,' 'hotel' and 'hospitality.' Linguistically speaking, guestpitality is part of hospitality. Christopher Logue offers a definition of the relationship in his *War Music: An Account of Homer's Iliad* thus: 'The host requires the guest to make himself at home. The guest remembers he is not.'

Traces of the tradition of sacred hospitality are visible everywhere — in British folklore people would leave a cake and a cup of wine for the fairies, as still today people leave a mince pie for Santa, and the idea lingers of laying an extra place at the table for the uninvited guest. In an old Gaelic tradition, the house door was unlocked and there would be food on the table for a passerby because Christ may walk in the guise of a stranger. In Germany, there was an old custom, still being practised in the 1930s, whereby wandering students, pilgrims and poor travellers were given supper, beer and a bed for the night while in the morning they could have bread and coffee to set them off on their way; all on the parish, as Patrick Leigh Fermor tells us. In a cruel inversion, in Thames Ditton in Surrey in 2014, the council declared it had 'cleansed' a site where Gypsies had been dwelling, with all the overtones of ethnic cleansing and racism that Gypsies have experienced for centuries.

Ancient Indian texts demanded five daily sacrifices, honouring the World Spirit, the ancestors, the gods, all living things and humankind. Honouring humanity happened through hospitality. In China, in the third millennium BC, one of the eight objects of government was 'the entertainment of guests,' presumably not quite the policy that contemporary English nationalism might support. 'They' are taking from 'our' hospitality, says the xenophobic line, stealing healthcare from our hospitals, ignoring the fact that it is migrant workers who keep the NHS on its feet.

When I was in Mongolia some years back, I struggled with one custom. To thank your host, I was told, is actually impolite in Mongolia. You can thank them at the end of a visit but not for every cup of tea or glass of vodka: that would be insulting to your host because it implies that there was even a shadow of a chance that they would not have been hospitable. I have never, but never, found any custom so difficult. I'm a polite kind of person (unless someone lies about me) and saying thank you was drilled into me from babyhood. Thank you for the salt. The bread. The days. Not saying thank you in Mongolia made me feel rude, over-entitled, a tourist of ruin with no coins of the heart to repay the hospitality of a host.

I want to introduce you to a word which might be a stranger to you, and I ask you to give it hospitality: *Xenia*. You are probably more familiar with the opposite word xenophobia, that hatred for foreigners which Britain is currently rehearsing. *Xenia* is a word to be treasured, to be welcomed into the home of your mind. It means the law of sacred hospitality to strangers, foreigners, refugees, wanderers. The god of *xenia* was Zeus, no less. '*Zeus xenios*,' Zeus the protector of strangers, embodying the religious obligation to be hospitable to travellers. In Greek mythology, the gods may disguise themselves as strangers seeking hospitality. When people offer this hospitality to strangers, the gods reward them.

Xenia is 'guest-friendship' and it comprises two rules, first a rule of hospitality — the host must offer food, drink, a bath if it is wanted and, interestingly, shouldn't ask questions until the guest has satisfied their needs. The second rule is the rule of guestpitality, that the guest must be courteous and not become a burden to the host. Also, the guest must offer the same welcome in return, to the host or another stranger.

When Odysseus returns home to Ithaca, he finds his house besieged by suitors to Penelope: these are guests who have not only outstayed their welcome (they have been there feasting for years), but have offended the code, demanding much more than they ought, and burdening their hosts. Xenia is also the name of a city in Ohio. Founded in 1803, the townspeople met and named it thus to suggest friendship and hospitality towards whoever arrived. In another example of hospitality, Sweden warmly welcomed guests by demonstrating the rights anyone has to camp and walk wherever they please across the land. They did this by registering the entire country of Sweden on Airbnb.

Legends and myths suggest the role of both guest and host is pregnant with significance, perhaps never more so than in the biblical story of Abraham and Sarah. It was a hot day in the desert, and Abraham was drowsy, sitting at the door of his tent in the heat of noon. Suddenly, he saw three strangers and ran to them, bowed and brought water so they could wash their feet, hot, dusty, and bruised. He offered them rest and food: bread, meat and milk. The strangers, as Genesis relates, were angels in disguise, and the reward for Abraham's hospitality was that he and his wife Sarah — though she thought herself too old to have children — were given a longed-for child.

Hospitality quickens life, the story suggests, so Abraham's glad and sudden generosity — he runs quickly to greet them and immediately gives them the best welcome he can offer — is rewarded with the best gift they could have asked for. A baby quickens in her womb. Kindness kindles life.

'Practise hospitality,' the New Testament commands. To receive, to give reception, in a hospitable sense, has a psychological counterpart; to be receptive to someone else's experience. Jesus, that subverter of the status quo, practised radical empathy, a hospitality of the heart so profound that he took on the identity of a homeless person: 'Foxes have holes and birds of the air have nests but the Son of Man has nowhere to lay his head.' Offering hospitality to strangers who are hungry, thirsty, migrant, unclothed, sick or in prison is, Jesus says, offering hospitality to Him. Offering asylum, sanctuary and refuge honours all that is divine.

From the fourth to the seventeenth century in English law, fugitives could not be arrested in a church: it was a sanctuary for forty days. This history was an eloquent backdrop for the Occupy movement, dwelling on the steps of St Paul's Cathedral in London, and offered temporary sanctuary there by those who understood their own religion.

Traditions of sacred hospitality can be found all over the world, and throughout history. The first place where it was noted that this tradition was lost was sixteenth-century England, and it happened because of that peculiar meanness which is often the concomitant of wealth. The bishops began restricting hospitality to just their friends and relatives rather than offering it to strangers. The wealthy put administrative barriers between themselves and the poor, as philosopher Theodore Zeldin says, they employed impersonal officials to deal with the dole, appointing almoners to deal out alms, keeping distress at arm's length. After that, says Zeldin, 'hospitality was never the same again.'

Street furniture is emblematic of society's sense of public hospitality. In even the very poorest parts of the world, there are public benches and shelters, and a traveller will be offered water at least. On the Camino there are water fountains everywhere along the way, and, beside one monastery, a fountain flowed with free wine. Where are the drinking fountains in Britain? The easy benches, the shelters on the waysides, the least of comforts? At train stations, you can hardly find a seat unless you pay for it buying a coffee. Need is turned into commercial opportunity. Street furniture, including bus stops, are designed with narrow little slats of sloping seats so you cannot be comfortable; public benches now have arm prongs (they're hardly armrests) purely to stop some desperate homeless person sleeping. No sanctuary, not even for a moment. Something peculiar happens to hospitality when wealth gets in the way.

The homeless, the sick, the disabled, the jobless, the hopeless are being treated as pests by the powerful, who see them as less-than-human, this 'poor, bare, forked animal' as King Lear describes. In London, wealthy property companies have erected 'anti-homeless spikes' in the recesses of pavements by posh properties to stop homeless people from sleeping there. It is how pests are treated — pigeons perhaps. Lying on a bed of nails: a proverbial punishment made real. When these spikes appeared in Manchester, one woman found it unbearable, and she covered them in warm, soft cushions as an eloquent protest to reverse the cruelty with kindness.

That image has at least pierced social conscience, so pointed a statement, knife-sharp and vicious towards those who have the least. The privileged have their knives out for the poor in the cuts, cutting welfare, that political version of sacred hospitality, and the poor have the knives out for themselves, as one vulnerable man did — in danger of losing the lifeline of benefits, he lined up his kitchen knives and stabbed himself to death. Cuts and cuts.

Shakespeare knew the solution: 'So distribution should undo excess/And each man have enough.' Those campaigning for the minimum of enoughness have been called 'vile sickness benefit extremists' by right-wing commentators. What was once considered a sacred duty to offer hospitality to strangers is rubbished, and in its place the cruel cuts, the racist refusal to receive other cultures, the spiked message to the homeless. Brexit brought out the worst in many Britons: a wave of loathing towards all immigrants, whether legal or illegal. By contrast, the brutal assault on Ukraine brought out the best in many people, and there was an outpouring of hospitality from people who wished to offer a home to Ukrainian refugees. The UK government, though, made the system so complicated and slow that it was hard for that hospitality to materialise.

Who is it, this person? Pest. Scrounger. Alien. Stranger. Immigrant. Asylum-seeker. Refugee. Sojourner. Traveller. Guest. Pilgrim. Angel. Beware of showing hospitality to strangers, for thereby some have entertained scroungers unawares, as the Bible does not say. If you want to watch the savage and heartbreaking reality of refugees, the documentary film *Fire at Sea* directed by Gianfranco Rosi in 2016, reveals it: the way in which people fleeing in terror for their lives arrive at Lampedusa, and the mercy of those who rescue and try to care for them when they arrive. Fleeing because of a geopolitical system that everyone is responsible for, they are the least to blame. And they are killed for their need.

Sacred hospitality suggests that everyone should develop the qualities of a host: geniality, congeniality, generosity, all generating life and liveliness in regenerating generations, as Abraham and Sarah were given quickening life and generations were born in honour of their hospitality. No matter who this stranger is, the host-society is influenced and its own life is shaped by its hospitality. Or lack of.

The churches have set up food banks, and church leaders have strongly criticised welfare cuts, but the tide is against them. A former Work and Pensions Secretary was known for mewling his Christianity, ignoring the fact that the penalty for inhospitality, according to Jesus's radical politics, is damnation. And Jesus was absolutely specific. Those who refused to help someone hungry, thirsty, a stranger, unclothed, sick or in prison, in other words someone who refused to help the unemployed, the poor, those on welfare and sickness benefits, in prison, needing the NHS and immigrants, would be damned in punishment.

Of all the old stories of sacred hospitality, my favourite is Philemon and Baucis. Zeus, *Zeus-xenia*, and Hermes, protector of travellers, visited a village to test its hospitality. No one would welcome them except Philemon and Baucis, an old, poor couple. (As so often, in legend and folklore, it is the poor who are generous.) The rich neighbours turned the strangers away, 'the doors bolted and no word of kindness given, so wicked were they,' writes Ovid. 'A thousand homes they came to seeking rest; a thousand homes were barred against them.' But Philemon and Baucis gave the guest-gods sanctuary, little knowing their identity. They brought a rug, built up the fire, offered a bed and warm water to wash their feet. They gave their guests cabbage and pork, olives, plums, endives, radishes, cheese, eggs, nuts, figs, dates, apples, grapes, honeycomb and wine. The wine never ran out; 'the wine welled up all of its own accord within the bowl.'

The hosts went to kill their goose, but they could not catch the bird which ran to the guest-gods. 'He seemed to flee for sanctuary to the Gods themselves.' Their identity revealed, Zeus and Hermes take Philemon and Baucis up a mountain, telling them not to turn back until they reach the top. When they do, they see their village has been destroyed in a flood: the community which doesn't offer hospitality is destroyed by its own meanness. Hospitality offers food to the hunger of a stranger: inhospitality consumes itself. The one remaining thing from the village is the cottage of Philemon and Baucis, and it has become a temple, a sanctuary sacred to hospitality, salvaged by hospitality.

★

In Bali, traditionally, the home is created in accordance with the organic proportions of the owner. The layout, size and scale of all the buildings within the home compound must be harmonious with the physical body of the dweller. It is a touching idea, and one which has a fractal resonance. The world as a whole, the home of hummingbirds and koalas, of water boatmen and honeyguides, of humans and coral, orangutan, porpoises and laughingthrushes, exists in elegant and exact proportion to each creature that sings its way into life. As the human needs a home, so the sheep is hefted to its own hill. The limpet has a 'home scar' for, as the tide ebbs, a limpet out grazing will turn for home, returning to its chosen rock where over time the shape of its shell has grown corroborate with its rock. The limpet has written its story on the rock, and the rock on the limpet.

The most sacred of all sacred hospitality is the one we have been given, as guests, and are bound to share. And we don't. In his *Diary of a Young Naturalist*, Dara McAnulty writes of his aghast pain at hearing a male corncrake, keening and crexing with no mate to return his call. The isolation, the cruelty of loneliness making the keening all the more tragic. The reason is that harvesting rhythms have been altered, meaning that corncrakes no longer have nesting habitat. In another act of bird cruelty, house martins cannot nest on many new-build houses because there is insufficient texture in the beams. They need good wood, and are deterred by plastic and metal. By sweet contrast, on Bardsey Island, off the Llŷn Peninsula, roofing work was carried out on a building with ancient slates, covered in lichen that had lived there for decades. The roofers carefully numbered each slate so they could be repositioned after repair without disturbing the lichen colony.

The Celts believed there were gods in lakes, so they threw into them gifts and gems: we throw in microplastics and poison. In the oceans, plastic kills sea creatures, and the reproductive systems of whales and dolphins are damaged by toxic industrial chemicals while the use of low-frequency sonar underwater causes anguish, pain, injury and death to these creatures. Nemesis watches, unsmiling. We are overstepping the mark, disobeying the laws of sacred hospitality that means no one should take more than their due, and no one should suffer because of the excess of others.

Chief Oren Lyons of the Onondaga people, says: 'We humans stand somewhere between the mountain and the ant' and our decisions and ways of life need to reflect that we are just one part of the whole. In order for humans to be truly at home, everything else has to have its place. 'Nothing in this world is indifferent to us,' wrote Pope Francis. They cannot be: we wield too much power over them. If we humans are making other creatures cruelly homeless, the only answer is a politics of kindness, a chivalric devotion to the Earth, and an honouring of the most ancient laws of sacred hospitality that extends to everything: a slate for the lichen, a home-scar for a limpet, a sett for a badger, a form for a hare, an eyrie for an eagle, a nest for a house martin, a roost for a bat — and a fork for a robin.

Acknowledgements

Smokestack Books published 'Compass' in *The Long White Thread of Words: Poems for John Berger*. Little Toller Press first published 'The Grace Notes of Birdsong' in *Arboreal*. Aeon Magazine published a version of two essays: 'Rituals at the Doorway of the Psyche' and 'Sky-grandmothers Hurling Stars.' Country Life published a version of 'The Language of Flowers.'

Artevents published a version of 'A Trouserful of Wantonness' in *Towards Re-enchantment: Place and Its Meaning.* Inque Magazine first published 'Prague.' The Film and Video Umbrella commissioned 'Hearth: A Thesaurus of Home,' 'A Beggarly Account of Empty Boxes' and 'Sacred Hospitality' for their project *Stay Where You Are*. Orion Magazine published a version of 'Artifice and Pastoral.' Gareth Evans commissioned 'Twilight and Otter' and it was first published by Hedgespoken. Lapham's Quarterly published a version of 'Skate Fever.'

Thank you to all the above.

Thank you to The Society of Authors and The Royal Literary Fund for financial support. In particular, I would like to thank the following individuals: Gareth Evans, friend and instigator, for first guiding me towards creating this book. Steven Nightingale for lending me his beautiful house while I was working on it. Thank you to Tom Bullough and others who read this collection in its drafts. Anita Roy for giving it such intelligent editorial attention. Adrian Cooper and all at Little Toller for such imaginative work in bringing it into the world. Jessica Woollard, whose confidence in this gave me so much strength, and whose sensitivity and sincerity make her the ideal agent. Mike Parker, with whom I have walked for miles, talking over the themes of these essays. Your thoughts and friendship enrich my life and my work.

Little Toller Books
w. littletoller.co.uk e. books@littletoller.co.uk